Games in the Global Village

Games in the Global Village:

A 50-Nation Study of Entertainment Television

Anne Cooper-Chen

Bowling Green State University Popular Press
Bowling Green, OH 43403

Library of Congress Catalogue Card No.: 93-73820

ISBN: 0-87972-598-2 Clothbound
0-87972-599-0 Paperback

Cover design by Laura Darnell-Dumm

CONTENTS

DEDICATION

To my parents

George H. Messerly, 1911-1981

Dorothy P. Messerly, 1911-1988

Introduction

FOREWORD

David Manning White

The creative moment when a writer makes a decision to explore *terra incognita* has always intrigued me. Most authors, I'd venture, would be hard pressed to remember the exact week, let alone the very day or hour when a certain work began to percolate. Not Anne Cooper-Chen, though, for she recalls the very minute her quest began. One evening during the autumn of 1985 she chanced to see a short segment superficially comparing television game shows in various countries on *Entertainment Tonight.* Voila, the project that would engross her for the next eight years was planted. As she wryly notes, what eventually became this comprehensive and engaging 50-nation study of a mass culture phenomenon was itself inspired serendipitously by a popular American syndicated television program. She surmised, correctly, that a thorough and systematic global study of television game shows might provide a revealing window through which to look at Marshall McLuhan's so-called "global village."

Her collection of data started in December 1987, during a trip to England and France. Utilizing a personal video camera, she taped portions of some 20 game shows directly off the screen. By 1988 when she traveled to Taiwan, Tunisia, and Japan, the quest was in full bloom. Through local contacts in these countries who videotaped the shows directly she was able to get better quality tapes. Finally, in 1990, her data collection shifted from tapes to monitoring. In order to increase the number of countries, and also decrease the costs to collaborators, she sent a simple monitoring form and covering letter to personal contacts in nearly 60 countries. International students at Ohio University, where Dr. Cooper-Chen directs the Center for International Journalism, helpfully suggested names of home-country contacts. A number of them, notably in Saudi Arabia, Korea, Peru, Switzerland, and Poland, not only answered her query but sent tapes as well.

Early in this project, she decided that she ought to examine the dynamics of actual game shows by attending some in person and, if possible, be a contestant on one or more. Her account of an exhausting trip to Los Angeles in 1989 and how she tried (unsuccessfully) to become a contestant on several game shows is as pertinent as it is revealing. It sheds some insight on why 15,000 people a year try out for *Jeopardy*, or why anyone is willing to stand in line for hours on the remote chance of hearing "come on down" on *The Price is Right*. For every person who is chosen to be on a game show there are at least 20 others who can vent their frustration in not being chosen.

Nevertheless, a sizable number of people do get on these shows. As Dr. Cooper-Chen points out, there are 30 game shows daily televised in the United States, with an average of four contestants each. That's 120 winners (and losers) five or six times a week, or more than 30,000 people a year. If only a quarter of that number of players appear on shows in each of the other 50 nations in her study, there are still more than 375,000 contestants outside of the United States. Four hundred thousand aspirants a year competing in the spectrum of global game shows amount to quite a substantial figure!

I happen to know, quite well I might add, two people whose lives were ameliorated considerably by becoming contestants on a game show. One of my sons, Richard G. White, has shown quite a proclivity for solving puzzles and excelling in word games ever since he was ten years old. This knack did not diminish during his undergraduate years at Harvard, or when he was completing a law degree at George Washington University. In the early 1980s he tried out for *Wheel of Fortune*, was accepted, and won easily the first night. The next show his luck turned sour and the "bankrupt" tick did him in.

Then, about 1986 he tried out for *Sale of the Century,* and it also accepted him, but this time his knack at games paid off exponentially. By winning ten consecutive times he acquired about $120,000 in cash and prizes, including a Ford Taurus sedan he still drives. A few months later the originator of *Sale of the Century*, an Australian game show lord named Reg Grundy, invited Richard and two other big winners to Sydney to compete against the top Aussie achievers. Even though the lads from Down Under prevailed, Richard was treated royally during a splendid two weeks there and came back home with yet more prizes.

In 1988, Richard's wife, Rani (also a whiz at solving puzzles), applied to the very same show and was accepted. During *her* ten successive victories she logged up nearly $140,000 in merchandise and money, including a Volkswagen convertible and $50,000 cash. They may hold some kind of record for the total winnings by a couple but, if not, $260,000 (even after paying Uncle Sam a capital gains tax) is still nothing to sneeze at.

Professor Cooper-Chen discovered that most of her acquaintances were a bit sheepish about answering whether they watched game shows regularly, although most of them did. Forgoing any bashful reservations I will not hide in any culture-closet and pretend that watching game shows is beneath my behavorial precepts. My wife, Dr. Catherine White, and I have been spending the 7 to 8 p.m. hour for at least the past ten years watching *Wheel of Fortune* and *Jeopardy*. That means that we've devoted more than 3,500 hours helping Merv Griffin, Pat Sajak, and Alex Trebek become even more affluent. Do we watch it out of "habit" or because it diverts our minds from the exigencies of the day (slaughter in Sarajevo, starvation in Somalia) or because we like to see if we can do better than the night's contestants? Perhaps a little of each of the above. The excoriators of mass culture will shake their heads and with a sad grimace tell me that I am micturating away too, too many precious hours. Well, I'm quite aware that Dmitri Shostakovich composed his extraordinary Eighth Quartet during an intensive 72-hour burst of sheer creativity, but let's face it, I (and most of the 47 million who watch *Wheel of Fortune*) couldn't compose music a la Shostakovich, write novels a la Alice Walker, conjure theories like any of the Nobel laureates if we avoided every vestige of popular culture. I wouldn't be writing the Great American novel during my usual dinner hour, even if I had the ability to do so. I may sometimes ask myself why I've spent several thousand hours watching game shows, but I certainly do not hold them responsible for the books I might have—should have ?—written.

I learned any number of engrossing items through reading Ms. Cooper-Chen's assiduously researched data in this book. For example, more women (55.4 percent) than men appear on American game shows; blacks (12.5 percent of the players) are fairly represented, but Hispanics (1.4 percent) are under represented when compared to the U.S. census figures.

Or that in the Muslim world all contestants in Saudi Arabian game shows are male, which one might expect, but that in Tunisia, Egypt, Turkey and Lebanon there is nearly an equal proportion of male and female players.

Game shows have endured (and will probably continue to do so) since the beginning of television's history. Their non-controversial, apolitical nature appeals to advertisers and their very high ratings verify their strong appeal to viewers. Perhaps Dr. Cooper-Chen's most significant finding in examining game shows in 50 countries was that McLuhan's "global village" is really comprised of *many* global villages in which indigenous cultural patterns are superimposed on the same type of show; in other words, the medium is *not* the message.

When Bernard Rosenberg and I first seriously examined the social implications of the media in *Mass Culture* more than 35 years ago, I hopefully envisioned that compelling studies such as Professor Cooper-Chen's *Games in the Global Village* would be forthcoming. Today, with the invaluable help of the Popular Press in Bowling Green, Ohio, and other publishing houses, this happily has come to pass.

Author's note: David Manning White died in December 1993 as this book was going to press.

PREFACE

> Since formal popular culture study is less than a few decades old, then, it is not surprising that the body of knowledge it has amassed contains a variety of lacunae. One of the more significant of these is comparative popular culture studies. (Rollin 3)

Comparative popular culture studies, according to Rollin (3), is "scholarship that makes a deliberate effort to compare and contrast the culture consumed by masses of people in two different countries or world regions." This book compares and contrasts popular television offerings in 50 countries—an impossibly gargantuan task without a window to aid our understanding. The window I have chosen is the game show genre.

Game shows have a "blank slate" quality that makes them ideal for comparing entertainment television across borders. Some pull in home viewers to play along; others treat viewers as spectators. Game shows can emphasize mental capacities or physical skills. They can test esoteric, "bookish" knowledge or "popular culture"/common-sense savvy. They can involve intense time pressure or proceed more leisurely. They can be based on skill or luck, or a combination of the two. They can humiliate losers or let them off easily; they can award winners glorious, costly prizes or token awards amounting to pride and honor. They can appeal to children, young adults, or the older generation.

Game shows can run the gamut of many subject areas or focus on one, such as rock music (MTV's *Remote Control*) or football (ESPN's *NFL Trivia Game*). They can spotlight dazzlingly high IQs (the BBC's erudite *Mastermind*) or dazzlingly nude bodies (Germany's *Tutti Frutti*). They can limp along in mid-morning time slots or smash the competition in prime time (France's *La Roue de la Fortune*).

Almost any country can afford to produce these budget-friendly shows, and almost every country does. Five half-hour game shows cost about one-third the total of five half-hour soap episodes (Graham, *Come* 7) and 1/15th the total of five half-hour situation comedies. Yet some countries choose to produce pricey game shows, such as Japan's *Let's Go! The World*, which features a studio host and a traveling hostess who asks questions from locations all over the world.

Japan, like the United States, exports game show formats outside its borders, as do a few European countries. Of the 260 shows that this study identified, about one-third use transferred formats. Thus a TV-watching traveler can find similar shows on small screens scattered all over the world. On the other hand, shows based on like-sounding concepts may differ dramatically; for example, dating shows exist in countries from Taiwan to Germany and Japan to France, but modes of matching couples in a TV game are as diverse as these nations' cuisines.

An understanding of cultural similarities and differences lies at the heart of this book. Writing in another context, Geertz (23) refers to anthropology's "deepest theoretical dilemma: how is such variation [of cultural forms] to be squared with the biological unity of the human species?" We hope this book may shed some light on that dilemma.

When a book sets out to survey global television, the TV sets of the world do not automatically beam signals to an author's VCR. Nor could this author travel to 50 countries equipped to tape each nation's game shows in approximately the same season. More than 75 monitors sent back coding sheets and in some cases tapes and TV schedules so that this first comprehensive comparison of TV content could get into print. Those who helped include:

CANADA: Herta Rodina, Virginia Watson-Rouslin.

CARIBBEAN/LATIN AMERICA: Gene Bigler, Vibert Cambridge, Lucia Castellon-Aguayo, Connie Messerly Kehoe, Caryn Lindsey, Louise Montgomery, Tatiana Ramirez, Gilda Rota, Josep Rota, Regina Silva, Weinar Silva, Sonia Sweek, Roberto Winsberg, Alma Mock Yen.

EUROPE: Margaret Churchman, Nathalie Dandache, Amy Graves, Ralph Kliesch, Alvi McWilliams, Franco Messerli, Matt Mueller, Jackie Mulhern, Mischa Nedeljkovic, Devote Ngabriano, Jerzy Oledski, Stanislas Perkner, Paul Reece, Paul Talbot, Pilar Vicente, Paul Van der veur, Lois Vines and Jan Servaes and students at Catholic University, Njimegen, the Netherlands.

NEAR AND MIDDLE EAST: Ali Alanazi, Mahmoud Hammoud, Belinda Hopkinson, Laura Lande, Yorgo Pasadeos, Deb Traynor, Ayseli Usluata.

AFRICA: Mounir Adhoum, Hussein Amin, Paul Chakalisa, Jerry Domatob, MaryAnn and Don Flournoy, Ahmed Lamnadi, Mitchell Land, Janet Macharia, Moulaba Abu

Mada, Themba Mbjeje, Abubakar Mu'azu, Lamlenn Samson, Tantoh Thomas, Ojogum Tellson, Mohamed Wafai.

ASIA/PACIFIC: Debashis Aikat, Radkhika Balasubrahmanian, Zhao Bin, Ni Chen, Yunhee Choe, Singh and Naresh Fernandes, Kath Filmer, Errol Hodge, Bukhory Ismail, Youichi Ito, Hiroshi Kawakami, Anil Kumar, Teruyo Kuramoto, Suzanna Layton, Tojun Oh, Bonnie Peng, Sivagami Natesan, Zennedy Que, Susan Quimpo, Sankaran Ramananthan, Hochang Shin, Arvind Singhal, Manhong Song, Noi Sripun Tiam, Candy Wong, Li-fen Zhang, Wei-hong Zhang.

VARIOUS COUNTRIES: Diane Campbell, Robert L. Stevenson, Robert Stewart, Dorothy Zhang.

David Manning White, my first mass media teacher, has done me the great honor of writing this book's foreword. I met him in 1976 when I took his theory seminar at Virginia Commonwealth University. Through reading his Course by Newspaper in 1978 on popular culture, for the first time I learned that this subfield had a name. Only later did I learn of his part in creating the subfield. I treasure the enthusiasm that radiates from the foreword, one of his last publications.

My husband, Charles Chen, is the spiritual coauthor of this book. He went with me to California on the great game-show tryout; photocopied pages at midnight to meet convention deadlines; solved numerous software quandaries; translated Japanese and Chinese videotape dialogue and TV schedules; and kept me going over the eight years of this project. His family, especially Lie-chiou and Ming-shi Chen, were most helpful, too.

My colleagues at Ohio University helped in large and small ways. I appreciate especially a research leave in fall 1990 arranged by Ralph Izard, Guido Stempel and Paul Nelson.

Without Pat Browne, director of the Popular Press, and Ray Browne, its founder and advisory editor, this book would not be in your hands. They have my enduring gratitude. (And Bowling Green State University library has 25 of my game show videotapes! Anyone reading this study can see the real thing.)

Finally, I'm thankful to my parents, who brought me to the light of day at just the right moment to observe TV history. Having arrived on this planet in 1944, I had already learned to read when they bought our first television, a Dumont, in 1950. So I saw the box as a new friend, but I had known life without it as well. I had access to the pivotal first TV season of 1948, living in New York City and watching the sets of neighbors.

Although *Captain Video* on Dumont stole my heart, I also vividly remember the game shows: *Break the Bank*, *Stop the Music*, *Quiz Kids* and especially *Pantomine Quiz*. The tugs on the earlobe ("sounds like"), the fingers on the forearm ("how many syllables?"), and all the other charades body language provided my friends and me years of life-imitates-TV art activity.

The quiz show scandals, which marked the end of Americans' innocent romance with television—yes, content existed solely to deliver viewers to advertisers—ironically happened just as I entered my new phase as a teenager. Before the scandals, I watched the games, *Ed Sullivan*, *Mickey Mouse Club*, *Lassie*, and later *Ben Casey, M.D.*, *Man with a Camera* and *American Bandstand* with gusto, and without apology. Then about 1960, I started to tune it all out. Only *Password* could capture my attention—but summers only. Therein lay game shows' beauty: constant, ever forgiving, heaping no blame upon us fickle college students in the form of summer replacements.

As I write this on a Fulbright sabbatical in Japan, enchanted all over again by a new type of travel question quiz, I remember the democratic arms that U.S. television spread in the 1950s. In Japan everyone watches all kinds of shows unapologetically. It has not hurt students' scores on high school achievement tests. Neither did it damage those of us born in the 1940s, who watched television and had record high SAT scores. But that thorny issue remains for others to address. This book belongs to play.

Kasugai City, Aichi-ken, Japan

Chapter 1

THE WORLD OF TV GAMES

Enough has been said to ask for far more serious regard of play, and not of information, as the primary concern of any communication theory. (Stephenson 206)

The logo fills the television screen. It's the *Wheel of Fortune* wheel, seen by 46 million Americans on the show's daytime and syndicated versions—the same wheel that graced the cover of *Newsweek* and was featured on *Nightline* and *60 Minutes*.

But a French-language voiceover welcomes viewers to *La Roue de la Fortune*. Then an unfamiliar host bounds on stage, and a dark-haired hostess spins into view. The popular American program has not been dubbed for export; rather, only the format has been licensed. After all, how would "R U B B E R D U C K Y" translate into French?

1. Game shows' popularity

Whether formally licensed from abroad like the top-rated *La Roue de la Fortune*, informally adapted from abroad, or originated at home, game shows have universal appeal. "Worldwide Gameshows: They're Hot & Priced Right" declared a special six-page report in *Variety* in 1992. *Wheel of Fortune* has emerged as possibly the most-watched TV show in history, with a weekly audience of about 100 million (Tempest).

In Spain, according to the *Variety* report, four game shows regularly make the top ten rated programs. Indeed, one show, *El Precio Justo* (licensed version of *The Price Is Right*) holds the all-time Spanish record for advertising sales—more than $200 million in 18 months in 1990-91 (More 42). In Germany, where game shows constitute "the fastest-growing programming area" on television, a recent hit record was titled, *Life Is a Quiz Show and We're Just the Contestants* (Lieb 38).

The United States surpasses all nations in the number, variety, and subject-specificity of game shows (see Ch. 8). For example, in 1990 a viewer in the Columbus, Ohio, area could watch 34 different such shows every week. Even the nation of Belgium, with fewer than 10 million people, boasted an astounding 13 different game shows on its weekly TV schedule.

A TV game show may be defined as a program featuring civilian, that is non-celebrity, contestants who compete for prizes or cash by solving problems, answering questions, or performing tasks following prescribed rules. The contestants may include celebrities, but these celebrities are "playing themselves" while participating in the game rather than performing. The prizes may range from astronomical sums of cash to little more than token mementoes. The definition does not include "amateur" contests, many of which feature semi-professional performers trying to break into show business. It does include student quiz contests.

Game shows have endured since the beginning of television's history in many nations. Their noncontroversial, apolitical nature appeals to advertisers (Wally and Magiera 4) while ratings attest that they likewise appeal to viewers (see Ch. 7). Then what makes the shows so compelling, even turning some viewers into "quiz addicts" (Goodson 415)? The limited amount of audience research on game shows (see Ch. 5) cannot give definitive answers. But theories abound.

On a *Nightline* program (1987), Merv Griffin, creator of *Wheel of Fortune*, said game shows give audiences relief from the depressing nightly news. Psychiatrist Carole Lieberman told *Newsweek* that game shows "allow people to return to the playfulness of childhood" (Waters, "What" 64). Semiotician Marshall Blonsky believes the "game show squeal" epitomizes "the addictive euphoria of TV's speed and greed" (Germani 13).

The interactive shows—those that let viewers play the game before answers are revealed—offer viewers relief from one of television's most criticized drawbacks: passivity. (Quick!! what's B _ _ B L _ S _ N _ B _ N G L _ S?)

Beth Fiance, contestant coordinator for *Scrabble* wrote to the author that "people like to...play along—they like to feel smart." One friend of the author's faithfully tapes all *Jeopardy* episodes—not so she can shift the viewing time, but so she can hit the pause button and give herself time to remember the answers.

The author's friend, aged 65, lives in central Ohio. In fact, in the United States and certain other countries, the 55+ female viewer remains the mainstay of game shows' audience (see Ch. 7). As far back as the 1950s, Glick isolated five types of appeals, noting especially the role of gender: the excitement of watching a competition; women's vicarious identification with female players; the fun of testing one's own knowledge; women's fondness for male hosts; and the release of relaxing as "giggling girls again" (128-29).

Later (see Ch. 4), we will present the premise that TV game shows ("mind sports") function for female viewers in much the same way that TV athletic contests function for males.

Game show producer Mark Goodson explores the "win/win" complexity of game shows' appeal to both sexes (415). On the one hand, if a player misses a question that the viewer knows, the viewer can feel proud and smart. On the other hand, if the player wins, the viewer can celebrate "a victory for 'our side.'" The quick pre-game interviews with players color the viewer's identification and affect this "self-measuring process" (Goodson 415).

Goodson furthermore believes that game shows' "reality gives a special edge to the experience" (415). Except for sporting events (see Ch. 4), nothing else on television offers the similarly spontaneous tension of an undetermined outcome. Talk shows, while real, lack movement toward a final climax. Dramas, while compelling, require suspended disbelief.

But game shows offer both reality and drama believes Paul Talbot, whose firm controls about 75 percent of U.S. games that are licensed overseas. "Every game has a different cast of characters and a different progression of action," he told the author. "You get to know each character, even if briefly."

The quiz show scandals resulted because producers failed to perceive this dual appeal. According to the testimony of Charles van Doren before Congress in 1959, the producer of *Twenty-One*, Albert Freedman, saw big-money quizzes as scripted dramas. Freedman coached van Doren to pause, hesitate and build suspense and "thus increase the entertainment value of the program" (Barnouw 244). But the producers clearly knew the shows' compelling nature rested on their perceived honesty—as witness the isolation booths and bank trust officer who "would certify to the inviolability of the proceedings" (185). Even President Eishenhower called the deception "a terrible thing to do to the American people."

Thirty years later, Mondrad and Martinat, who analyzed the 1980s' game show fever in France, concluded that the "passionate rapport" that game shows elicit requires "absolute honesty of the games" (14). Perhaps the era of scandals has tarred all game shows with the same 1950s brush. Compared with the deception of that era, today's shows seem more inane than sinister. Yet criticism levelled at TV game shows has vitriolic intensity.

2. Game show bashing

In June 1955, *The $64,000 Question* made its debut on CBS in the slot just before Edward R. Murrow's *See It Now*. Less than a month later, the weekly *See It Now* was cancelled. "If *See It Now* signified television at its best," writes TV historian Sally Bedell Smith, "the quiz show represented the worst of the new medium" (26).

Yet Smith may be confusing cause and effect. As Barnouw points out, in 1955, "The atmosphere of television was changing" (186). As the number of sets grew, television's power as an advertising medium soared. Sponsors "wanted television time and programs, but generally not of the *See It Now* type" (184).

The more commercial a broadcast system becomes, the more it seeks to maximize profits through high audience ratings. The four commercial U.S. networks cater to the lowest common denominator by broadcasting "predominantly entertainment programs" (Singhal 80). To some critics, that is precisely the problem.

Australian John Fiske sees game shows as "bearers of capitalist and patriarchal ideologies" (*Television* 271). Further, Fiske sees game shows as a metaphor for the West's elitist educational system, which acknowledges differences in natural ability, while (wrongly) assuming equality of opportunity. The host (schoolmaster) presides over a class of students (contestants) engaged in competitions based on skill and luck (206-07). As in life, "luck provides an ideologically accepted explanation of success or failure" (270), masking the true roles of wealth, gender, and race in creating elite and subordinate classes.

Himmelstein singles out specific shows for criticism: *The Dating Game* and *The Newlywed Game* symbolize for him a "disdain for human relations," making of the audience "video voyeurs" (269). Some game shows, says Himmelstein, such as *The Gong Show* and *The $1.98 Beauty Show*, represent

> the purest form of exploitation of one's fellow human beings—that which preys upon their feelings of insignificance or inadequacy in their everyday lives and allows them a moment of video exposure in exchange for their naive complicity in their own exploitation for their owner's profit. This is nothing other than a slaveowner-slave relationship, where exploited ephemeral television celebrity is purchased and displayed as a commodity, as a fool, before the invited guests—the millions of television viewers. (270)

Himmelstein lambastes contestants and watchers alike (272). Contestants on giveaway shows that require little or no skill want something for nothing. Everyone, it seems, is deceived, even the viewers at home who must take a secret joy in watching greedy contestants lose...while they simultaneously fantasize that they were "there," on television gunning for the big deal. The prizes [are] right out of the suburban middle-landscape catalogue...wall-to-wall carpets, trash compactors, gas bar-b-ques..."You have just won a replica of Ward Cleaver's house." Applause.

The shows that emphasize mind over greed are hardly better, says Himmelstein, in that, beginning with the radio version of *The Quiz Kids* in 1940, "knowledge was equated with memorization of facts and rapid recall under pressure" (273). How, concludes Himmelstein, "can a television executive with a conscience allow these travesties to air on his station?" (274).

Although Himmelstein is probably the most bitter and mean-spirited of game show critics, he has plenty of company. David Gergen, former editor of *U.S. News & World Report*, categorizes game shows as television that sinks to the lowest common denominator—along with "violence, serial comedies, blood and thunder, and most of all, boredom" (Hamblin).

Meyer calls *The Price Is Right* and other big-prize, small-skill game shows the "cynical exploitation of middle-class greed" (37). Holbrook likewise decries the materialism and consumption ethos of *The Price Is Right*. What, asks the author of a *Newsweek* cover story on game shows, "could be more in sync with our hyper-acquisitive ethos?" (Waters, "What" 64). Waters sees an appeal to the "lottery mentality—the flourishing conviction that luck, rather than acuity or hard work, determines whether Joe Prole will strike it big" (64).

The first children's game shows (as distinct from quiz shows) made their debuts on the Nickelodeon cable network in 1986, prompting a new vein of criticism. The glorification of "exhibitionism, voyeurism and rampant acquisitiveness...just may hook them for life," worried *Newsweek*'s TV critic (Waters, "Much" 72). Peggy Charen, president of Action for Children's Television, says this type of show represents "greed taking over America. I think it teaches young people that what you have determines who you are" (Waters, "Much" 73).

Another charge relates to the rising frustration that the sight of vast riches and prizes may create (Nam 214). None of these fears can be summarily dismissed. However, more benign views of game shows also exist.

3. Praise and pervasiveness

As one former contestant pointed out on *Nightline* (1987), game shows "don't cause cancer and don't circumvent Congress." Several other commentators discount the alarmist views of how game shows affect values.

"The greed of game shows sounds like what's taught in business schools," says Merrill Brown, former editor of *Channels* magazine. "It's reality. So is the competition of game shows. It's hard to get into college. TV reflects outside issues; the successful shows touch a nerve."

Jeremy Gerard, TV critic of the *New York Times*, believes that the greed factor "is no worse now than it ever was" and that other facets of television are much more a cause for concern. To counter the theory that greed attracts viewers, Monte Hall notes that the ratings of *Let's Make a Deal* did not go up as dollar amounts of prizes increased; conversely, shows with small amounts at stake have had excellent ratings (*Nightline* 1987).

Likewise, for contestants greed seems not to be a motivating factor. According to the host of the British show *You Bet*, Jeremy Beadle, "On our show, we give each participant a little plastic token to commemorate their visit, and in a funny way they value that more than the money because it means they haven't been bought" (Ferry 28).

"I equate game shows with the American dream," states *Jeopardy* host Alex Trebek. "...on a particular day you have an opportunity to be a TV star and make a lot of money. You can be rich and famous for an hour" (Graham, "Game" 7-8).

Film critic Jeffrey Lyons states the benign view of game shows this way:

> I wouldn't dream of proclaiming that *Super Sloppy Double Dare* is good for your child. But what's wrong with watching an admittedly dumb—but hilarious—program just for fun? My son dissolves into spasms of laughter watching the contestants climb chocolate slides, wade through mountains of plastic foam chips or get covered with green goo. (14)

TV creator-writer-producer Christopher Cerf, a member of the Children's Television Workshop, finds game shows "a good way to be didactic" (see Ch. 10). He believes the genre can overcome television's main drawback, passivity; not only can parents and kids actively play the game, but they can interact with each other.

Cerf's father, Bennett Cerf, hosted *What's My Line?* in the 1950s (top prize: $50). When the elder Cerf died in 1990, game show producer Mark Goodson credited that and other early conversational game shows with giving birth to another genre as well: the TV talk show.

Although *What's My Line?* left network television in 1967 (and was in syndication 1968-75), many U.S. shows from the 1950s have endured to the 1990s (debut dates from Graham, "Come"):

Blind Date (1949); later *The Dating Game* (1965)
Concentration (1958)
Family Feud (1976), as spinoff of *The Match Game* (1962)
Jeopardy (1964)
Name That Tune (1953)
The Newlywed Game (1966)
Password (1961), to which a clock was added as *Pyramid* (1973)
Sale of the Century (1983)
To Tell the Truth (1956)

By the 1970s, game shows had so ingrained themselves into the American psyche that viewers of *Saturday Night Live,* which made its debut in 1975, could easily appreciate endless parodies of the genre (see Ch. 8). By 1985, when Vanna White and Pat Sajak led the Fourth of July parade in tiny Nelsonville, Ohio, the game show had reached folk culture status: "game shows and the USA go together like apple pie and vanilla ice cream," wrote Graham ("Game" 7) of the Nelsonville celebration.

On February 9, 1987, Vanna White appeared on the cover of *Newsweek* under a headline that read: "Game Shows: America's Obsession*TV Cashes In." On March 6, 1987, Ted Koppel devoted his entire *Nightline* show to the genre.

Now many of the active parlor games that led to spectator TV games have reverted to real-people games, but their TV names have stuck. In the university town of Athens, Ohio, the author has observed the following phenomena in 1990 alone:

Jan. 25, 1990	Ohio University holds College Bowl finals; We Knew That beats out The Roughriders and will advance to the regional tournament March 3-4.
Feb. 27-28, 1990	Phi Mu sorority stages *Family Feud* game featuring fraternity and sorority teams to raise money for charity.
April 26, 1990	Phi Alpha Delta sorority stages *Win, Lose or Draw* tournament also to raise funds.
May 29, 1990	Journalism professor gives *News Jeopardy!* current events quiz, featuring such answers as "Fernando Collor de Mello." (Q-Who is Brazil's new president?)
Sept. 27, 1990	Communications students produce first episode of a local access TV program, *Quiz Me*, for fifth and sixth grade students.
Nov. 11, 1990	Provost's office invites 24 high schools to compete in a double-elimination quiz tournament, open to the public.

While life was imitating art in the United States, television overseas began imitating U.S. television. "The wonderful world of the American game show," wrote Ferry, "is taking Europe by storm" (26). Indeed, all of the 1950s and 1960s game show warhorses listed above and many more have successfully traveled overseas (see Ch. 6).

Wheel of Fortune, which made its debut on CBS in 1975, has spawned more local versions than any other U.S. game show (it runs in 25 countries under names such as *Lykkehjulet* in Norway, *Rad von Fortuin* in Germany and *Carkifelek* in Turkey). Ironically, some shows, like the short-lived *Child's Play* (CBS 1982-83), have scored better with British, Belgian, and German audiences than the U.S. viewers for whom they were originated.

B

Global Television: That's Entertainment

Chapter 2

THE PLAYFUL TUBE

Television remains to this day a medium of entertainment, first and foremost, not only in the Western world but throughout the world. (D. Browne, "Media" 193)

The worldwide ascendance of television from the 1950s to the 1980s makes it "by far the fastest developed medium in human history," according to Ray Browne ("Repressive" 118), founder of the Center for Popular Culture at Bowling Green (Ohio) State University. Today more than one billion TV sets dot the globe, a 50 percent jump over the previous five years (Lippman). Merrill Brown, former editor of *Channels* magazine, calls television "the centerpiece of our entertainment lives." In the Persian Gulf, the average person watches that centerpiece six hours a day; in French-speaking Belgium, 4.5 hours; and in Japan, 3.44 hours (Lippman).

1. Television entertains the world

After pre-war experiments in industrialized countries during the 1930s and 1940s, World War II halted the expansion of television. Then in the 1950s, some 50 countries began TV services (D. Browne, *Comparing* 15). By 1954, the United States and Britain began to fine tune their distinctly different systems, moving closer to each other: in the United States, the first "educational," noncommercial station went on the air in Houston, while in Britain, a commercial system was authorized as a counterpoint to the British Broadcasting Corporation.

Similarly, in Japan, the U.S. Occupation in 1950 authorized a commercial system to compete with the noncommercial Nippon Hoso Kyokai (NHK), which had been modeled on the BBC. The Soviet Union greatly expanded its state-controlled system in the early 1960s.

Early adopters of television also included a number of Third World countries. Mexico, Cuba and Brazil began TV operations in 1950. The Philippines followed suit in 1953, as did Algeria in 1956 and Egypt in 1960. By the end of the 1960s, half the world's nations had joined the TV age.

Because two-thirds of the world's people live in the Third World, a large number of sets exist in Third World countries, despite a lower percentage of penetration. The Third World's share of the planet's television sets increased from 5 percent in 1965 to 10 percent in 1975 to 14 percent in 1980 to 20 percent in 1984 to 40 percent in 1990. Part of the dramatic increase resulted from China's and India's relatively late expansion of television—in China after Mao Zedong's death in 1976 and in India after the Satellite Instructional Television Experiment (SITE) broadcasts of 1975-76.

In India, between 1984 and 1985, the number of TV viewers jumped from 37 to 60 million, then increased again to 90 million in 1988. During that year, sets were sold at the rate of one every five minutes, even though a black-and-white set costs $200 to $250, or about two months' salary. For those who still cannot afford this relatively high cost, the practice of community viewing increases access to television. By the year 2000, India will have an estimated 63 million sets, with an audience of some 378 million people (Singhal and Rogers, *India's...* 67).

The story of China's romance with television in the 1980s shows dramatically the phenomenal pull of the medium. In 1980 the country had about 630,000 sets. By 1985, there were 12 million sets, and by the end of the decade, about 118 million (about one set for every ten persons). Bishop (108) found that smugglers who paid $500 for a set in Hong Kong could sell it for $1,000 (109).

According to BBC statistics for 1989, television reached at least 600 million of China's 1.1 billion population (55 percent); about 125 million of India's 880 million people (15 percent); and about 70 million of Mexico's 80 million people (87 percent) (Singhal, "Entertainment..." 78). Compare these high figures to the almost complete (98 percent) penetration in the United States.

Whether enough TV sets exist for almost everybody to have one all his own, as in North America, or the ratio means that a roomful of people would have to share one, as in Africa, television is an entertainment medium. Donald Browne defines an entertainment mass medium as "that which appears to have as its *primary* purpose the amusement, distraction and/or relaxation of its audience" (188).

In 1983, Varis found entertainment to account for these percentages of TV minutes: US, 40 percent; Canada, 36 percent; Latin America, 44 percent; Western Europe, 35 percent; Eastern Europe, 36 percent; Asia, 48 percent;

and the Arab region, 42 percent. In only two areas, entertainment was the second rather than highest-percentage category: USSR, informative content, 30 percent and entertainment, 27 percent; Africa, informative, 39 percent and entertainment, 30 percent (150).

Recent statistics from UNESCO and the BBC World Service confirm what Varis had found: entertainment constitutes the largest category of TV content almost everywhere in the world. For example, the percentage of TV time devoted to entertainment in Mexico is 74.2 percent; former Soviet Union, 49.5 percent; and Portugal, 70.8 percent (Lippman 7).

In the words of Fiske and Hartley, television fills the "bardic function" that contemporary societies need. It takes its place in a plethora of media that have filled social needs.

2. Theories of mass entertainment

The Latin *tenere*, root of the word "entertain," means to hold or keep. Webster's New World Dictionary gives "to amuse; divert" as the word's first meaning. Barnouw and Kirkland (102) define the term in its modern mass sense as an "experience that can be sold to and enjoyed by large and heterogeneous groups of people." Mendelsohn uses a functionalist definition of mass media entertainment: "gratification of human needs for pleasure via television, radio, the cinema, popular novels, newspapers and magazines" (15).

Fischer and Melnik see the entertainment field, including the subfield of television, as characterized by passive participation and lack of feedback (xiii-xv). Donald Browne defines an entertainment mass medium as "that which appears to have as its *primary* purpose the amusement, distraction and/or relaxation of its audience" ("Media" 188). While these and other definitions and descriptions of mass entertainment may abound, "theories of entertainment per se are practically nonexistent" (Fischer and Melnik xvii).

Social science theories, says Reynolds, explain why things happen (4). Knowledge is expressed in the form of existence statements (an object is identified as an example of a concept) and relational statements (describing how concepts are associated or causally related to each other). Collections of statements form theories (Reynolds 67-68). "Any idea is 'theory' until it is supported by empirical data, whereupon it becomes 'fact' or 'reality'" (11).

Existence statements resemble definitions. By contrast, relational statements lie squarely at "the heart of scientific knowledge" (Reynolds 69).

Since mass media include newspapers as well as film, radio, and television, mass media entertainment stretches back to the 15th century in Europe and the 8th century in China. To make theories more relevant, we could limit the time frame to the 20th century, and make ever more concrete statements about the television medium: pleasure and TV programs, pleasure and non-drama TV programs, pleasure and TV game shows.

Needless to say, no one has developed a theory so precise that it relates only to game shows. Nor would such a theory have much value. Thus, instead of reaching down to TV game shows through deduction, in this section we will examine through induction two theories about TV entertainment. To test their applicability, we will set them against the specific game show genre.

TV ENTERTAINMENT AS STORYTELLING. Mendelsohn believes that "fantasy is the key to the entertainment puzzle" (95). Thus his analysis of mass media concen-trates on fiction and drama rather than nonfictional, nondramatic but still entertaining types of programs—such as television game shows. The same premise informed a 1970s conference on television and entertainment and a subsequent book (Tannenbaum) based on the proceedings.

Similarly, Barnouw and Kirkland believe that entertainment represents "an escape from reality ...entertainment in all its forms constitutes a storytelling environment that operates by principles at once implicit and widely shared" (103). Their idea, though not so labelled, contains the elements of a causal process theory. They present a classic existence statement, identifying an object (storytelling) as an instance of a well-established concept (entertainment); they then imply causation (storytelling creates escape). But how does their "theory" of entertainment hold up? Not well, when applied to the game show genre.

Indeed, game shows do have a certain dramatic appeal, thanks to their "cast" (contestants), who create dramatic tension by their words, actions, and interactions; the "bit players" (prize fondlers, hostesses, and letter turners); the "hero," or protagonist (host), who day after day hurls the characters into a tension-filled contest; the formulaic "plot" (the game's rule structure) that features a buildup, climax, and denouement; and a happy ending, as the winner comes center stage and the losers retreat.

But one does not need to fantasize while watching game shows in the way that one "loses oneself" in a televised drama depicting scenes removed from the viewer's life. Furthermore, the fantasy thought that "that could be me" can fairly easily translate into reality, given the tryouts in various cities and the notifications at the end of each show about how to audition when one travels to California.

Zillmann deals solely with suspense in drama. However, the "state of uncertainty" and "state of pleasant excitement about an expected event" (133) that characterize an Alfred Hitchcock or "Murder, She Wrote" episode also characterize game shows on at least two levels. Each segment leaves the viewer wondering "Which contestant will beat out the other(s)?" and at the same time "What is the answer?" In the final "winner's circle" round common to many games, the tension of a real-time clock ticking off the seconds combines with the viewer's uncertainty about answers to the fast-paced questions and whether the contestant will finish with enough points in the allotted time.

One could hypothesize the distress to be even greater in game shows than in dramas, since one's own straining to think of the answers is added to the distress of watching a man/woman in the street come up with the answers under the glare of TV lights, in front of an audience, and at risk of losing major prizes or sums of cash.

We limit our understanding of communication if we simply equate entertainment with drama and storytelling. Game shows, which resemble sports more than they resemble soap operas, have a certain here-and-nowness that differs from the escapist experience of stepping into the Huxtables' (Bill Cosby's) living room or JR'S ranch in Dallas. The active participation that game shows invite goes beyond simple story/drama definitions of entertainment.

Thus, the storytelling theory of entertainment must be made more genre-specific to hold up.

TV ENTERTAINMENT VS. INFORMATION. A second non-labeled theory tackles the false dichotomy between entertainment and informational TV programs. This well-entrenched distinction has bureaucratic roots: first, the institutional division within commercial television; and second, the industry-wide division between commercial and non-commercial ("educational") television.

In the dual system of the United States, the United Kingdom, Israel, Australia, Japan, and other countries, one or more "educational" networks coexist with one or more commercial, entertainment-oriented networks. These "institutional barriers help to...encourage depart-mentalized thinking" (Melnik 145). However, the "myth that 'pure entertainment' exists is one that is slowly but surely being dismantled" (Fischer and Melnik xix).

Indeed, the false division of programs into "information" and "entertainment" means little to researchers, such as George Gerbner's Philadelphia group, who study *television's* (rather than situation comedies' or news shows') long-term effects. Similarly, the enter-education movement ignores the entertainment/information dichotomy by combining the two functions (see Ch. 10) and manipulating the learning function to prescribed ends. The arguments against separating entertainment from information take three forms.

First, a chorus of voices contends that TV entertainment does indeed inform (e.g., Barnouw 102; D. Browne, *Comparing* 58). Viewers may turn to television as a medium of entertainment, relaxation, and enjoyment, but inadvertently—and consistently—they learn from it. Berman states that

> nearly everything we see on television is a form of news. We get enormous amounts of social information dispensed by soaps and sitcoms. And we are continually advised, exhorted, and persuaded to live our lives in certain ways. (103)

Lull confirms that in his interviews with Chinese TV watchers, the inadvertent content (e.g., the scenes shown where the news was taking place or the lifestyle shown and products used in comedies) meant more than the intended content ("Freedom"). Barnouw and Kirkland caution that the enjoyable experience "may indeed inform or persuade, but it is generally presumed that these effects are secondary or incidental and will not interfere with the real function of pleasant diversion" (103). In sum, in the words of FCC Commissioner Nicholas Johnson, "All television is educational. The only question is: what does it teach?"

Second, and conversely, "all media have properties of entertainment" (Fischer and Melnik xiii). Even the nightly TV news is "entertainment and mythology under the respectable guise of 'reality'" (Kaminsky and Mahan 165). As Melnik notes, "A documentary is or can be entertaining...Conversely, entertainment can be informative and can influence" (145).

At a conference on televison's entertainment functions, Bogart discussed TV news as entertainment (Tannenbaum). Berman agrees, arguing that news ("nonfiction programming") is really about ourselves, not outside events (10).

Third, given its complex nature, TV entertainment has complex effects. "Entertainment fulfills a variety of social functions and hence cannot avoid being political in the widest sense of the word" (Fischer and Melnik xix). According to Barnouw and Kirkland, entertainment "has informational content that usually cultivates conventional themes, outlooks and perspectives" (102).

Of all TV genres, game shows best demonstrate the artificial nature of news vs. entertainment boundaries. Some shows (*The Dating Game, Tutti Frutti, Double Dare*) walk and talk like entertainment division products; others (*High Q, College Quiz Bowl*) have the feel and smell of educational television. A few (*Where in the World Is Carmen Sandiego?*) purposefully exploit television's dual nature, entertaining in order to inform (see Ch. 10).

Furthermore, game shows form a microcosm of all TV genres. As we have seen, they somewhat resemble dramas. Like talk shows, they have a host who interviews celebrity and civilian guests-of-the-day. But as we shall see in the next chapter, they resemble most closely televised team sports.

3. Mass entertainment studies: the 1950s and 1960s

According to David Manning White, co-editor of "the first significant contemporary text on the subject in 1957" (Merritt A-6), defining popular culture is like "asking a fish to define water.... [It] is made up of the things that we eat, that we wear, that we listen to, that we read...popular culture is something somebody is willing to pay for" (A-6). But despite or because of their pervasiveness, popular culture in general and mass entertainment in particular have had to fight for academic recognition (R. Browne, "Against").

If Wilbur Schramm "was *the* founding father" of the field of mass communications (McAnany, "Wilbur" 109), he also set the field's direction: political rather than popular or entertainment communication. Schramm worked during World War II with the Office of War Information, 1941-43, and with "the cold war propaganda of the 1950s" (115). This work coalesced with the postwar "ideological struggle with the Soviet Union that would color the remainder of the century with a new peacetime political role for communication" (112).

McAnany even believes that "we can be somewhat precise about the date" that Schramm founded the field: 1948, the year he created the Institute of Communication Research at the University of Illinois ("Wilbur" 112). The subsequent "preference schools or departments of journalism showed for the vast field of political communication" provided "a subject with which they could also legitimize their existence" (Fischer and Melnik 2).

Ironically, 1948 also stands as a landmark in the history of mass entertainment communication. In that year, television established itself in the United States as a true mass entertainment medium. Television's expansion in 1948 "was nothing short of miraculous" (Castleman and Podrazik 37). By fall 1948, the number of stations nearly tripled, to 37 in 22 cities (with another 86 FCC-approved stations about to sign on). For the first time, in fall 1948, the four networks offered full prime-time schedules.

The fall 1948 lineup already included five game shows: *Face the Music* and *What's It Worth?* on CBS;

Charade Quiz on Dumont; *Americana Quiz* on NBC; and *Break the Bank*, which became ABC's first top ten show. An FCC freeze on new stations due to signal interference problems enabled networks to work on programming and production techniques until the freeze ended in 1952.

The Television Age ushered in a new phase of the mass culture debate, which Rowland and Watkins trace back to the Renaissance, when the "rise of commodity culture engendered a series of arguments whose terms remained remarkably common over three or four centuries" (12). By the mid-1950s, as postwar America contemplated "our future as we go into the era of extended leisure," the academy joined the debate (White 21).

David Manning White, who has written this book's foreword, "holds the title as unofficial 'dean' of popular culture studies" (Merritt A-6). White and Rosenberg compiled *Mass Culture* because "no traditional source books were available" on the subject (v). In it, White decries the "rehearsal of all that is ugly and bathetic in our popular arts by critics" and asserts "that it is time that the other side of the coin be examined" (21).

White does not mention quiz shows per se. But another author in his edited text does. Lang uses game shows to stand for the stereotypical "lowbrow" program that by definition attracts a mass audience (380). But labeling, cautions Lang, runs up against "the vagaries of taste" (381), making one generation's vulgarities the "esthetic discoveries" of its children. Mass appeal, concludes Lang, "does not simply reflect an 'average' taste of the general public devoid of a particular slant. It is better visualized as a 'modal' taste.... The lowest common denominator is far from common to all" (384).

White's own defense of television is based on its "promise to the 'average' man that a cultural richness no previous age could give him is at hand"; if television "allowed the majority taste to mandate every taste, then I would agree with these critics" (17). Rowland and Watkins call the text "commentary that grew out of the traditional literary curricula" (12).

White points out that on March 11, 1956, 50 million people watched all or part of "Richard III" on NBC (16). And that in 1955, "youngsters set a record for borrowing books from public libraries" (17). White was writing during the TV Golden Age, before the advent of PBS, when Shakespeare existed side-by-side with big-money, prime-time quiz shows on the commercial networks. But soon television's Golden Age ended, when the power of "the majority taste" (Barnouw 186) changed the nature of commercial television.

Schramm likewise observed television's appeal to the majority, which prompted his search for alternatives. After helping to establish public station KQED in San Francisco in the late 1950s, Schramm began 20 years of "serious written contributions to the field of educational communications" (McAnany, "Wilbur" 116). A lone voice or two reacted *against* Schramm's reactions. In *Mass Entertertainment*, Harold Mendelsohn takes on Schramm's "neo Calvinistic" (24) *Television in the Lives of Our Children*, lambasting "the distinctions that Schramm and his associates make between 'reality orientation' (substitute 'proper behavior') and 'fantasy orientation' (substitute 'improper behavior')."

"At best," writes Mendelsohn

> entertainment receives peripheral attention when communications' effects are investigated.... entertainment is considered to be too frivolous for serious pursuit...because entertainment involves all facets of human activity, the complexity of the problems involved discourage their systematic exploration. (17)

Drawing on history, anthropology, sociology, social psychology, and psychoanalysis, the book explores the reasons that "entertainment is generally equated with evil in our society" (18).

The good vs. evil world view, according to Ray Browne in *Against Academia*, was "a confrontation between the Past and the Present, the Old and the New, the Sleepers and the Wakers, the Knowers and the Learners" (2). Browne meets all the criteria that McAnany applies to Schramm in assessing his impact: editor/publisher, academic institution builder, and prolific writer ("Wilbur" 110). As Mendelsohn was writing his major work in the mid-1960s, Browne embarked on a series of major works and accomplishments.

In 1965, Browne organized a popular culture conference at Purdue University. In 1967, he established the Center for the Study of Popular Culture at Bowling Green (Ohio) State University and created the *Journal of Popular Culture*. In 1970, he founded the Popular Culture Association and established the Popular Press, which that same year published its first book.

Despite this flowering of activity in Ohio, Fischer and Melnik saw entertainment as an

> area of mass communication research in which there is an enormous deficit.... Such neglect was (and still is) perhaps due

to the stigma attached to such products, a lack of awareness as to their possible functions and far-reaching significance and a lack of adequate and common conceptual tools (at least until fairly recently). (2)

Fairly recently, a subfield of voices has grown in the field of entertainment television research.

4. Entertainment TV studies: the 1970s and 1980s

By the 1970s, in the words of social scientist Elihu Katz ("Can Authentic..."), it was time "to take entertainment seriously." "One wonders," agreed Tannenbaum, "how it [television's entertainment function] has been neglected so long" (2). Tannenbaum specifically decries the "paucity of research on the significance of entertainment in everyday life...Scholars of television, particularly, avoid this phenomenon at their own peril" (1).

Like observers of game shows (see Ch. 1), observers of mass-mediated culture seem to fall into two groups: critics and "celebrators" (Real 31). From 19th-century commentator de Tocqueville to Allan Bloom, pessimistic critics "wring their hands over the deplorable state of the popular arts" (30). Social philosophers such as Jacques Ellul lament mass media's depersonalized technology. Humanist Daniel Boorstin sees an aversion to televsion on the part of academics, who "are troubled by the way television trespasses on the book. Of course, TV is 'vulgar'—because it's not in their control" (70).

In *Amusing Ourselves to Death*, one of television's critics, Neil Postman, presents a "lamentation about the most significant American cultural fact of the second half of the twentieth century: the decline of the Age of Typography and the ascendancy of the Age of Television" (8).

Postman, a student but not a disciple of Marshall McLuhan's, believes that public business has been "recast in terms that are most suitable to television" (8). The political functions of television bother Postman, but not its entertainment function:

> I raise no objection to television's junk. The best things on television *are* its junk, and no one and nothing is seriously threatened by it.... television is at its most trivial and, therefore, most dangerous when its aspirations are high, when it presents itself as a carrier of important cultural conversations. The irony here is that this is what intellectuals and critics are constantly urging television to do. (16)

Postman would, thus, not object to game shows, which he would surely define as "junk," but to a political TV advertisement using a game format:

> But what I am claiming here is not that television is entertaining but that it has made entertainment itself the natural format for the representation of all experience.... The problem is not that television presents us with entertaining subject matter but that all subject matter is presented as entertainment, which is another issue altogether.
>
> To say it another way: Entertainment is the supraideology of all discourse on television. (87)

The celebrators of mass-mediated culture include those who praise the access and vast marketplace that television has created, as well as the academic "scholar-fan" (Real

32). Enter-educationists (see Ch. 10) form a special subgroup of celebrators.

A watershed academic conference on television and entertainment took place in the mid-1970s, after which the proceedings appeared as a book titled *The Entertainment Functions of Television,* edited by Percy Tannenbaum. The phrases "game show" and "quiz show" do not appear in the index, nor does the title to any particular game/quiz show. "Entertainment program" in this volume is equated with drama and fiction; even news programs are analyzed in terms of drama, fantasy, and fiction.

Tannenbaum's one-time conference could not match for number and variety the academic papers on TV entertainment presented at the meetings of the Popular Culture Association and the American Culture Association. By the same token, the journals that emanate from the Center for the Study of Popular Culture have carried far more papers on TV entertainment than the single Tannenbaum volume, especially the *Journal of Popular Film,* which added *"and Television"* to its name in 1978.

According to Ray Browne, the Center was "created to cover the publication of the *Journal of Popular Culture* and other publications and activities, some of which I foresaw in 1968 and some of which I did not foresee" (*Against* 78). Browne launched the *Journal of American Culture* in 1978 to capture all facets of Americana—"from 'elite' to popular and folk culture on a continuum" (59). Consequently, in 1979, "the creation of a national association that would parallel the purpose of the magazine seemed warranted" (61).

The Popular Culture Association's first national meeting at Michigan State University in 1971 featured 42 sessions, including three (7 percent) on television (topics: black stereotypes, soap operas, and "reshaping the mind"). The American Culture Association's first meeting, held jointly with the PCA's ninth annual convention in Pittsburgh in 1979, featured 49 sessions, including three devoted solely or partly to television.

By 1990, at the PCA's 20th annual meeting in Toronto, combined with the ACA's 12th annual meeting, the number of sessions had increased to 538, of which 20 (3.7 percent) had "television" or "soap opera" in their titles. Thus about 5 percent of ACA/PCA papers 1970-90 have dealt with television. The PCA's publication, the *Journal of Popular Culture*, devotes about 10 percent of its articles to television.

In addition, other academic journals devote some space to TV entertainment studies (e.g., about 15 percent of articles in the *Journal of Communication*). Finally, certain divisions of other organizations' conventions (e.g., Association for Education in Journalism and Mass Communication, International Association for Mass Communication Research and International Communication Association) devote some time to TV entertainment studies, whether content, audience, or practitioner research.

Since the present volume is a content study of TV game shows, an overview of studies of all other TV content lies beyond its scope. (Ch. 5 will review previous research specifically on game shows.)

Chapter 3

THEORIES OF INTERNATIONAL MASS COMMUNICATION

The technology of communication is, generally speaking, universal; but the contents and functions of communication are culture-bound. (Kato, "Essays" 6)

Three sets of theories competing in the international communications marketplace might not seem relevant to game shows at first blush. Indeed, the first part of this chapter will not mention game shows very often. But the general context of these communication theories will embrace game shows as a particular manifestation eventually. As we noted in Chapter 2, sometimes positions and statements carry all the elements of theories, even if no one has actually labeled them as such.

Theory Set 1 deals with the matter of domestic vs. foreign television. One camp (the cultural imperialists) says that Western (especially U.S.) TV programs have the power to overwhelm local cultures; the working concepts include a powerless audience and powerful mass media. Another camp (the localists) says the opposite; its working concepts include an active audience and strong local cultures.

Theory Set 2 deals with the effects of technology on local societies. The unification proponents have a common ancestor in McLuhan, who wrote that "electrically contracted, the globe is no more than a village" (20). The national village proponents contend that persons within a country may watch some of the same news events and entertainment programs, but persons in different countries have largely different mass media experiences.

Theory Set 3 more accurately could be called a question with three different answers: How can we best understand mass media in cultures outside our own? Anthropology stress a deep study of the forces that shape one culture. British cultural studies stress class differences as related to information access across societies. Comparative research, which measures similarities within one cultural aspect (e.g., the mass media) across societies, has generated the most concrete body of mass media findings. This chapter will look at each theory set in turn.

1. Domestic vs. imported television

In four separate trips covering seven months in Asia in the mid l980s, Iyer observed the "Coca-Colonizing forces" as "America's pop-cultural imperialism spread throughout the world" (5). Iyer, a former writer for *Time* magazine, describes more than he indicts, commenting that "the most remarkable anomalies in the global village are surely those created by willy-nilly collisions and collusions between East and West."

Because Iyer pleads guilty to parachute tourism rather than cultural immersion, he limits his examples primarily to pop music, movies, and visible storefronts—not television. Without a knowledge of the local languages, his observations cannot include game shows in indigenous languages, but rather include "the local bands in Socialist Burma that play note-perfect versions of the Doors' 'LA Woman' in Burmese;

the American tenpin bowling alley that is the latest nighttime hotspot in Beijing; the Baskin-Robbins imitation in Hiroshima" (Iyer 10-11).

Iyer sees contradictions rather than conspiracies when First and Third worlds meet, noting that "the Communist guerillas in the Philippines fight capitalism while wearing UCLA T-shirts" (12). Seeing the Third World as actively rather than passively consuming U.S. culture, Iyer comes close to reinventing the active audience idea in a rebuttal of media imperialism:

> To mention, however faintly, the West's cultural assault on the East is, inevitably, to draw dangerously close to the fashionable belief that the First World is corrupting the Third.... we often assert a kind of sentimental colonialism that would replace Rambo myths and conclude that because the First World feels guilty, the Third World must be innocent...This, however, I find simplistic—both because corruption often says most about those who detect it and because the developing world may often have good reason to assent in its own transformation. (13)

Empirical studies corroborate Iyer's observation. Liebes and Katz state, "The Japanese had a number of homemade choices to which they clearly felt greater affinity" than to the U.S. show, *Dallas* (131).

Herbert Schiller, on the other hand, has long disagreed with the active audience idea. He first blamed the U.S. government and, later, multinational corporations for imposing "colonial servitude" in their control of other nations' media choices (*Mass* 2). "Messages 'made in America,'" wrote Schiller, "radiate across the globe and serve as the ganglia of national power and expansion" (*Mass* 147-48).

In the 1970s, Schiller "articulated the tenets of a theology of an American information empire" (Stevenson 36). Schiller's *Mass Communication and American Empire* (1971) and *Communication and Cultural Domination* (1976) were followed by Jeremy Tunstall's *The Media Are American*, Anthony Smith's *The Geopolitics of Information,* and Thomas McPhail's *Electronic Colonialism.*

Stevenson groups Schiller with "an impressive list of Marxists and neo-Marxists": Kaarle Nordenstreng of Finland; Juan Somavia of Chile; and Mustapha Masmoudi of Tunisia, "who, more than anyone else, brought the new world information order [NWIO] issue before the UNESCO" (36).

TV entertainment programming played a part in the NWIO debate, chiefly as an example of imbalanced North-to-South communication flows (Varis). But the very phrase INFORMATION order betrays the news/technology orientation of the debate, which raged most intensely 1974-84 (see Table 3.1). As transnational entertainment issues grew more prominent, information issues quieted down.

THREE TRENDS. In the mid-to-late 1980s, three trends emerged. *First,* research began to prove or discount many of the NWIO charges. *Second,* the concept of information was partially replaced on the international communication agenda by the concept of culture, which relates more closely to entertainment. *Third,* U.S.-to-Europe TV entertainment flows joined U.S.-to-Third World TV entertainment flows as an arena of political and academic concern.

Table 3.1

The New World Information Order Debate, 1970-90

1970	UNESCO 16th General Conference, Paris. The first resolution regarding mass media is placed on conference agenda.
1972	UNESCO 17th General Conference, Paris. The first resolution on the "use" of mass media is presented.
1974	UNESCO 18th General Conference, Paris. Amadou Mahtar M'Bow of Senegal is elected new director-general.
1976	UNESCO 19th General Conference, Nairobi. MacBride Commission appointed; IAMCR multi-country media study requested. (First UNESCO meeting in Africa.)
1978	UNESCO 20th General Conference, Belgrade. Resolution on "contribution" (NOT "use") of mass media is passed.
1980	The MacBride Commission report, *Many Voices, One World* is released.
1981	Western media representatives, meeting at Talloires, France, issue declaration support-ing free flow of ideas.
1984	The United States withdraws from UNESCO.
1985	UNESCO 23rd General Conference. The United Kingdom and Singapore withdraw from UNESCO; absence of these three members costs UNESCO 1/3 of budget.
1987	UNESCO 24th General Conference, Paris. M'Bow steps down; Federico Mayor of Spain is elected director-general, vowing to deemphasize NWIO.
1989	UNESCO 25th General Conference, Paris.
1990	State Department report affirms U.S. decision to stay out of UNESCO: United Kingdom also affirms decision.

Although most of the research dealt with international news flows (e.g., Stevenson and Shaw; Larson), some dealt with entertainment. Varis, who studied TV programs in 69 countries for two weeks in 1983, found imports to account for one-third or more of total programming time. But individual countries varied greatly. In Latin America, for example, Ecuador imported 66 percent of total programs, but Brazil, only 30 percent; in Asia/Oceania, New Zealand imported 72 percent of total programs, but China, only 8 percent. Varis found that "the bulk of imported programs originate in the United States and—although to a lesser extent—in Western Europe and Japan" (150).

But what about the actual effects of imported TV entertainment on indigenous cultures? Wang and Dissanayake, who reviewed a large number of studies relating to Asian media, conclude that "whether indigenous cultures disintegrate under the dominance of television is debatable" (25). Mondol, concurring, states

> The impact of TV on the culture of Third World nations in Asia is a complex blend of ingredients. It is only one of the "spices" in a rich Asiatic (electronic) "curry." As the Asian viewer watches a program, he or she filters and reprocesses the images and actions according to his or her own perceptions and values. (36)

The theme of the 16th Biennial Conference of the International Association for Mass Communication Research in Barcelona in 1988, "Social Communication and Cultural Identity," struck a nerve in countries as diverse as the Netherlands (Servaes), Ghana (Ansah), and Ivory Coast

(Land). Both Western and Third World critics of Western television may confuse WESTERN ideas and technology with inevitable MODERN ideas and technology. Neither need threaten a local culture.

As Ansah (18) points out, "If the cultural base is solid, foreign imports will mean an enrichment rather than a dilution of the essence of a national or ethnic culture." To shore up that base and avoid dependency, more local programming should be done. Ansah cautions, however:

> Entertainment should not be seen merely as trivial or neutral, with the functional objective of providing diversion and escapism from the harsh realities of existence...but as a potent force in the inculcation and dissemination of values. (26)

Land argues that an active audience exists in the Ivory Coast, where citizens "are not passive recipients of First World culture.... assimilation depends more on the one 'being assimilated' than on the one doing the assimilating" (1273). In Malaysia, Muslim families watch the depiction of sex between unmarried couples and use the shows to tell their children what not to do (Mondol 36).

In the 1980s, just as in the 1970s, Schiller's works may exemplify changing academic emphases. After *Who Knows: Information in the Age of the Fortune 500* (1981) and *Information and the Crisis Economy* (1984), Schiller turned from information to culture.

In *Culture, Inc.* (1989), Schiller argues that beginning about 1985, privatization of mass media accelerated "as global capital brushes aside public need and social obligation" (145). The old "limited effects" paradigm reemerged, but this time applied to the international arena and bolstered by the idea of an audience empowered to choose from a limitless media array. "Yet what is the actual diversity that is available over multichannel systems?" asks Schiller (*Culture* 147). "Has not cable television, no less than the networks, been swallowed by the big information-cultural combines?" Both the active-audience and limited-effects ideas are myths, he believes.

With the jury still out on television's precise effects, the critical theorists like Schiller and the empirical researchers continued on paths that still remain separate to this day (Wartella). Politicians and voters, however, heed the more compelling cultural imperialists rather than the less alarmist empiricists—not just in the Third World, but in an advanced country like Canada as well. In 1983, the Canadian Radio and Television Commission stated:

> ...if Canadians do not use what is one of the world's most extensive and sophisticated communications systems to speak to themselves—if it serves only for the importation of foreign programs—there is a real and legitimate concern that the country will ultimately lose the means of expressing its identity. (Artwick 4)

The 1988 Canada-U.S. Free Trade Agreement included a cultural exemption that enabled Canada to regulate trade in cultural products.

In Europe, two factors in the late 1980s created apprehension over U.S. programs. First, privatization in Italy, France, and the United Kingdom created a sales boom in programs as new channels filled their schedules, with prices increasing by as much as 300 percent a day. Second, pan-European satellite channels "swooped down on Hollywood with bulging checkbooks," ready to buy (Beck 46).

The European Community's argument for quotas on imported programs reflected cultural worries:

> [the] fear that homogenized programming from the outside would drown out European cultural diversity and provide no reflection of separate national cultures, and of concern that alien values would dominate television schedules. (Bjork 1 4)

The American argument against quotas cited restraint of trade while dismissing the cultural concerns. Jack Valenti, president of the Motion Picture Association of America, could not see how an "American television program is going to collapse 2500 years of culture or somehow stunt and atrophy all of the great legends, myths, and truths and triumphs of French culture."

On Oct. 3, 1989, after years of debate, the Council of European Communities adopted the following directive:

> Member States shall ensure where practicable and by appropriate means, that broadcasters reserve for European works, within the meaning of Article 6, a majority proportion of their transmission time, excluding the time appointed to news, sports events, games, advertising and teletext services. (No. L 298/26)

The directive had as its source a green paper, *Television Without Frontiers*, which reviewed the cultural and social aspects of television within the EC. It stressed the themes of European integration and freedom from outside influence:

...most of the films shown come from one single non-member country—the U.S.A. As a result there is already a certain uniformity in the range of films screened on television in the Community. Programmes such as *Dallas* are carried by almost every television channel in the Member States. The creation of a common market for television production is thus one essential step if dominance of the big American media corporations is to be counterbalanced. (33)

Without quite using the phrase "media imperialism," Jean-Michel Gaillard, head of France's Antenne 2 state-owned TV network, says, "We can't any longer be invaded by programs from abroad, which threaten to submerge us" (Revzin B3).

Apart from the cultural issues, the directive aims to build up Europe's own program production industry. The United States "now sells programming to European television stations at a price European producers can't compete with" (Artwick 5). In 1993, France was still asking for restrictions on U.S. feature film imports in General Agreement on Tariffs and Trade negotiations.

"Stop the Global Village," Europeans seem to be saying. "We want to get off!" But are between-nation forces really stronger than within-nation forces?

2. Global vs. national villages

Are we moving together or farther apart? (Hachten 146). The debate over which force pulls more strongly ensues in various disciplines (Hachten 8-13). Cousins, for example, comes down on the side of "togetherness":

...a world geographic unit is moving toward a world community. The world's people still live inside national

> borders, but human consciousness is being stretched to embrace a sense of common challenge and common destiny. (18)

By contrast, Berry contends that "global thinking is not possible," because it is too abstract (62). Similarly, Boulding cautions:

> We are so much in the middle of the development of world communication systems that it is difficult to predict its consequences. But we must be careful not to exaggerate its consequences, for the world is not a "global village"—it just has too many people in it. (151)

NEWS

Among mass media scholars, Real contends that mass media ("supermedia") celebrate human solidarity:

> the media provide us access to and participation in our collectively shared symbols and acts. These media celebrations reflect and reinforce many of our most cherished moments and values—in the signing of an arms control agreement, in the launching of a space flight, in the selection of a president. (256)

Like Real, we think of the same international events over and over because so few rank as truly significant worldwide: a moon walk, a royal wedding, the Olympics, a devastating earthquake, the fall of the Berlin Wall. However, Cooper-Chen in a five-country study of TV news September 1-5, 1986, found agreement on only two major stories: the Aero-Mexico jet/private plane collision in California and the Pan Am jet hijacking in Pakistan ("A Week"). Other major events made the evening news in some nations but not others, and with differing emphases. For example, Sri Lanka covered the Non-Aligned Summit in Zimbabwe extensively; Japan, not at all.

The global village idea applies to technical possibilities; yes, satellites can permit almost every country to transmit in timely fashion scenes of the Armenian earthquake and the opening of the Brandenburg Gate. But even the so-called global networks take differing slants, as anyone who has watched BBC-TV's international service, CNN International, and CNN domestic can attest.

The Olympics comes to U.S. viewers over NBC from Barcelona—quite a different Olympics from that seen in Japan. Granted, the golden long jumping of Carl Lewis or the missteps of Kim Zemaskal look the same (except perhaps for camera angles) in Japan and the United States. Yet the anchors and sports-specific commentators and obviously their dialogue will differ from country to country. And aside from the Gold Medal competitions shown in their entirety, selection of what portions of what competitions at what level of the elimination process will differ according to each country's gatekeeper-editors.

Thus Real lacks a much-needed phrase to complete his lofty sentiment: "Popular media today operate on a scale of inclusiveness unimaginable in earlier generations. The earth's population is drawn ineluctably toward media dependency"—IN THEIR OWN COUNTRY, THROUGH THE LENS OF THEIR OWN COUNTRY'S MEDIA (15).

Condry, a national village proponent, notes:

McLuhan's prediction was too broad. He should have noted that the first effect of television would be to turn nations into villages, to make them more aware of themselves. When President John F. Kennedy was shot, an entire nation watched on television. As if we were in a single village where a leader had been murdered, we reacted to events as they happened. We saw them happen, we listened as our elders (Walter Cronkite, Chet Huntley, etc.) told us the mournful story. (273)

If McLuhan's prediction was too broad, Condry's assessment is too narrow. The news perspective he takes masks possible commonalities that cross borders. Localities produce *local news* shows.

Most nations have one or more nationwide newscasts (government-controlled, government-advised or independent) that sums up national and international happenings. A nation's people need to know about tax law changes, border disputes, elections, college entrance exam results, problems with the train system, and weather—in the language(s) of the country.

A better gauge exists to help us see communication patterns, whether local, global, or something else. To best see patterns, we should consider TV entertainment.

ENTERTAINMENT

A cultural anthropologist's work in Brazil confirmed others' observations about preference for local entertainment programs:

...the most popular network relies heavily on native productions. *Dallas* and *Dynasty* draw minuscule audiences...American programming that is culturally alien and inappropriate for local conditions will not do very well anywhere when a quality local choice is available. (Kottak 16)

Furthermore, Kottak confirms the national village idea—especially germane in the case of Brazil, a diverse nation with many hitherto isolated populations which now constitutes the world's single largest national audience: "It isn't North American culture but a new pan-Brazilian national culture that Brazilian TV is propagating...The programs that attract this horde are made by Brazilians, for Brazilians" (16).

In studying European TV entertainment, Tapio Varis found that 30 percent of programs in Western Europe were imported—44 percent of them from the United States ("International"). Thus 13 percent of European televison originated in the United States. However, Varis does not discuss the popularity of this 13 percent, which would tell us whether audiences were flocking to them by choice or whether they were used as filler in a medium that devours material and always hungers for more. In fact, most U.S. shows rate no higher than in the top 20 to 50 rather than the top 10. Citing examples from West Germany and Brazil, Artwick asserts that audiences "prefer their own sitcoms and action shows which include jokes and situations closer to home" (19).

Goonaskera cites studies from Indonesia, Taiwan, and Sri Lanka showing that rural audiences do not like foreign programs because they cannot relate to the experiences and events portrayed. A growing body of evidence shows that, when well-produced indigenous programs compete with imports, audiences prefer the local product (Wildman and Siwek).

Furthermore, "indigenous" need not necessarily conform to political boundaries. Varis notes a "trend toward greater regional exchanges" ("International"

150). In Arab countries, about one-third of imports come from other Arab states; in Latin America, about ten percent of imports come from regional neighbors. But unofficial "imports" make assessments of influence difficult. "Cross-border broadcasting, or signal overspill, also complicates the task of correctly identifying importing and exporting" (Wildman and Siwek 38). Spillover signals from West Germany surely played some role in East Germany's revolution and reunification.

Writing more recently, Sepstrup, a professor in Denmark, documents which programs of what sorts flow from which nations in Europe. Contending that Euro-regionalism is growing, he argues against the theory of cultural imperialism, which he thinks lacks academic rigor.

Linguistic and cultural minority groups form another network of potential audiences for films and TV programs. Indian productions in Hindi and Tamil now reach these linguistic groups throughout Southeast Asia. Hong Kong exports Kung Fu action dramas to Chinese populations throughout the world. Conversely, language can act as a barrier to programs from close neighbors with different cultures. "Why," asks Artwick, "should one expect a French audience to accept Italian programming, or Spanish viewers to watch British television?" (22). The predilection for TV programs made in one's home country by and for one's compatriots seems clear. Some contrary evidence indicates that U.S. programs cross borders better than those of any other country, which may simply indicate their "nowness" rather than the intrinsic appeal of U.S. culture. Perhaps U.S. programs cross borders because they must appeal to the broad, many-cultured (or non-cultured) U.S. public.

Artwick cites three examples indicating that non-U.S. audiences like U.S. programs. In Italy, the three private networks, which run schedules heavy on U.S. shows, do well against RAI, the public network (20-21). In Viet Nam, in the late 1960s, millions of urban Vietnamese preferred the U.S. armed forces network to the Vietnamese-language network with indigenous content (the opposite of villagers' preferences). In Saudi Arabia, students said they preferred U.S. videocassettes over other nations' programs, including those from Egypt. Rebuttals to these phenomena argue *for* preference for one's own programs (Artwick 21). High production values and diversity of content may account for the popularity of U.S. shows rather than wholesale disdain for one's own cultural products.

One arena that U.S. firms do better in than anyone, it seems, is the commercial feature film. Indeed, "better than half of Hollywood's income derives from business abroad, a large percentage of it from the continent" (Hift 14). In the future, "more production companies may simply hire Hollywood consultants" to help give European television and films that "American commercial touch." When it comes to game shows, format transfers (see Ch. 6) offer foreign-proved production values combined with local cultural values and personalities.

3. Cultural anthropology and cultural studies

"A nation's culture," writes Simon Hoggart of the *London Observer*, "is always more interesting than its politics, as every foreign correspondent knows." And within an interesting, "foreign" culture, TV entertainment is surely its most acessible aspect, aside from its cuisine.

But what is "culture"? Definitions vary widely. According to Martin,

> Culture, like communication, may be thought of in terms of a continuum. Culture ranges from an individual's unique patterned ways of behaving, feeling and reacting to certain universal norms that are rooted in common biological needs of mankind. (430)

Servaes, also a mass media scholar, defines culture as

> a phenomenon whose content differs from community to community. Therefore, as each culture operates out of its own logic, each culture has to be analyzed on the basis of its own "logical" structure. (843)

To Real, author of *Supermedia*, culture is "the systematic way of construing reality that a people acquires as a consequence of living in a group" (36).

The deepest understanding of culture, however, comes from the field of cultural anthropology, one of four approaches to studying non-Western cultures, along with linguistics, physical anthropology and archaeology (Ulin 2). According to noted cultural anthropologist Clifford Geertz, culture is the concept "around which the whole discipline of anthropology arose" (4). Geertz defines culture as "the webs of significance [man] himself has spun" (5).

E.B.Tylor in his *Primitive Culture,* published in 1871, defined culture as that "complex whole which includes knowledge, belief, art, morals, customs and many other capabilities and habits acquired by man as a member of society" (qtd. in Briggs 437).

Similarly, Kottak defines culture as "knowledge, beliefs, perceptions, attitudes, expectations, values, and patterns of behavior that people learn by growing up in a given society." To an anthropologist, "not just university graduates, but all people are cultured" (Kottak 8). Enculturation is "the process whereby one grows up in a particular society and absorbs its culture" (8).

"All anthropological approaches to culture center, however, on regularities within cultural patterns, explicit or implicit," writes Briggs (437). "Culture is seen as being transmitted from one generation to the next through symbols and through artifacts, through records and through living traditions."

Traditional cultural anthropology does not deal with mass media. In Ulin's *Cultural Anthropology*, for example, the words "media" and "television" do not appear in the index. Nor does Bernard mention these topics as avenues of inquiry in *Research Methods in Cultural Anthropology.* Bernard does caution, however, against "a danger that anthropologists will be relegated to the role of curiosity hunters, and that we will play an even smaller role in the future of social science" (25-26).

Kottak specifically wonders

> how my more traditional colleagues in anthropology have managed to avoid being interested in television—so striking are the behavioral modifications it has wrought in the natives we see and talk to most frequently: our fellow citizens in modern society....
>
> Psychologists are still debating the precise effects of television on *individual* behavior and psycho-pathology.... However, television's *cultural* effects are indubitable. (7-8)

Anthropologists pursue this central question regarding culture: *"How is cultural diversity both influencing and being affected by larger forces?"* (14). One such force, television, has influence comparable to the family, the church, and the school. Specifically, culture affects television in these areas: 1) program content; 2) viewer preferences; 3) viewer interpre-tations; and 4) impact of messages on viewers (14). Kottak summarizes his thesis regarding television as follows:

> New culture patterns related to television's penetration of the American home have emerged since the l950s. As *technology*, television affects collective behavior, as people duplicate, in many areas of their lives, habits developed while watching TV. Television *content* also influences mass culture because it provides widely shared common knowledge, beliefs, and expectations. (9)

Kottak's inspiration came from a researcher who studied not television, but pre-media society in Bali: Clifford Geertz. Geertz ranks as one of 21 "late 20th century theorists" that Beniger isolated in the 1,800-page *International Encyclopedia of Communication* (710). However, comparative mass media studies have not heretofore relied on anthropology, nor has Clifford Geertz had much influence on mass media scholars. The plumbing of other disciplines to find relevant insights for mass media research is a hallmark of the field. The present study aims to give what Geertz calls "thick descriptions" by watching the recorded behavior of persons on TV game shows (6).

> Culture is public because meaning is. You can't wink (or burlesque one) without knowing what counts as winking or how to

contract your eyelids...But to draw from such truths the conclusion that knowing how to wink is winking...is to betray as deep a confusion as, taking thin descriptions for thick, to identify winking with eyelid contractions. (12)

All anthropological writings are second- or third-order interpretations. "By definition, only a 'native' makes first order ones; it's *his* culture," explains Geertz (15). Furthermore, says Geertz

it is not necessary to know everything in order to understand something.... Cultural analysis is (or should be) guessing at meanings, assessing the guesses, and drawing explanatory conclusions from the better guesses. (20)

The problem as Geertz sees it is "how to get from a collection of miniatures...to wall-sized culturescapes of the nation, the epoch" (21). He elaborates:

The great natural variation of cultural forms is, of course, not only anthropology's great (and wasting) resource, but the ground of its deepest theoretical dilemma: how is such variation to be squared with the biological unity of the human species? (22-23)

This study will aim to follow Geertz's cautions. Game shows are rituals of behavior, highly refined by rules and time constraints. An observer sees miniatures (one type of TV show) of natives of a culture behaving. Some game shows would not work except in their own culture. Either the content or the length differs—no ten-hour show could survive in the United States, but one does in Brazil. The game shows on TV have made it—either by ratings or someone's decision in a noncommercial system that is a top-down culture. They are part of the culture.

The use of video "records" of how people function in a culture-bound situation has a long history in anthropology. Franz Boas (1858-1942) used both photography and film in his field work, one of the first anthropologists to do so. His student Margaret Mead made many films with her third husband, Gregory Bateson, including the comparative ethnographic work "Bathing Babies in Three Cultures."

Recently communication researchers have found insights by employing anthropological methods. James Lull, who suggested the approach in the late 1970s, used it in both his *World Families Watch Television* and *Inside Family Viewing: Ethnographic Research on Television's Audiences*.

Conversely, a few anthrolpologists have begun to study communication. From 1983 to 1987, Kottak studied television in Brazil, using content analysis; interviews with experts and TV personnel; archival and statistical research; and field study at six rural communities.

Cultural studies tried and rejected ethnographic research such as that of Margaret Mead because that approach "offered no easy route to the study of relations *between* cultures and subcultures; it tended to obscure...the relations between classes" (Streeter 77).

The Birmingham Centre for Contemporary Cultural Studies "questions what seems to be obvious" (Streeter 75). Raymond Williams and Richard Hoggart, key figures in British cultural studies, grew up in the working class without any disdain for popular literature. As an antidote to quantitative social science, the center turned to Western

Marxists and European Structuralists such as Levi-Strauss, who study patterns and relations.

Raymond Williams, who died in 1988, used "inductive cultural analysis derived from the tradition of close reading of literary texts" (Garnham 123). Although a socialist intellectual, he took a positive view of popular, commercial culture. For him, "communication and culture... were in his work almost interchangeable" (Garnham 126).

4. Comparative TV studies

From all manner of voices comes a call for comparative mass media research. Schramm called it "a promising field of study within the larger field of international communication" (Edelstein, *Comparative* 7). Schramm added, "In the decades to come, it may actually prove one of the best investments for all of us" (Edelstein, *Comparative* 11).

Wartella wants more comparative audience research. But comparing mass media audiences (individuals) has many potential pitfalls, points out Schramm:

> For example, when an American and a Bolivian are asked to rate, on a 10-point scale, their satisfaction with standard of living and each records a 6, one might mean that he is able to buy a yacht and send his children to an expensive private school, and the other might mean simply that he can afford to buy enough food and clothing for his family—in other words, functional rather than absolute equivalence. (Edelstein, *Comparative* 10-11)

In addition, language equivalence and meaning equivalence can make research with questionnaires difficult. Behavior equivalence (behavior that looks similar but has different meanings in different cultures) can cause misinterpretation in observational research. "Difficulties like these are one reason why theory is scant in the comparative field," concludes Schramm (11). In reviewing comparative studies from the 1950s to 1980, Edelstein concludes that

> there were very substantial commonalities across social groups in the several cultures that were studied...That is, when one compared age, sex, and education groups across cultures, there were great similarities among individuals in their uses of mass communication; but within cultures, there were great variations among social classes in their media utilities. (*Comparative* 7 6)

Ten years later, Edelstein asserted:

> As comparativists, you should identify and discuss the common bases of societies. The real question is the influence of the larger culture [on mass media]. Don't make comparisons if [situations] are too similar or too different. Our goal in comparative research is looking for commonalities but expecting differences. ("Comparative")

Rollin defined comparative popular culture as "scholarship that makes a deliberate effort to compare and contrast the culture consumed by masses of people in two different countries or world regions" (3).

Ray Browne, who writes of "Internationalizing PCA/ACA," received an enthusiastic reception in Japan, China, Russia, and Mexico (*Against* 70-77). Browne states:

> ...popular culture is an international language. American popular culture scholars should be interested in and should study those cultures of other countries. In doing so we can remove some of the provincialism that seems to permeate our culture and especially our students' lives. Popular culture studies can and should be a two-way street with mutual education along the way and reaped at the end. International understanding is too important not to be sought in every possible way. ("Against" 76-77)

Regarding television specifically, comparative research can help us isolate "television's impact as technology (relatively constant) from the impact of its content (much more cross-culturally variable" (Kottak 15).

Despite all the calls for more comparative research, relatively little exists. As Edelstein points out, journals of comparative studies exist in many fields ("Comparative") (e.g., *The Journal of Cross-cultural Psychology*). Why not in mass media? Or why not in popular culture? Articles could come from any country, as long as they compared two or more cultures on some popular culture dimension.

Schramm himself carried out one of the earliest true comparative content studies (of the 1956 Hungary and Suez crises). Like the Schramm study (*One*), much comparative content analysis deals with news, either in print media or, less commonly, on television (e.g., Cooper-Chen "A Week"; Straubhaar et al.) or even both print and television (Sreberny-Mohammadi et al.). Little deals with entertainment television, most of that with drama (e.g., Iwao, Pool, and Hagiwara). Now and then comparative studies on journalists themselves appear (e.g., Noelle-Neumann, E.R. Kocher, and P. Elliott).

Some entertainment TV research compares audiences. Liebes and Katz explored differing interpretations of *Dallas* in six cultures (the United States, Japan, and four ethnic groups in Israel). Kubey and Csikszentmihalyi get to the heart of the anthropological dilemma that the unified human species has so many variations in culture.

> ...the consistency of the patterns we have found may suggest the anthropological notion of the so-called "psychic unity of humankind." At least as far as television viewing is concerned and the samples studied, human consciousness operates in similar ways irrespective of differences in age and culture. (94)

When looking at the similarity of effects, we must remember that these 1980s' studies did not concentrate on content. For example, older people may watch more news and Italian teens watch more MTV-type of programming. What evokes relaxation in one country may differ from what evokes it in another.

More to the point: what constitutes a playful game show in one culture may (and does) differ from that kind of playful show in another. The macro view says, "Human beings react similarly to the experience of TV." The micro, anthropological view says, "See how different the TV creations are that entertain people in this culture when you compare them with what entertains people in this other culture."

Szalai and colleagues, using time diaries from 25,000 subjects, conducted a 12-nation study on leisure and media use in 1965-66. Unfortunately, in those years fewer than half of those surveyed in some countries had TV sets.

Since 1965, television viewing has taken over more free time and seems to have displaced to some extent newspaper reading. But "television does not increase disproportionately with greater amounts of free time" (Robinson 414).

Most research on TV's influence has dealt with children; except for "uses and grats" approaches, little has dealt with adults (Katz, Gurevitch, and Haas). Rating service data tell us that, worldwide, women watch more than men do; in the United States, weekday viewing (10 a.m.-6:30 p.m.) accounts for 17 percent of women's total viewing week, but only 6 percent of men's (Newton and Buck 290-91).

Women's use of broadcast soap operas has been well studied—starting even before the age of television (Herzog). Japanese women's soap opera viewing has also been studied (Muramatsu). Game shows are even more popular and consume more TV hours than soaps, yet remain unstudied except for ratings data, which tell us that more women than men watch them in some cultures.

In a study of adults in five countries—Japan, Korea, the Philippines, Britain, and the United States—Newton and Buck found "more differences on specific variables related to gender than to culture" (302). In all five cultures, women watched more than men did.

Other cross-cultural differences also exist; "it appears that exposure to television does not operate in the same way across cultures" (Newton and Buck 305). For example, in the United States, individuals who watched television heavily had less egalitarian attitudes, whereas in Asia the opposite held true. Except for education, most variables did not correlate with exposure, considering men and women together:

> the social/psychological importance to an individual viewer is more than simply the amount of time he or she spends in front of the screen. (304)

Salomon believes that cross-cultural TV studies should involve more than individual psychological effects:

> the introduction of a commodity or technology into culturally different communities easily leads to differential effects.... The meaning each culture attributes to the novelty, the way it perceives it and thus *experiences* it, makes this "common" commodity far from common. (382)

In his summary chapter in a book comparing six broadcast systems, Browne emphasizes that all six exist "to distribute programming, but it is quite easy to lose sight of that purpose in the thicket of structural considerations that surrounds broadcast systems" (*Comparing* 385). Depending on whether one stands far back or close enough to see detail, the six countries' TV content looks either quite similar or quite different. All six provide news and entertainment, points out Browne:

> One can go a step further and state that every system provides national and international news, "serious" and "light" entertainment, programming intended particularly for adults, particularly for children, and so on. Every system also forbids certain sorts of program content...And there are some overall similarities in scheduling, especially in the placement of major newscasts and most of the more expensive programs in the evening hours... (*Comparing* 385-86)

Schedules in the various countries devote similar percentages of time to these categories, including some high culture entertainment, which universally rates lower than light entertainment. Differences in entertainment programs, according to Browne, include pacing, appreciation of satire, tolerance for sentimentality, amount of violence, roles of women and minorities, urban/rural emphasis, and social/political messages (e.g., a negative view of Communism in U.S. dramatic shows) (*Comparing* 387-91). Differences may be due to ideology, legislation, or the vague notion of "national taste." Similarities (aside from the basic unity of the human species) may derive from international marketing or producers' observations of programs in other countries.

Chapter 4

GAMING, LEISURE AND MIND SPORTS

It has long been my conviction that we can learn far more about the conditions, and values, of a society by contemplating how it chooses to play, to use its free time, to take its leisure, than by examining how it goes about its work. (Giamatti 1 3)

A. Bartlett Giamatti, former president of Yale University and, at the time of his death, the commissioner of baseball, brings a unique perspective to understanding the cultural meaning of sports and play. Leisure "is so important, as a concept, as an index to a culture's condition, because it is a form of freedom and is about making choices" (22). The Greek word for "leisure" is "schole," the root word of "school"; conversely, the world of "business" is "a-scholia" (un-leisure). Thus, elaborates Giamatti

pure play and schooling that pursues knowledge for its own sake, and leisure or free time, are all at least connected conceptually.

They are *all* autotelic activities—that is, their goal is the full exercise of themselves, for their own sake, because in them is achieved a condition that is active, not idle; entertaining, not simply useful; perfecting of our humanity, not merely exploitative of it.

Giamatti sees "not a dualistic opposition between work and play [but] a progression from one to the other" (29). Concludes Giamatti:

> In short, whether classical or Christian, leisure as an ideal was a state of unforced harmony with others; it was, ideally, to live fully amidst activity, which activity has the characteristic of free time. (30)

1. Play, sports and leisure

Despite his own qualifications, Giamatti nominates Allen Guttmann as "our most distinguished contemporary thinker on the nature and role of sport in society" (14). Play, according to Guttmann, is

> any nonutilitarian physical or intellectual activity pursued for its own sake.... Play is autotelic. Pleasure is in the doing and not in what has been done. One might say that play is to work as process is to results. (*Nature* 3)

Play is in its ideal sense "the most human of activities" (Guttmann, *Nature* 4).

If Guttmann stands out in our own times, few would argue that Johan Huizinga wrote the seminal work on leisure and play, *Homo Ludens*, first published in 1938. Huizinga defines play as "a free activity standing quite consciously outside 'ordinary' life as being 'not serious,' but at the same time absorbing the player intensely and utterly" (13). Huizinga dignifies play with these words:

> You can deny, if you like, nearly all abstractions: justice, beauty, truth, goodness, mind, God. You can deny seriousness, but not play. But in acknowledging play you acknowledge mind, for whatever else play is, it is not matter. (3)

Play "sustains an even greater cluster of meanings than either 'sport' or 'game.' Kittens and puppies, babies and children are said to play.... Soccer and hockey are played," notes sports philosopher Paul Weiss (133). All these activities "have in common the idea of being cut off from the workaday world" (134).

Sport likewise means different things to different people at different times. Weiss notes that sport "covers whatever is dealt with in sports pages of newspapers and magazines," including reports on bridge and chess (132). Giamatti points out that "sport" for Shakespeare "meant what 'play' or 'recreation' means for us, as opposed to 'work,'[which] is allied with tedium" (19). In modern times, as leisure expanded and mass media developed to entertain us, play became differentiated.

RULES OF THE GAMES. Play encompasses both rule-free and organized play, or games. Games, which are rule-bound,

> symbolize the willing surrender of absolute spontaneity for the sake of playful order.... One must obey the rules one imposes on oneself.... The rules are quite often designedly inefficient. (Guttmann, *Nature* 4)

Huizinga concurs that rules "determine what 'holds' in the temporary world circumscribed by play...Indeed, as soon as the rules are transgressed the whole play-world collapses" (11). Rules are indeed an integral part of games. "Where its rules begin, there the game begins; where its rules end, there the game ends. When the game is over those rules are left behind," states Weiss (146).

Child developmentalist Piaget has observed that games with rules appear at Stage II, ages 7-11. Piaget defines Stage II play as

> games with sensory-motor combinations (races, marbles, ball games, etc.) or intellectual combinations (cards, chess, etc.), in which there is competition between individuals (otherwise rules would be useless) and which are regulated either by a code handed down from earlier generations, or by temporary agreement. (113)

Noncompetitive games (having rules but no won-lost outcome) do exist, but are far less common than competitive games (contests). Leapfrog, ring-around-the-rosie, *kemari* (a Japanese game in which players work together to keep a ball in the air) are all noncompetitive games (Guttmann, *Nature*).

Most adult games, according to Piaget, have "regulations imposed by the group, and their violation carries a sanction" (113). Of course, contests exist outside the realm of play; legal proceedings and wars are competitive but hardly aimed at playfulness, although lawyers and generals may in fact enjoy them (Guttmann, *Nature*).

UNIVERSAL GAME TYPES. Anthropological studies of sport can help us understand our own sports culture, which in turn can help us know ourselves. In the words of Huizinga:

> Play is older than culture, for culture, however inadequately defined, always presupposes human society, and animals have not waited for man to teach them their playing. (1)

Huizinga believes that "genuine, pure play is one of the main bases of civilisation" (5).

French anthropologist Roger Caillois, in explicating his "sociologie *a partir* des jeux" (as opposed to a "sociologie des jeux") includes everything from coin-flipping to mountain-climbing in his games typology (142). Caillois writes that primitive societies tend to mimickry (e.g., use of masks) and vertigo games (e.g., possession by spirits); by contrast, other societies lean toward contests (e.g., merit exams) and chance (e.g., an aristocracy based on accidents of birth):

> the Incas, the Assyrians, the Chinese or the Romans are examples of ordered societies with offices, career codes, calculations, and controlled hierarchical privilege... (169-70)

Roberts and Sutton-Smith isolate three main types of games: 1) games of physical skill, which may involve strategy and chance; 2) games to strategy, which may involve chance; and 3) games of chance.

Using large data bases, they study the relation of games and culture. Games can help people overcome psychological conflict; Sutton-Smith and Roberts see games as

> models of ways of succeeding over others, by magical power (as in games of chance), by force (as in physical skill games), or by cleverness (as in games of strategy)...[children learn] necessary arts of trickery, deception, harassment, divination, and foul play that teachers won't teach them, but which are most important in successful human interrelationships in marriage, business, and war. (86)

Freud, in *Beyond the Pleasure Principle*, similarly stresses the element of mastery when people play games.

Regarding broad social schemes based on games, Guttmann cautions that

> it is doubtful that the kind of game, determined by anthropologists, matters as much as the cultural perception of the game on the part of the players themselves. We can learn a great deal from careful attention to the games a society emphasizes, but the "same" game is likely to vary greatly in its meaning from one cultural context to another. (*Nature* 11)

Still, the roles of chance, intellect, and physical prowess do seem universal in the world's games. As Weiss states:

> There is always an element of luck in every game.... it could be argued that luck is but a way of describing the overall effect of the contingencies which are essential to the very existence of a game. The athlete is to show what he is and can do in a game as it actually unfolds, peppered with the unexpected.... (191)

Weiss adds that for gamblers, unlike athletes, "luck is not a grace note, an addendum to what they are or do. It is an integral part of their lives and of their performances" (187).

GAMES AND NATIONAL CULTURE. In their study of culturally distinct Mayan descendants in four rural Mexican communities, Rota and Tremmel made a discovery about TV sports (11). They found that the amount of time children watched television "is not related to their sense of cultural and national identity." The content, rather than number of hours, may better predict identity:

> exposure to specific television programs has some effect, even if that effect is somewhat weak.... Among categories of TV programs,

sports is the one with the largest number of significant correlates. (13)

Rota and Tremmel further discovered that "the level of Traditionalism/Nationalism is higher among children whose use of television is more controlled by their parents" (14).

Some play activities in U.S. culture—hiking, recreational swimming, and cycling—are not competitive. But generally U.S. culture has "a powerful tendency to transform noncompetitive games into contests," such that the gentle game of frisbee turned into Ultimate Frisbee (Guttmann, *Ball Game* 3). Says Guttmann:

> Provided the situation is not excessively stressful, subjects in psychological experiments do better when the task is made into a contest. Beyond that, psychologists discovered, nearly a century ago, that the physical presence of a human competitor stimulated subjects to higher levels of achievement than they were able to attain when measured only by a stopwatch or a speedometer. (4)

Conversely, "we have a marvelous ability to transform almost any tedious or unpleasant task into a game" (Guttmann, *Nature* 13).

Guttmann isolates seven characteristics of modern sports: secularism, equality (same rules apply to everyone), bureaucraticization, specialization, rationalization (e.g., scientific fitness training), quantification, and an obsession with records (*Ball Game* 5-6). TV game shows exhibit secularism, equality, bureaucraticization and quantification; contestants in some games also train scientifically (i.e., practice systematically) and, in the 1950s when ever higher sums were being won on prime-time quizzes, TV audiences were obsessed with the record-setting dollar figures. Finally, just as distinctions have developed between rugby, American football, and soccer, specialization occurs in that certain TV games draw on shopping skills, others on word skills, others on math skills, and so on. By analogy, game shows have much in common with modern sports.

Beyond these traits, a bias against unequal matches and against grandstanding characterizes an informal code of conduct in modern sports. "Fair play," according to Guttmann, "requires that participants seek out opponents who can challenge them to rise to their highest level of achievement" (*Ball Game* 4). In most TV games, the contestant selection process ensures that players have skill at the game and can match the degree of skill to avoid matches that are doomed from the start to be lopsided.

2. The play theory of mass communication

In a broad sense, writings on sport form the basis for understanding *all* entertainment enterprises. In a narrower sense, an understanding of sports gives us insights into the game show genre. Taken together, the writings trace the three-strand evolution of mass media entertainment as a field of study.

Strand 1, "observable play" (Sutton-Smith, *Play Theory* ix) includes observations on children's games (e.g., Piaget), athletic contests (e.g., Caillois; Guttman, *Nature* and *Ball Game*) and sports spectators (Guttmann, *Sports Spectators*). The seminal modern work on the role of sport and play in society, *Homo Ludens* by Johan Huizinga, appeared in English in 1950. Huizinga greatly influenced William Stephenson.

For *Strand 2,* psychological or "subjective play," the seminal work is Stephenson's *Play Theory of Mass Communication*, first published in 1967 and reissued in 1988. *Strand 3,* "interactive media play," explores alert, active audience participation in radio or television programs (see Ch. 10).

More than 20 years ago, Stephenson had already anticipated the benefits of non-educational, escapist entertaining TV programs. Although he did not refer to uses and gratifications theories that had arisen in the late 1950s and early 1960s, his ideas foreshadow findings later reported by Katz, Gurevitch, and Haas (169) that television gives pleasure. The resurgence of game shows in the late 1980s calls for another look at his play theory.

On his book's first page, Stephenson comes down clearly on the side of game shows and other forms of "mass pap." Stephenson draws from the book *Homo Ludens* by J. Huizinga the idea that culture "depends on play" (40). Rather than being a waste of time, play "teaches loyalty, competitiveness, and patience" (46).

Play is *voluntary*, a stepping aside from one's duties; *secluded,* taking place in a particular time or place; *temporary*, an interlude having a beginning and an end; *absorbing,* letting the player escape completely into it; and *unproductive,* except for the satisfaction and fun created (Stephenson 46). Work, on the other hand, "deals with reality, with earning a living, with production" (45).

Applying these ideas to mass communication, Stephenson says that some content deals with work (informational and educational programs), while some deals with play. To date, information theory has been "all about work and not about fun." Since "play is of primary importance" in communication, the study of entertainment—"all the popular and humanistic arts—is of first importance in every theoretical aspect" (Stephenson 198). A role of mass communication should be to "maximize the communication-pleasure in the world...I would like to see more play, rather than less" (205).

Turning to audiences and media effects, Stephenson argues that low-culture television benefits its audiences in addition to providing enjoyment. It

> is characterized by absence of involvement in deeper belief systems and socially controlled internalized values. Somewhere in such entertainment, we must suppose, there are moments of self-enhancement, of self-existence, a break-through into communication-pleasure.... Communication-pleasure is always self-enhancing, and this gives us hope for the future of entertainment. (206)

Sutton-Smith, in his introduction to Stephenson, says that to Stephenson, "communication-pleasure" (*Play Theory* ix-xx) has a passive, sedentary character, although the "mind is constantly at work freely translating or transforming this [media] material" (xiv).

3. TV games and spectators

In Guttmann's opinion, "the athlete who displaces his attention from the activity to the audience, who performs for the fans, violates the code of sports" (*Nature* 12). But Giamatti draws a more charitable parallel between performing athletes and performing artists:

> They share the need for impeccable and split-second timing....and as nearly an absolute *concentration* as possible so

that all externalities are integrated, all distraction absorbed to the self... (40)

"The artist needs his audience," points out Gutt-mann (*Nature* 12). "Play, however, needs no audience."

When an audience does form, it gets its share of criticism. Weiss, for example, comments that "spectators live through a game in one way, and players in another. Sometimes there is action between them, but on the whole it is what the players do that helps determine how the spectators will behave, rather than conversely" (164). Weiss adds with some disparagement that "he who sits on the sidelines of a football game neither participates in nor is active in the game" (173).

No one denounces museum "spectators" for failing to paint pictures, but condemnation such as Weiss' of sports spectators is rife, points out Guttmann (*Sports* 147). According to Guttmann:

> The most detailed criticism of sports spectators comes, however, not from the churches, which have generally made their peace with whatever happens in sports, but from the Marxist tradition, which has, especially in its Neo-Marxist variant, developed a full-scale indictment of the alleged dehumanization of both athletes and spectators. (147)

Marxists condemn the racism, commercialism, militarism, nationalism, and imperialism in sports, but they enthusiastically endorse sports and athleticism. Neo-Marxists, however, indict sports on several counts (Guttmann, *Sports* 148-49). Regarding spectators, sports serve capitalism as a kind of opiate, draining away the repressed sexual energy that cannot serve the economic system.

STUDIES OF SPORTS SPECTATORS. Regarding sports spectators, still only "meager scholarship" exists (Guttmann, *Sports* 1). But some of it can be marshaled to counter the critique of the neo-Marxists. Supporting studies have been done in Europe, such as one in Switzerland that found that "the athletically active are more than ten times as likely to attend sports events as are the inactive" (150). Conversely, spectators are more likely to belong to the (admittedly small) group of participants than non-spectators.

Why then do people watch sports? Duncan and Brummett argue for three types of pleasures: 1) voyeuristic, or watching without being invited; 2) fetishism, or the pleasure of watching a spectacle; and 3) narcissism, or identifying with the object being viewed.

Becker and Creedon tested the ideas that viewers 1) "want to learn about that sport so as to enhance their own play" and/or 2) "might be interested in sport because they enjoy its excitement and activity for its own sake. The uncertainty of the outcome and the opportunity to cheer and ride the crest of enthusiasm are key" (2).

After showing 122 undergraduates tapes of sporting events and asking them questions, Becker and Creedon conclude

> the modeling motivation is a rather pure one. Those high in this motivation seem generally interested in and willing to learn from athletes regardless of gender....
>
> Spectating, on the other hand, seems to be a more traditional orientation. It seems plausible now that those high in this motivation may see sports rather traditionally and

associate the spectacle of sport with male activity and male domination. (7)

Giamatti idolizes the "magical" experience of live spectating, while disparaging "those indoors in front of a screen" (77). Giamatti toasts "the average fan whose presence is crucial to the public presentation of sports" and salutes "the happy camaraderie" of "the stadium holding paradise" (78). But for professional sports, many more fans attend to the screen outside the stadium than venture inside it. TV sports have almost replaced radio-mediated sports, so that mass-media sport has become synonymous with TV sport.

TV GAMES. Figure 4.1 shows how the philosophers of play and sport have explained the place of athletic contests within human activities. Mass mediated (televised) games can tell us as much about contemporary societies as ritual games could tell about premodern societies. Instead of limiting the last branch of Figure 1 to stadium sports, we can add made-for-television, nonathletic sports: TV game shows.

Most television content falls under the rule-free play on Figure 4.2. TV game shows fall between TV sports and rule-free television. Depending on the nature of the game (I-chance-based, II-intellectual or III-physical), an expanded version of the branching diagram would look like Figure 4.3.

This writer believes that TV game shows resemble rule-bound, competitive sports, but that some go one step beyond: some games permit (type II, Fig. 4.3) the viewer to "jump into the tube" and play along. Aside from this interactive quality, sports and game shows both share seven characteristics:

Figure 4.1
Athletic Contests within the Context of Human Activities

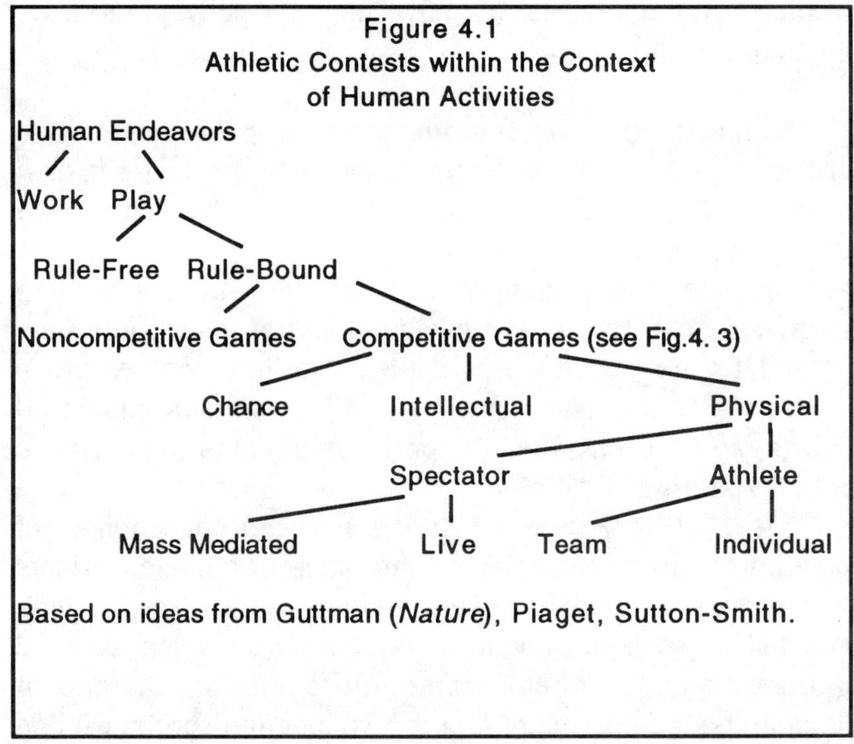

Based on ideas from Guttman (*Nature*), Piaget, Sutton-Smith.

Figure 4.2
Entertainment within the Context of Human Activites

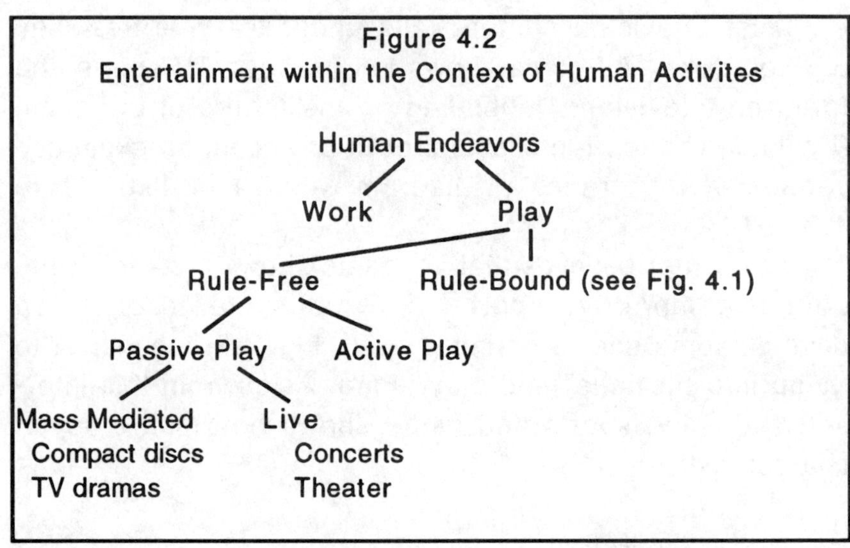

Immediacy	the action unfolds in real time, unlike drama or comedy, which can compress hours, days or years into minutes;
Independence	the action unfolds on its own accord, adhering to established rules, beyond the control of sponsors, advertisers, scriptwriters, or producers;
Purity	the outcome is not predetermined, and when game-fixing scandals do occur, fans feel betrayed;
Luck	present in varying degrees, ranging from near absence in chess to paramount importance in a show such as *Let's Make a Deal*;
Skill	present in varying degrees, ranging from near absence in a show such as "Card Sharks" to paramount importance in gymnastics;
Closure	the outcome results in a winning player or team and a loser or losers;
Escape	the game unfolds without relation to the world's events, only an adherence to internal rules.

Game show spectators are a small, semi-related segment of TV sports spectators. They have been quantified by ratings services but not studied psychologically. They differ from sports spectators in these ways:

* game show spectators are not apathetic, at least not when they watch the interactive games;
* the stereotype of violent spectators (though more relevant to those in the stands than those watching TV) has nothing to do with game shows;
* the lure that some spectators feel toward a blood sport (e.g., bullfighting, boxing) has nothing in common with the appeal of TV games;

* the possibility of catching up and vicariously experiencing the televised game does not exist (you can't "read all about it" when it comes to TV games; you have to watch for yourself);
* there is no loyalty to a team, favorite players (TV game show contestants usually play for one segment, or at most a champion may last for several days);
* there is no season, no closure (except for some final tournaments on some TV games, TV games have no World Series, no sense of "real time" day or season being evident).

4. Women, sports, and mind games

Since game shows share traits with TV sports, the gender differences in their respective audiences can lend insights to understanding these two genres. (See also Creedon.)

WOMEN AS SPORTS SPECTATORS. In 1963, when Nielsen ratings began to provide data on sports programs, 50 percent of adult men watched football; 46 percent, boxing; 44 percent, both baseball and bowling; and 38 percent, golf. Comparable figures for women were 27, 37, 33, 37 and 29 percents. By 1983, the ratings had finer distinctions but exhibited the same pattern; for example, 16.3 percent of men and only 7.4 percent of women watched NFL football. Also in 1983, more women than men watched the NCAA gymnastics championships. According to Guttmann, "men are more likely to watch men perform, while women are a more reliable audience for female athletes" (*Sports* 144).

This gender pattern persists worldwide. In Norway, 64 percent of men and 49 percent of women watch televised sports; women are more likely than men to to watch swimming and gymnastics. In Germany, 75 percent of men and 52 percent of women regularly watch TV sports.

Figure 4.3
Game Shows as a Bridge between TV and Athletics

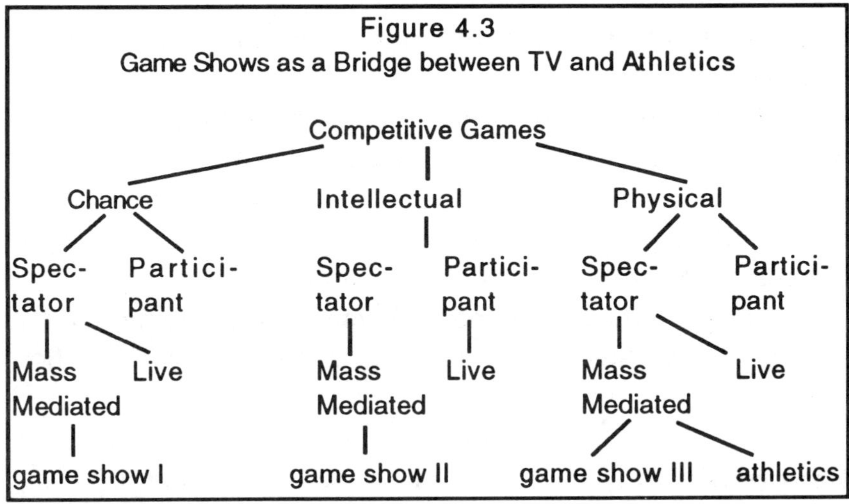

A survey released Feb. 20, 1991, revealed NFL football to be the nation's most popular spectator sport (cited by 39.1 percent of adults as a sport they loved or one of their favorites). Major league baseball was the favorite of 30.7 percent. Gender differences were evident, however. Three of five men, but only one of five women, loved NFL football. For baseball, two of five men, but only one of five women, cited it. A social class pattern holds true for sports. Baseball on television attracts disproportionately the poor and elderly. Since football attracts a younger, wealthier audience than bowling, commercial time sells for one-sixth as much as football. In the 1991 survey, the more money a household made, the more football was preferred over baseball.

The 1989 Super Bowl game on NBC attracted a 32.5 rating. No women's sports come close. An estimated 91 percent of U.S. men and 76 percent of U.S. women watch televised sports in an average week, according to a l986 *Sports Illustrated* poll. The same poll found men more likely to have watched televised women's sports than women.

NBC's ratings for the 1992 Barcelona Olympics suffered during the second week when fewer women watched. Sports that appeal to women—swimming, diving, and gymnastics—took place for the most part during the first week ("NBC's Olympics" 1992).

In a qualitative, personal analysis of why women watch men's sports, Australian video producer Beverly Poynton writes of Aussie football:

> Here were barely clad, eyeable Aussie male bodies in top anatomical nick.... With the commentary turned down and with some music the imagery may be released from its imposed fixity of meaning and the performance enjoyed as choreographed spectacle: lyrical, flagrantly masculine, erotic. ...that is a reminder of the original Grecian Olympics, where women were forbidden as spectators because the male athletes competed in the nude.

WOMEN SPECTATORS AND MIND GAMES. Ratings data other than that of sporting events suggests that women may seek more balanced spectating experiences than men. In addition to watching physical contests, women seem to derive satisfaction as well from watching contests based on intellect and chance.

Ratings data show some gender differences, both in the United States and abroad. Age and sex differences exist in hours spent viewing television. U.S. women watch more than men in every time and program category except one: sporting events. Among specific age groups, females over age 55 outdistance everyone else. The gender gap is most striking in the afternoon, peaking at about 3 to 4 p.m., after which children take over. During these "women's hours," soap operas, comedy reruns, and game shows predominate (Condry 39).

For example, of nine game shows aired in France in fall 1989, all drew more women spectators than men. The French version of *Jeopardy* had 1.6 percent of the men watching and 3.0 percent of the women.

The 1986 Cassandras (Nielsen syndication ratings) also revealed age and gender differences in viewing patterns: among the top five shows watched by women 25-54 were *Wheel of Fortune*, *Jeopardy!* and *New Newlywed Game*; by men 25-54, the only game show was *Wheel of Fortune*; and by teenagers, the top five were all comedies.

Game shows seem to assume for women—especially older women—the role that TV sports holds for men. It seems to take a cultural studies analyst, namely John Fiske, or a female game show fan, namely Maxene Fabe, to see the gender-based hypocrisy of TV game show bashing (see Ch. 1), cheek-by-jowl with delirious enthusiasm for televised (male) team sports. Fabe sees sexism in some (males') criticism:

> The critics were *really* condemning the sight of someone (women, maybe?) acting spontaneous and uninhibited while participating in a competition. Why not, I wondered, the same opprobrium for sports fans screaming at a hockey game? (xiii)

For his part, Fiske celebrates the freedom game shows give women "to be noisy in public; to escape from demure respectability, from the confines of good sense that patriarchy has constructed as necessary qualities for 'the feminine' (136).

Fiske equates the "low critical standing" of women's-interest game shows with "the disciplinary power of patriarchy to devalue anything that resists, threatens, or evades its power" (134). Or, by implication, the power to elevate in value anything that confirms its power, such as male team sports.

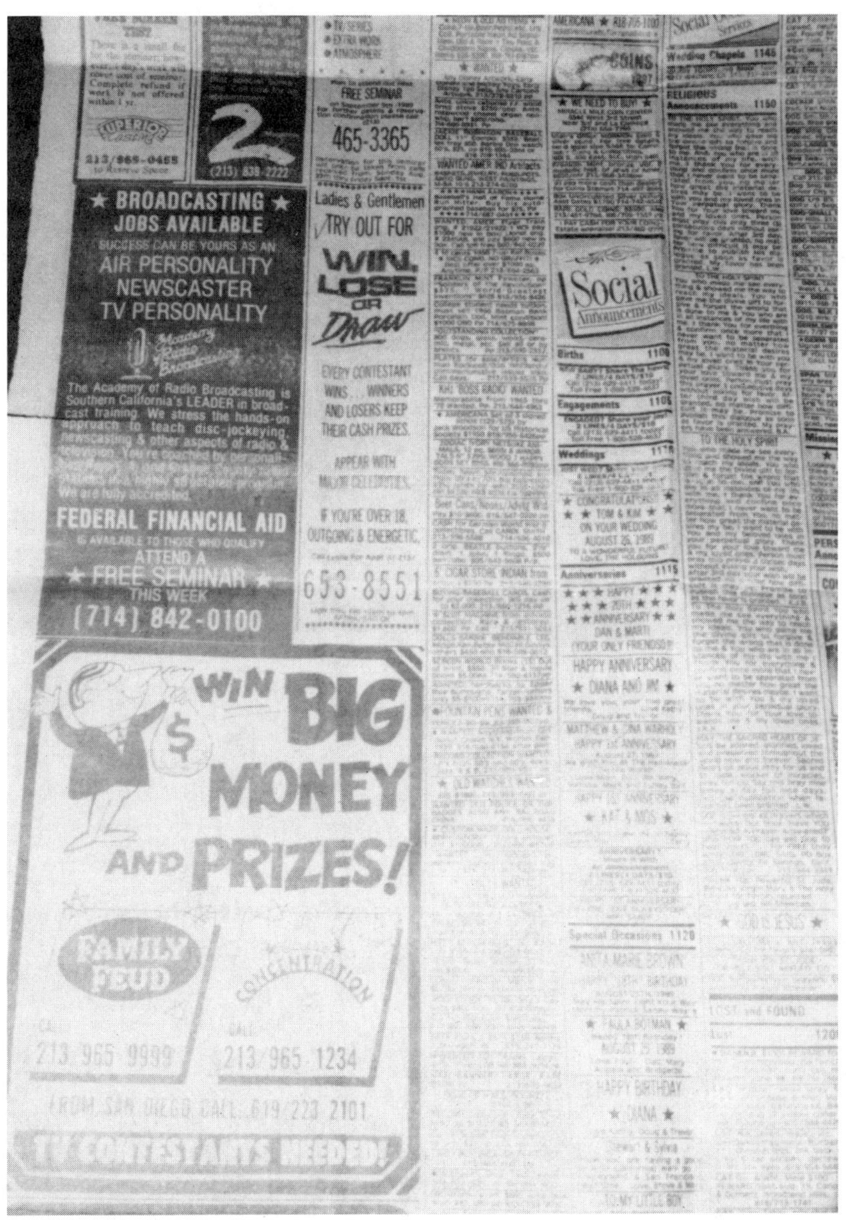

★ BROADCASTING ★
JOBS AVAILABLE
SUCCESS CAN BE YOURS AS AN
AIR PERSONALITY
NEWSCASTER
TV PERSONALITY

The Academy of Radio Broadcasting is Southern California's LEADER in broadcast training. We stress the hands-on approach to teach disc-jockeying, newscasting & other aspects of radio & television.

We are fully accredited.

FEDERAL FINANCIAL AID
IS AVAILABLE TO THOSE WHO QUALIFY
ATTEND A
★ FREE SEMINAR ★
THIS WEEK
(714) 842-0100

FREE SEMINAR
465-3365

Ladies & Gentlemen
TRY OUT FOR
WIN, LOSE OR DRAW
EVERY CONTESTANT WINS... WINNERS AND LOSERS KEEP THEIR CASH PRIZES.
APPEAR WITH MAJOR CELEBRITIES.
IF YOU'RE OVER 18, OUTGOING & ENERGETIC,
653-8551

WIN BIG MONEY AND PRIZES!
FAMILY FEUD
CALL
213 965 9999
CONCENTRATION
CALL
213/965-1234
FROM SAN DIEGO CALL: 619/223-2101
TV CONTESTANTS NEEDED!

Social Announcements
Births
Engagements
Weddings
★ CONGRATULATIONS ★
★ ★ TOM & KIM ★ ★
ON YOUR WEDDING
AUGUST 26, 1989
Anniversaries
★ ★ ★ HAPPY ★ ★ ★
★ ★ ★ 20TH ★ ★ ★
★ ★ ANNIVERSARY ★ ★
DAN & MARTI
HAPPY ANNIVERSARY
★ DIANA AND JIM ★
Special Occasions
HAPPY BIRTHDAY
★ DIANA ★
TO MY LITTLE BOY
Wedding Chapels
Religious Announcements
TO THE HOLY SPIRIT
LOST and FOUND

Family Feud and *Classic Concentration* advertise for contestants in the *Los Angeles Times*.

Dear Contestant:

Congratulations! I hope it pleases you as much as it pleases us to tell you that you are eligible to appear on "CLASSIC CONCENTRATION." Your name is now in our file of accepted contestants. (Of course, we cannot guarantee appearances.)

If we contact you for an appearance it will be approximately one week prior to the tape date. The wait for our call could involve several months. If you change address or phone numbers please let us know by calling (213) 965-1234.

You have invested a lot of time and effort with us. We recognize it and appreciate it.

Thank you,

Sincerely,

Howard Felsher
Producer

Letter of acceptance is sent to prospective contestants who have passed the Los Angeles-based tryouts of *Classic Concentration*.

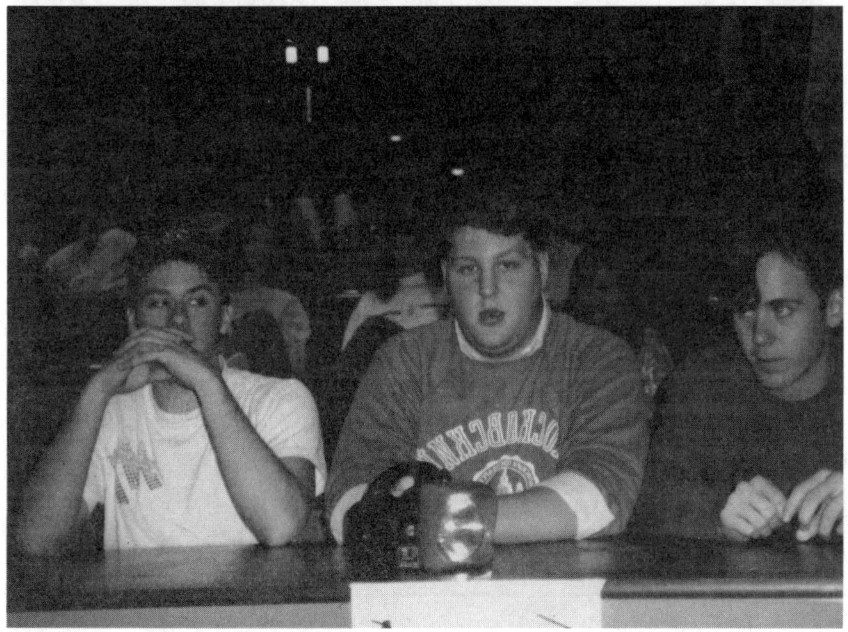

Ohio University teams play a low-tech version of *Jeopardy* featuring a hand-drawn game board (above) and flashlights that serve as buzzers (below). Photos by Anne Cooper-Chen.

The 1987 Iran-Contra Congressional inquiry, which coincided with *Wheel of Fortune's* popularity, inspired cartoonist Oliplant. Oliphant © 1987 UNIVERSAL PRESS SYNDICATE. Reprinted with permission. All rights reserved.

DOONESBURY

DOONESBURY GARRY TRUDEAU

Doonesbury strips from September 18, September 23 and October 6, 1989, reflect the late 1980s' U.S. game show craze.

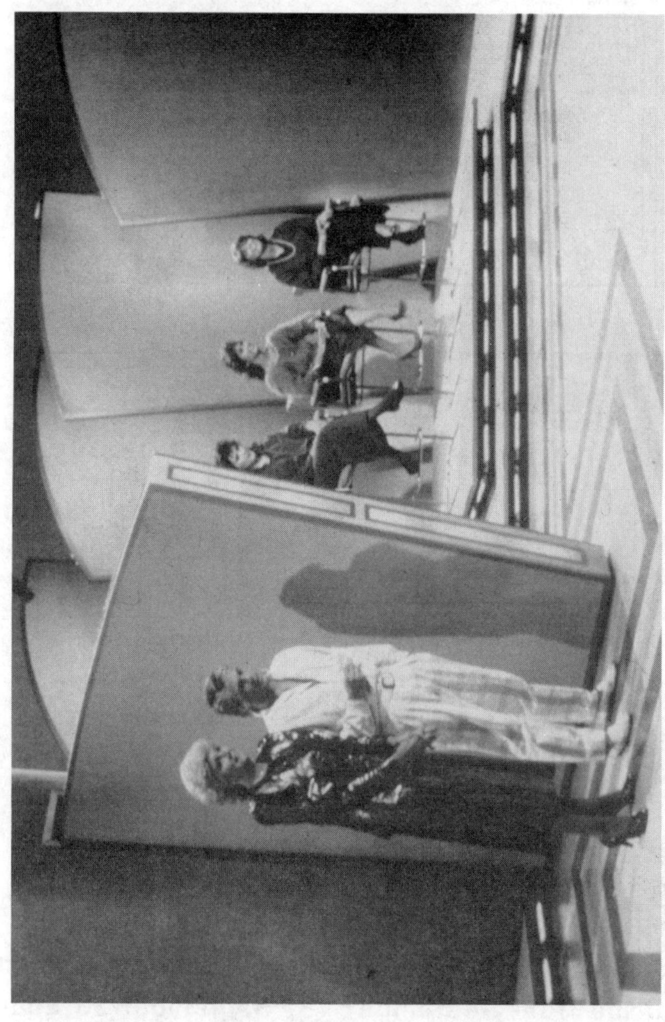

Hostess Cilla Black of ITV's *Blind Date* (UK show based on *The Dating Game*) waits with a bachelor who is about to meet his chosen bachelorette. Fremantle International, Inc.

Bernd Stephan (standing) of *Sag Die Wahrheit* (*To Tell the Truth*) on Germany's ARD Network hosts one of the relatively few Western game shows to feature celebrity panelists. Mark Goodson created the original U.S. version. Fremantle International, Inc.

Contestant on *OK! Il Prezzo E' Giusto* (Italy's Canale 5) chats with hostess, Iva Zannichi, as two models pose beside prizes. Mark Goodson created the original U.S. *Price Is Right.* Fremantle International, Inc.

Spain's *El Precio Justo* (TVE1) exemplifies the typical Western pattern of male host (Joaquin Prat) and silent, attractive female assistants. Mark Goodson created the U.S. original. Fremantle International, Inc.

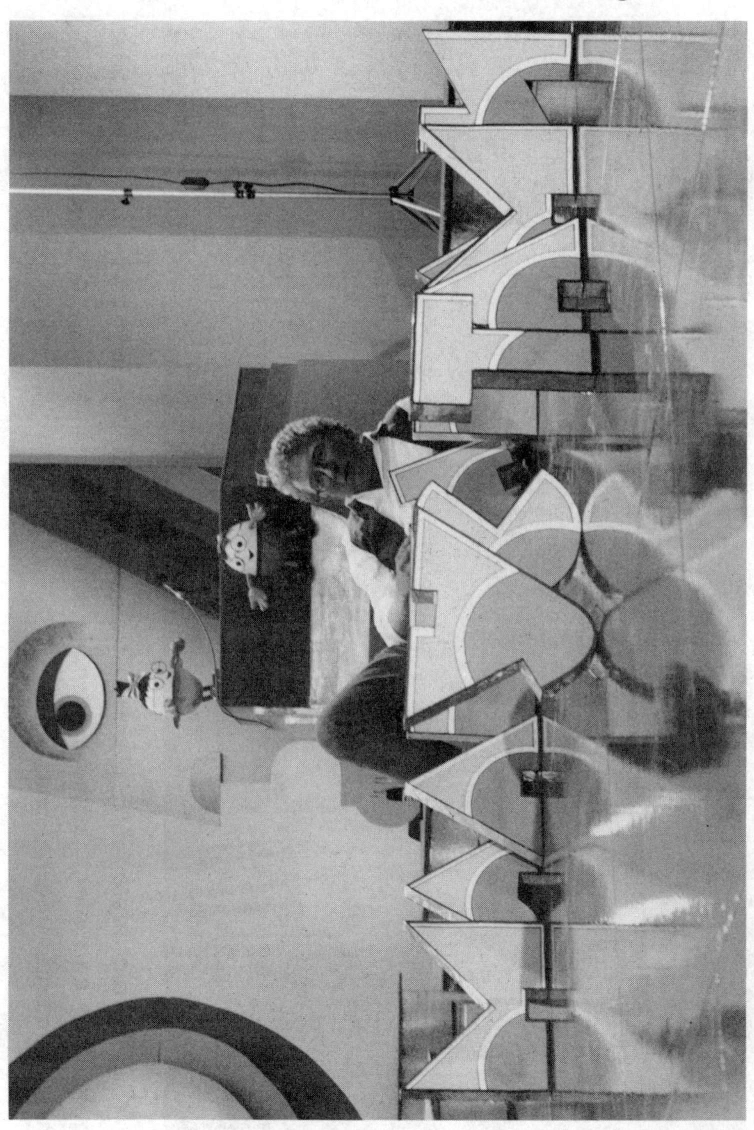

Fremantle executive producer, Richard Hearsey, relaxes on the set of *Ustamy Miadentsa* (*Child's Play*) as he prepares the show for production in Russia. Mark Goodson created the U.S. original. Fremantle International, Inc.

Above: the author meets the host of Taiwan's *Unlucky Strike* game. Below: Sylvie Nguiamba hosts Cameroon's *Cherchez le Mot*.

C

The Gamely Genre

THE GAMELY GENRE

In fall 1985, the author saw a short segment on *Entertainment Tonight* comparing various countries' game shows. That is how this project began. Most of Part C will draw from a 50-nation TV study that the author conducted—appropriately inspired by a TV program.

Data Collection

Data collection began in December 1987 during a trip to England and France. The author videotaped portions of about 20 game shows directly off the screen with a personal video camera. While not yielding broadcast quality results, the method avoided the problems of incompatible VCR systems.

In 1988 during trips to Taiwan, Tunisia, and Japan, local contacts videotaped shows directly, resulting in better quality tapes. Only the tape from Tunisia had to be made compatible with the NTSC system (using Ohio University equipment that translates non-NTSC tapes to NTSC). Contacts also provided tapes from Lebanon.

In 1990, the data collection shifted from tapes to monitoring in order to increase the number of countries and decrease the costs to collaborators. A simple monitoring form and one-page letter were sent to personal contacts in about 60 countries. The author distributed many forms at the International Association for Mass Communication Research convention in Bled, Yugoslavia, in

August. International students at Ohio University suggested names of home-country contacts. A number of contacts—notably in Saudi Arabia, Korea, Peru, Switzerland, and Poland—actually sent tapes. The author's collection of 25 videotapes showing games from 16 countries now resides at the Popular Culture Library, Bowling Green State University, Bowling Green, Ohio.

By spring 1991, data from 50 countries had been collected. The author tried to reconstruct a typical week from the monitoring forms, TV listings sent with monitoring forms, and TV listings in the Ohio University newspaper collection. However, OU, as do many libraries, tends to subscribe to international editions of newspapers, which do not include local TV listings.

The single most productive contact was Paul Talbot, president of Talbot/Fremantle Inter-national, Manhattan, whose firm licenses game shows in 14 countries. (Talbot's secretary calls him a man who truly loves the work he does.) King World International, Manhattan, provided data on licensees of *Wheel of Fortune* and *Jeopardy*.

In summer 1992, during a trip to Brazil, the author watched and analyzed that country's shows more extensively. In fall 1992, while in Japan, she did likewise.

Data Organization

This study did not include amateur shows—whether strictly amateur, such as Korea's *Housewife's Song Contest*, or near professional, such as the U.S. show *Star Search*. Nor did it include athletic competitions by near professionals such as the U.S. show *American Gladiators*. It did include shows that had game segments within a variety format if the game segments were prominent.

Data were organized into six categories and judged along two qualitative dimensions, inspired by Donald Browne (*Comparing* 386-91) but adapted to the game genre. The two qualitative dimensions, pacing and tolerance for senti-mentality, were subjectively determined. The six categories are: schedule placement (weekday strip, weekday prime and weekend), program duration (in minutes), presence/absence of celebrity panelists, gender of host, format origin (original or transferred from another country), and mode of play.

The mode-of-play typology, derived from watching taped shows, includes interactive, spectator, knowledge, and mixed format games. "Interactive" means that a home viewer can play along (e.g., guessing the phrase in *Wheel of Fortune*). "Spectator" means that contestants perform physical feats (e.g., running an obstacle course in *Double Dare*) or "perform" talk (as on *Love Connection*) for home viewers' enjoyment. "Knowledge" means that the average viewer at home, of the age level of the contestants, could answer only a few of the questions asked in the time allotted (e.g., England's *Mastermind*, France's *Des chiffres et des lettres* or any nation's quiz kid/College Bowl student faceoffs). "Mixed" means 1) a variety show that includes some game segments or 2) a game show with some interactive and some spectator portions.

The author studied U.S. game shows every other year, in 1986, 1988, 1990, and 1992. She traveled to California in 1989 to try out for and attend tapings of shows, interviewing producers and contestants in the process. However, she avoided duplicating the efforts of previous authors of books on U.S. game shows: Fabe, Graham (*Come*), Holbrook and DeLong. This book fills quite a different niche: a comparison of entertainment television around the world, with game shows as the window on that world. The four U.S. books provide a firm base from which to begin the globe-spanning adventure.

Chapter 5

RESEARCH ON GAME SHOWS

You can learn more about America by watching one-half hour of *Let's Make a Deal* than you can from watching Walter Cronkite for an entire month. (Fabe vi)

Maxene Fabe does not give a source for "Monty Hall's favorite quote" (vi), but the speaker has eerily echoed Giamatti, who sees a link between a society's values and its use of leisure (see Ch. 4). Are they sexist, classist, and capital-ist, as Fiske believes? ("Women"). Game shows stand as a ready-made case study for exploring these values.

After industry ratings and demographics had documented game shows' appeal (see Ch. 7), industry publications like *Ad Age* (e.g., Wally and Magiera) and *Variety* (e.g., Hardy) covered the phenomenon. But few popular culture or television scholars have focused exclusively on the genre. For example, no articles on game shows appeared in *The Journal of American Culture* 6.3 (Fall 1983), a special issue on daytime TV programming.

1. Books on U.S. game shows

Two mass-market and two social science books on U.S. game shows have appeared. Fabe calls her *Game Shows! A Behind-the-Screen Look at THE STARS! THE PRIZES! THE HOSTS! THE SCANDALS!* the "first book of its kind to embrace them affectionately, to take them seriously" (xvi).

Of some 700 radio and TV shows listed in the appendix, Fabe highlights 40 in the text, working chronologically up through the 1970s.

Short text segments, abundant black-and-white photographs, and generous samples of questions from well-known shows work together to "flicker and flash, to throw information and anecdotes at you zip, zip, zip, to have its varying textures and moods" (Fabe xvi). Fabe, a fan herself, admits to talking out loud to her television, "involuntarily, helplessly, unashamedly" (xv).

Graham in *Come on Down! The TV Game Show Book* identifies only 350 syndicated network shows produced since 1946, excluding many 13-week "specials" from the 1940s and early 1950s. More lavishly illustrated than Fabe, the book features color as well as black-and-white photographs, most taken by the author. Graham (1988) delves into the 1980s' *Wheel of Fortune* phenomenon, while Fabe merely mentions the pre-Vanna White, pre-Pat Sajak *Wheel*, which made its debut on NBC in 1975 in a morning time slot. While Fabe tracks the shows themselves, Graham concentrates on people; his book has chapters on producers, hosts, contestants, celebrities, and "elbow grabbers" (assistants).

Graham's last chapter, "The Game Show Hall of Fame," lists 20 great TV games (starting date on radio in parentheses):

Truth or Consequences	1950	(1940)
People Are Funny	1954	(1942)
Queen for a Day	1956	(1945)
Winner Take All	1948	(1946)
Pantomine Quiz		
(*Stump the Stars*)	1949	
You Bet Your Life	1950	(1947)
What's My Line?	1950	

The $64,000 Question (and *Challenge*)	1955
To Tell the Truth	1956
Concentration	1958
Video Village	1960
Password (*Password Plus*, etc.)	1961
Let's Make A Deal	1963
Jeopardy	1964
The Dating Game	1965
The Hollywood Squares	1966
The $10,000 Pyramid ($20,000, etc.)	1973
Wheel of Fortune	1975
Family Feud	1976
The Price Is Right	1956

(*Come* 161-87)

In an appropriate twist, since her whole book deals with the best shows, decade by decade, Fabe offers as her last chapter "The Ten Worst Game Shows":

Comeback Story	1953
Dream House	1968
Finders Keepers	1951
Make Me Laugh	1958
100 Grand	1963
Sense and Nonsense	1953
Supermarket Sweep	1965
Treasure Isle	1967
With This Ring	1951
You're In the Picture	1961

(289-92)

Graham agrees with Fabe's call on *Supermarket Sweep* (ABC 1965-67), "one of the most remembered game shows of all time, at least when the subject of bad taste comes up" (*Come* 200-01). Neither Fabe nor Graham (*Come*) discuss cable network game shows, such as those on Music TV, the Nashville Network, or Black Entertainment Television. *Supermarket Sweep* at this writing lives again as players run up and down grocery store aisles on The Lifetime Channel.

Delong offers the most recent book-length analysis of the phenomenon with his *Quiz Craze: America's Fascination with Game Shows*. He examines the shows' impact on U.S. society and the consumer marketplace.

Although his book was published in 1991, DeLong devotes less than one page to the entire 1980s decade. The word "television" does not appear in the book's title; indeed, more than half the text treats the pre-1950 (pre-TV) years. Clearly DeLong's interest lies in radio quizzes. He makes no mention of cable TV games such as *Double Dare* and *Remote Control*.

Holbrook analyzes *The Price Is Right* as the quintessence of consumption-oriented greed. His essay paints game shows as reflecting and reinforcing U.S. culture's obsession with merchandise, valued for its own sake. This slim volume resembles critical essays by Himmelstein and Fiske (*Television*) more than the histories written by Fabe, Graham (*Come*) and DeLong.

2. Audiences

The people who watch game shows have sometimes been studied in the context of large-scale audience projects. Sarrett and Messaris showed that young children reproduce versions of TV shows in games they create themselves. Similarly, as noted in Chapter 1, college students play versions of *Win, Lose or Draw*, *Family Feud* and *Jeopardy*.

Rubin and Rubin looked at one audience subgroup, people aged 55 and over, and 14 TV program types, including game shows. They found that game shows ranked fourth after news, sports, and music as most-liked programs. They also found that game shows ranked high along the following types of dimensions: entertainment, convenience, companionship, relaxation, arousal, "pass time," habitual, and escapist viewers, as well as females as a group. These shows ranked 3.10 (with 1 being "never watch" and 5 being "always watch").

Earlier, Alan Rubin discovered that game shows ranked only 2.2 (out of 5) with a quota sample of 300 adults, which seems to indicate the shows' special appeal for 55-and-over viewers. Rubin cited "the existence of both habitual and intentional viewing, with implications for the 'active audience'" (67). He also found a Pearson correlation of .65 for game shows associated with a cluster of motives, including companionship, habit, passing the time, economic reasons, entertainment, relaxation, and arousal.

Rubin found that increases in education level were related to decreases in watching game shows (75). However, his later study with Rebecca Rubin showed that for older viewers, low education was not associated with high game show interest (Rubin and Rubin).

Barwise, Ehrenberg, and Goodhardt used Arbitron surveys to study repeat-viewing patterns of programs that are "stripped" (shown five days a week in the same time slot). They found "a marked degree of program loyalty" to all shows, including game shows (27).

In October 1976, about 2.9 percent of adults in the New York City area watched "Tattletales" each day on WCBS, although the same people did not watch the show each day. (In fact, only 9 percent watched it all five days.) An average of 45 percent of those who watched any of the four game shows in the study also watched the same show the next day. Barwise, Ehrenberg, and Goodhardt conclude that "television fills the gap between other activities... (28). While people say they enjoy watching television, they tend to enjoy almost all other free-time activities."

Another type of audience study deals with mental and emotional states associated with TV shows. Bryant and Zillman found that game shows and situation comedies, unlike soap operas, arouse pleasant emotions; potentially stressful situations such as who will win are resolved by the awarding of some sort of prize to all contenders. Tan and Tan conducted phone interviews to measure both mental health and viewing habits of 446 adults. They found that game shows were positively related to a positive mental health state, while soap operas were related to a negative mental state.

3. Content: empirical studies

During nine weeks in fall 1986, Cooper-Chen monitored 13 game shows—each one twice a week ("Jumping"). These represented all the network affiliates' game shows available on the cable service in the author's area.

METHOD. "Game show" was defined in this study as a five-day-per-week program. All shows marked "game" in the local edition of *TV Guide* were included in the study, except for reruns of *The Best of Groucho* on the Christian Broadcasting Network. In addition, in fall 1987, 15 other shows were watched for format only. These included new network and syndicated shows: *Double Dare* on Nickelodeon, *Fandango* on the Nashville network and ten reruns on the USA network, making a total of 33 shows in the study.

Shows on which celebrities appeared were *$25,000 Pyramid*, *Super Password*, *Crosswits*, and *Hollywood Squares*. All others had civilian players.

RESULTS. A total of 929 contestants—414 males and 515 females—appeared on the 234 game show segments monitored in fall 1986. In addition, viewers saw or heard 39 hosts, assistants, and announcers (26 males and 13 females) as well as 182 celebrities (103 males and 79 females). Out of the 929, only one (a man in a wheelchair) was visibly handicapped.

a. *Proportion of network programming before 8 p.m.* On the network affiliates in this study, the hours of 6-9 a.m. and 6-7 p.m. were devoted to news. Thus game shows exist within a ten-hour period each weekday, 9 a.m.-8 p.m., excluding an hour for evening newscasts.

For fall 1986, 6.5 of the 30 daytime hours were devoted to game shows, or 22 percent. For fall 1987, the figure increased to 8 of 30 hours, or 27 percent. One half-hour show, *Crosswits*, had been cancelled, but five new half-hour shows had been added.

Austin had studied types of programming during local prime time 4-8 p.m. during 52 weeks in 1980-81 in Rochester, New York. He found that game shows made up 10.1 percent of the CBS affiliate's time and 8.3 percent of the ABC affiliate's. Looking at a shorter period, local prime time only, this study found higher figures than Austin had in 1980-81. Game shows were 12.5 percent of the four-hour block in 1986 and 21 percent in 1987.

b. *Contestants: age and sex.* Overall, the proportion of male to female contestants was 44.34 to 55.39 percent (see Table 5.1)—a slight overrepresentation of females compared to the U.S. population. However, the proportions varied greatly by show. The highest proportion of female players (87 percent) was on *Pyramid*, and the lowest (37 percent) was on *Dating Game*.

Table 5.1 also reveals that more than half of the contestants were aged 21-30, while only 2 percent were over 60. Despite the fact that 16.5 percent of the population in 1984 was 60 or older, only 5 of the 13 shows monitored had any contestants who appeared to be over 60 or referred to their age as over 60 during the game. Furthermore, 6 of the 13 shows had 5 percent or less of their contestants in their 50s, although 9.5 percent of the population in 1984 was aged 50-59.

The Cultural Indicators Project at the University of Pennsylvania (U.S. Commission on Civil Rights, 1979)

Table 5.1
Players on U.S. Game Shows—Age and Sex
Fall 1986

Age	Male (N=414) %	Female (N=515) %	Total (N=929) %
Below 20	.75	.96	1.71
21-30	24.54	28.84	53.38
31-40	9.58	14.53	24.11
41-50	3.76	4.62	8.38
51-60	2.26	1.82	4.08
Over 60	.75	1.29	2.04
Unknown	2.70	3.33	6.03
Totals	44.34	55.39	100.00

studied 5,042 characters on TV dramas and comedies. The project found about the same "invisibility" of the over-60s generation (2.9 percent), but more people in the 31-40 bracket (31.4 percent) and fewer in the 21-30 group (26.5 percent). Thus the "youth cult" is even more characteristic of game shows than dramas, particularly on two shows: *Dating Game* (with 94 percent of players in their 20s) and *Newlywed Game* (71.5 percent in their 20s). In reality, almost 20 percent of males and 22.5 percent of females aged 35-44 were single, as well as 30 percent of males and 76.1 percent of females aged 75 and older.

c. *Contestants: Race and Sex.* The racial makeup of the "player population" reflected reality much more accurately than the age makeup. Overall, whites were 85.03 percent of the contestants; blacks, 12.47 percent; Hispanics, 1.39 percent; and Asians, 1.07 percent (see Table 5.2). Only the

Table 5.2
Players on U.S. Game Shows—Race and Sex
Fall 1986

Race	Male (N=414) %	Female (N=515) %	Total (N=929) %
White	38.21	46.82	85.03
Black	5.59	6.88	12.47
Hispanic	.53	.86	1.39
Asian	.21	.86	1.07
Totals	44.54	55.42	100.00

Note: totals may not add up to exactly 100 due to rounding.

conspicuous absence of Hispanics mars an otherwise representative microcosm of the U.S. population.

Blacks (II.8 percent nationwide) are even slightly over-represented on game shows. The highest percentage of blacks was on *Newlywed Game*, which almost always had one black couple out of the four. Twice during the nine weeks there were two black couples on the same show (50 percent).

Although blacks have broken the numbers barrier, certain taboos remain. On *Dating Game*, where a player "interviews" three potential dates whom he or she cannot see, there was no instance in which the "interviewer" and the group of three were of different races. In other words, a white player was assured of having a white date. On *Newlywed Game*, a few couples included a white person and either an Asian or Hispanic spouse, but no black/white couples appeared.

Asians represented 1.07 percent of players, compared with 1.45 percent of the population. *Jeopardy!* had the most Asians (6 percent), while *Wheel of Fortune* had 4 percent and both *Hollywood Squares* and *$25,000 Pyramid* had 3 percent. Seven of the 13 shows had no Asians on in the nine weeks monitored.

Some of the underrepresentation of Hispanics might be explained by difficulties in identifying ethnicity based on appearance and surnames. Still, the only show that came close to the percentage of Hispanics nationwide (6.5 percent) was *Crosswits*, with 6.25 percent. Other shows had 2 percent or less, with six of the 13 having no Hispanics at all.

Given that California has the largest Hispanic population in the nation (more than 4.5 million in 1980), it seems unusual that the representation is so slight. Most contestants must live in or travel to Los Angeles to try out for the shows, since only a few programs conduct tryout searches around the nation. According to *Sale of the Century*'s producer, George Vosburgh, who answered a questionnaire for this study, contestants "must speak intelligible English"—a criterion that works against many Hispanics.

Minority females are much better represented on game shows (8.6 percent when aggregated) than minority (black, Hispanic and Asian) males. Native Americans would obviously be easier to identify on dramas than on game shows; in any case, none was observed during the nine-week monitoring period.

d. *Talent and celebrities: race and sex.* As Table 5.3 shows, of the l3 shows monitored, only one (8 percent)—*Dating Game*—had a female host (Elaine Joyce). Similarly, only one—*Crosswits*—had a female announcer. All hosts,

Table 5.3
On-air Talent on U.S. Game Shows—Race and Sex
Fall 1986

	Male (N=26)		Female (N=13)		Total (N=39)
	Black	White	Black	White	
Hosts	0	12	0	1	13
Voice-Overs	12		1		13
Asst.'s	0	2	1	10	13

assistants, and models except one were white. *Sale of the Century*, the only show that had a black model, was also the only show in which males were cast in a secondary role. The show has five models who act out vignettes to illustrate the prizes; of the five, one is a black female, while two of the white models are males. We should note that not all shows had assistants. Indeed, Vanna White was the only assistant on the local prime- time syndicated shows.

Table 5.4 reveals a gender split for celebrities just about the reverse of that for contestants—56 percent male. Likewise, the ethnic breakdown (88 percent white) moves away even slightly more from the U.S. population figure of 83.2 than did the contestant population. However, most striking is the chasm between all three groups and the persons in charge—the hosts. U.S. game show hosting was in 1986 a white male preserve.

Table 5.4
Celebrities on U.S. Game Shows—Race and Sex
Fall 1986

	Male (N=103) %	Female (N=79) %	Total (N=182) %
Race			
White	51.09	37.36	88.45
Black	4.94	6.04	10.98
Hispanic	.50	—	.50
Asian	—	—	—
Totals	56.53	43.40	100.00

4. Content: qualitative assessments.

WOMEN AND MEN. The gender differences on game shows have caused considerable comment. Any habitual watcher can verify the observations of several scholar fans. Fiske puts gender issues in the starkest, most stereotyped terms, based on his viewing of U.S./U.K./Australian shows:

* a male host holds control;
* a subordinate female partner (or a harem of subordinate females) speaks little and smiles much, displaying "total happiness with her subordination";
* the glamorous "showgirl" assistants contrast jarringly with the real-life female contestants;
* the fantasy-female assistants represent the dominant cultural ideal: white, young, attractive and slim. ("Women" 142)

Fiske argues that "the role of game shows in women's culture is problematic" ("Women" 134) and contradictory: the shows embody "patriarchal values," but "in a feminine way" (135).

The subordinate groups in society may be criticized for their low-culture tastes, but they are in a Catch-22 situation: "'high' culture is available and of interest to a minority only (within which women have difficulty establishing a place for themselves) and no alternatives exist" (Fiske, "Women" 135). They simply have to make do with the cards they are dealt.

In analyzing the raucous, carnivalesque *Price Is Right*, which critics call crass and greed-ridden (e.g. Holbrook), Fiske points out that "the essence of carnival was the inversion of the rules of everyday life" ("Women" 136).

Women on the show expressed not only the freedom to make noise, but "to give public, noisy acclaim to skills that are ordinarily silenced"—spending and managing the household's money. On the show, the (work) skills honed when women scrimp to buy necessities turn into a form of leisure: shopping for fun.

Family Feud requires players to guess the most-mentioned responses that 100 people gave to questions such as, "Where do people leave their umbrellas?"—a televised version of co-orientation theory (how does A think B will react to X?). The game represents to Fiske a skill that women possess:

> a bottom-up knowledge, not a top-down one. It is also an 'inferior,' domestic form of knowledge and is thus a particularly feminine one.... It is knowledge of people and how they are thinking and feeling that enables women to manage and smooth relationships within the family. ("Women" 138)

In stark contrast stands masculine, "'factual' knowledge, which can be gauged as right or wrong against external, public criteria" (Fiske, "Women" 143). *Jeopardy!*, the British show *Mastermind* (note the masculine title), and the 1950s' *$64,000 Question* represent this non-intuitive, objective knowledge.

Perfect Match (an Australian show that combines *The Dating Game* and *Love Connection* concepts) strikes Fiske as the most progressive, egalitarian game show of all ("Women" 140). After the televised arrangement, the couple returns to talk about the (often disastrous) date:

> The women tend to comment freely about the men's shortcomings.... the women feel no guilt at all at the 'failure' of

the date. They are freed from the feminine responsibility to manage the emotional life of the couple (or family).

Fiske sees the above three shows as embodiments of patriarchy's modes of female subordination—consumerism, the family, and romance—but at the same time "they offer great opportunities for these discourses to be subverted, inverted and turned back on themselves" ("Women" 143). Fiske's class-based analysis lacks exhaustiveness, omitting as it does the many shows that do not fit a gender-based interpretation, such as history's most successful game show, *Wheel of Fortune*. Likewise, data contradict some of Fiske's "facts," such as the assertion that females predominate and adult males rarely appear on *Family Feud* ("Women" 138). Furthermore, he could not have known that the egalitarian *Love Connection*, at least in its U.S. version, was scripted, prehearsed, and rigged (*TV's Love Connection* 1993).

HOSTS. Fabe and Graham (*Come*) note the following women who have hosted or co-hosted shows:

Arlene Francis	*Blind Date*	1949 New York
Vera Vague	*Follow the Leader*	1953
Denise Darcel	*Gamble on Love*	1954 Dumont
Eloise McElhone	*Quick on the Draw*	?
Kathy Godfrey	*On Your Way*	?
Sarah Purcell	*The Better Sex*	1977
Betty White	*Just Men*	1983
Elaine Joyce	*All-New Dating Game*	1986
Vicki Lawrence	*Win, Lose or Draw*	1987

Mark Goodson explains the lack of women hosts in one word: "control." He elaborates that on one extreme women may end up "sounding like a third-grade teacher or a gym coach," and on the other "she comes over as mousy or saccharine or like a B-girl" (Fabe 38).

Vanna White contends she nor any other woman could make it as a host: "If a woman hosting a game show was right, they'd be doing it. It doesn't work. I don't know why it doesn't work, but it doesn't." Research flies in the face of these stereotypes, but they persist. In 1955, a pilot with Betty White as a host tested higher than a pilot with a male. But the networks said it would not work in the long run, and a man was given the job.

Women, the majority of the population, have had somewhat more success than minorities as hosts. One black male, Cab Calloway, hosted a radio musical game, *Quizzical*, in 1941, but could not find a sponsor (DeLong 247-48). Two black males have hosted U.S. network TV shows: Adam Wade on *Musical Chairs* (1975) and Nipsey Russell on *Your Number's Up* (1986). In fall 1992, Bill Cosby began hosting a syndicated game, *You Bet Your Life.* No U.S. network shows have been hosted by Asians, Arabs, or Hispanics (Graham, *Come* 79). Cable channels with game shows, such as Black Entertainment Television, Nikelodeon, and Galavision, do have minority hosts.

STORYTELLING. A creative bridge between literature and game shows requires a switch of terms to remove the 1950s sexism. Kaminsky and Mahan use Northrop Frye's categories of protagonists—gods, heroes, men, and fools—"to organize and type game shows and discuss what they might mean." They approach the dilemma that the storytelling theory of television (see Ch. 2, 34) could not solve—namely, how to fit TV game shows into the largely narrative medium of TV entertainment.

Gods. Personalities endowed with more power (i.e., knowledge) than viewers include those who appear on *Jeopardy*, *The $64,000 Question,* or the British *Mastermind*, as well as child-gods (*The Quiz Kids*) and resident gods such as Dr. Bergen Evans of Northwestern University, host in the 1950s of *Down You Go*. The 1950s' scandals reversed god/man roles so jarringly that "the public wanted public execution. Contestant Charles Van Doren became the scapegoat" (Kaminsky and Mahan 47). The network gods turned out to hold the power, contradicting who we thought were gods, the (seemingly) all-knowing players.

Men. Kaminsky and Mahan change Frye's designation from "men" to "poised common person," such as players on *The Price Is Right*, *Double Dare*, *Win, Lose* or *Draw,* or *Family Feud* (47). For these momentary celebrities, "work is involved, not just answering questions." The key attribute is quickness, either in delivering common-sense knowledge or performing physical tasks.

Fools. Viewers can feel superior to these unpoised players: for "the reward of temporary social recognition, they willingly play the fool," such as on *Supermarket Sweep*, *Let's Make a Deal* or *Truth or Consequences* (Kaminsky and Mahan 47). *Queen for a Day* and *Strike It Rich* represent confessional variants, wherein the "fool's misery or punishment confirm the superiority of the audience" (50).

Chapter 6

RULES OF THE GAMES

We create a new sport, but we can't afford to have all the rules that baseball has. When you make a game show, you have to come up with a game that plays well, with amateurs playing it, not professionals...

Producer Reg Grundy
quoted by Graham (*Come* 5 0)

1. Themes, types, and peripherals

Televison writers who think about game shows try to reverse engineer the programs created by Grundy and other noted U.S. producers: Chuck Barris, Jack Barry/Dan Enright, Louis Cowan, Ralph Edwards, Mark Goodson/Bill Todman, Merv Griffin, Merrill Heatter/Bob Quigley, and Bob Stewart (Graham, *Come* 60-67). With such a plethora of U.S. game shows alone, no writer can resist the urge to create typologies to try to understand what makes the shows tick. In doing so, the game's core vs. its peripherals can easily get tangled up. And the theme/motif can often obscure the true nature of a game's mode of play.

For example, the core of *Concentration*, its title to the contrary, involves solving a word-and-picture rebus rather than memorizing prizes' positions. Player A can use Player B's turned-over clue squares to solve the phrase and win. When this author tried out for *Concentration* (see

Appendix), the first elimination separated out those who could from those who could not solve partially obscured rebus puzzles. In the second elimination, memory loomed as less important than an animated persona.

Likewise, its title to the contrary, *Wheel of Fortune* uses gambling as a motif rather than the core of its mode of play. Players rack up dollars as they spin, but the dollars mean nothing wihout a win. A phrase gradually emerges as each player "contributes" letters; to win, one must solve the word puzzle, not excel (or be lucky at) roulette.

Various authors have identified a gambling motif as characteristic of TV game shows. Kaminsky and Mahan, who adopt a literary view of game shows, think that an element of chance "suggests the protagonist is determining his or her own fate" (52). Players on *Let's Make a Deal* decide whether to keep the status quo or risk it for something better, creating an illusion of control over their (prize-winning) fate. Shows with the aura of a gambling casino include *High Rollers*, *Card Sharks*, *Press Your Luck,* and *Wheel of Fortune*.

Other themes characteristic of game shows, in addition to gambling, include a fascination with celebrities, others' love/sex lives, shopping and striking it rich; some shows even incorporate more than one of these obsessions. Shows featuring celebrities are *The $25,000 Pyramid*, *Super Password*, *Crosswits*, *Hollywood Squares*, *Win, Lose or Draw*, and *Fandango*. Those trading on love or sex are *Studs*, *The Personals*, *Score 1*, *The Dating Game*, *Love Connection,* and *The Newlywed Game*. Shows simulating shopping expeditions are *Wheel of Fortune*, *Let's Make a Deal*, *Sale of the Century,* and *The Price is Right*.

Througout her book, while describing the best shows of given decades, Fabe pulls together similar shows in a sidebar, thus creating a thematic typology inadvertently. She identifies these types:

1. Act-It-Out	*Pantomime Quiz* 1949 + six others
2. Stunt	*Beat the Clock* 1950 + seven others
3. Comedy	*You Bet Your Life* (Groucho Marx) 1950 + 11 others note: add *Whaddya Know?* on American Public Radio
4. Cartoon	four note: add *Win, Lose or Draw*
5. Music	*Name That Tune* + 11 others (not incl. radio)
6. Tearjerk	*This Is Your Life* + 10 others (*Queen for a Day* has its own entry)
7. Beauty	four including a parody, *$1.98 Beauty Show*
8. Bluff	*To Tell the Truth* + 10 others
9. Pricing	*The Price Is Right* + 10 others
10. Word	*Password* + 31 others
11. Love/marriage	*The Newlywed Game* + 16 others
12. Children's	*Storybook Squares* + 18 others
13. Family	*Family Feud* + 12 others
14. Sports quizzes	*Pro-fan* + 17 others (add *NFL Trivia Game*)
15. Gambling	*New High Rollers* + 26 others

Fabe mixes modes of play (e.g., act-it-out) with question topics (e.g., sports) and motif/themes (e.g., gambling). Clearly, surface similarities between shows with the same theme—for example, the casino-like *Card Sharks* and *Wheel of Fortune*—fade when one starts to watch and play each game. The process of guessing whether the next face-down card will be higher or lower than a four of hearts (*Card Sharks*) differs markedly from the process of mentally supplying the missing letters in the phrase "j__rn_l_sm st_d_nt" (*Wheel of Fortune*).

Graham, who has eight more years of shows from which to draw conclusions, makes a conscious typology:

1. Q and A	*Uncle Jim's Question Bee* (1936), *Sale of the Century, Jeopardy!*
2. Words	*Wheel of Fortune, Scrabble, Million Dollar Chance of a Lifetime, Crosswits*
3. Word Communication	*Password, $100,000 Pyramid, You Don't Say*
4. Puzzle	*Concentration, Tic Tac Dough, The Face Is Familiar, Catch Phrase*
5. Celebrity Panel	*What's My Line? To Tell the Truth, Call My Bluff*
6. People	(embarrassing personal facts revealed) *Newlywed Game, Dating Game*
7. Stunts	*Beat the Clock, People Are Funny, Truth or Consequences*
8. Gambling	(simple questions lead to games of chance) *Card Sharks, High Rollers, Pay Cards*
9. Charades	*Pantomime Quiz, Body Language, Showoffs*

(*Come* 54)

But most of these types, like most of Fabe's themes, have nothing to do with the interaction itself. For example, the members of a celebrity panel could be replaced by a civilian without affecting the nature of the game. And a celebrity panel can involve any type of play (*Hollywood*

Squares, where civilians win or lose, differs greatly from *What's My Line?*).

Furthermore, neither typology is exhaustive. For example, *The Price Is Right*, which requires knowledge of current market values, and *Name That Tune*, which requires a musical memory, do not fit in Graham's categories (*Come* 54). Similarly, Fabe has no place for the black culture Q-and-A of *Family Figures*.

Fabe, with insight, identifies these types of formats:

"the hard quiz"	questions with a right/wrong answer a) hard facts b) fifth-grade facts c) common knowledge/pop culture facts
"hunch and happenstance"	second-guessing answers that others might give, psyching out a bluff
"gut instinct"	yes/no decision (door #1, 2 or 3)
chance	dice roll, turn of wheel

(55-56)

However, this typology leaves out physical games like *Double Dare* and "evolving phrase" puzzles like *Bumper Stumpers*, *Concentration*, and *Wheel of Fortune*.

Fiske constructs a single-principle typology that gets at the core game rather than peripherals, based on type of knowledge required of players.

Quiz Show

factual knowledge		human knowledge	
" academic"	"everyday"	of people in gen.	of specific indiv.
Mastermind	*Price Is Right*	*Family Feud*	*Newlywed Game*
$64,000 Q	*Wheel of Fortune*	*Play Your Cards Right*	*Love Connection*
Sale of the Century			

(*Television* 269)

But his schema leaves no room for stunt shows or clue-giving shows, which rest on the ability to form associations rather than any kind of knowledge.

Graham identifies a typical basic game form, helpful but not a substitute for an overarching typology:

Main game
Second round
Bonus round (endgame, lightning round) (*Come* 5 4)

The next section presents this author's typology that throws a net large enough to catch all U.S. as well as international shows.

2. Passive vs. interactive formats-United States

A simpler, two-group typology can encompass all the game shows that producers' fertile imaginations can create. Table 6.1 divides games into two types: spectator and interactive. "Interactive" means that viewers can "jump into the tube" and play along (Schiffres 55). "Spectator" means that contestants "perform" while viewers watch passively, albeit enjoyably.

Table 6.1 shows that game shows—in this case those in the Game Show Hall of Fame—can be subdivided into eight categories based on mode of play (Graham, *Come* 161-87).

The top-rated game show of all time, *Wheel of Fortune*, belongs to the Alphabet Puzzle category. Viewers have time to figure out the solution, as each round of play reveals progressively more clues, words or letters.

The use of a timer or buzzer (Buzzer Q and A) means viewers have to answer quickly to "beat" the studio contestants. Yet the pressure doesn't turn off viewers, as

Table 6.1
Categories of Top 20 U.S. Game Shows Based on Problem Type and Means of Solution, 1948-88

Category	Format	Shows
INTERACTIVE		
Alphabet puzzle	Solve word, phrase or name puzzles as more information emerges with each round	*Wheel of Fortune* *Concentration*
Buzzer Q and A	Supply correct response before the competitors or before clock runs out	*Winner Takes All* *$64,000 Question** *Jeopardy**
Q and A	Supply correct response to an open-ended or multiple-choice question	*You Bet Your Life* *Hollywood Squares*
Player's gamble	Pick one of two or three possible choices, based on little or no information	*Let's Make a Deal*
Coorientation	Intuit how other(s) will (have) respond(ed) to a Q or set of choices	*Family Feud*
High/low	Give a numerical answer close to target number, without going too high	*Price Is Right*
Clue giving	By actions, words or pictures, prompt partner(s) to give the correct response	*Password* + *$25,000 Pyramid* + *Pantomine Quiz* +
Probe	Panel tries to ferret out truth by close questioning	*To Tell the Truth* *What's My Line?*+
SPECTATOR		
Voyeur	Audience listens to players describing details of their personal lives	*Queen for a Day* *Dating Game*
Stunt	Players act like perfomers as audience watches physical (often amusing) exhibitions	*Truth/ Consequences* *People Are Funny*
Chance	Skill plays no role; dice, roulette wheel determines outcome	*Video Village*

+Semi-interactive; answer is revealed to viewers
*Specialist knowledge

Top 20 games from Graham (*Come*, 161-87)

quick-paced *Jeopardy!* with its highly knowledgeable players, attests. *The $64,000 Question* started out at most viewers' knowledge level with a $64 question, but then gradually left more and more of them behind. At the $64,000 level, the show stepped partly into the spectator realm, as sweating players "performed" for a watchful audience—a scripted performance, as the scandal investigations revealed (see Ch. 8).

While Q-and-A games require some outside knowledge, games in the category Player's Guess involve no knowledge. They turn on a classic human dilemma: bird in the hand vs. two in the bush. On *People Are Funny* (1954-60), Art Linkletter used the idea of sure cash vs. boom-or-bust boxes long before *Let's Make a Deal.* Viewers at home, having mentally made their choice, could get instant feedback from Monty Hall.

The Coorientation category involves intuition rather than facts. *Family Feud* lets viewers play along at second-guessing average Americans' responses to questions like "Where do people say they misplace their umbrellas?"

In the High/Low category, *The Price Is Right*, network television's longest-running daytime game, involves pricing products or groups of products. Players (and home viewers) must come as close as possible without going over the real price.

In the Clue-giving (semi-active) category, viewers know what word or phrase the clue-giving player must elicit from other team member(s); yet viewers find themselves particpating by pretending to give clues. Furthermore, while viewers know the six clue words on *Password*, they must guess at the final solution. And viewers can add another dimension to charade games, whether *Pantomine*

Quiz or *Win, Lose or Draw*, by closing their eyes to avoid seeing the target phrase. For some rounds, the producers encourage interaction by NOT revealing the target word or phrase.

Similarly, viewers could close their eyes to the guest's occupation in the Probe game *What's My Line?* Based on panelists' probes, they can guess who's telling the truth in the classic Probe game *TTTT*.

American viewers' tastes have changed over the years, from spectator to interactivity. More accurately, producers gradually learned to exploit the interactive potential of the TV medium. By 1987, 93 percent of shows let the home viewer play along. On Table 6.1, all four spectator games—*Queen for a Day*, *Video Village*, *Truth or Consequences*, and *People Are Funny*—date from the 1950s (see Ch. 8). One might also argue for *You Bet Your Life* (1950-61) as a spectator game, carried as it was by Groucho's personality; yet despite the comedy, it had a question-and-answer format.

The tearjerking *Queen for a Day* gave the role of voyeur to the viewer, learning intimate secrets about someone who could be a next-door neighbor. *People Are Funny* had some interactive elements, as noted above, but like *Truth or Consequences*, performances with seltzer bottles and pies in the face dominated the format.

The spectator category Chance (represented by *Video Village*, 1960-62) appeared briefly but did not persevere into the 1980s. U.S. viewers seem to enjoy an element of chance in their games, but not an outcome determined solely by chance. An unlucky spin on *Wheel* can cost a player a turn; a *Price Is Right* pricing game based on roulette numbers determines the winner from among finalists.

However, the finalists get to the magic circle on their pricing skill merits (or the fumbles of others).

Table 6.2 describes one recent year, 1987. Although no 1987 show fit in the Probe subgroup, the Probe show *To Tell the Truth* later came back to the small screen. The biggest change occurred in the spectator Voyeur category, where the sexual innuendo of *The Dating Game* and *Love Connection* replaced the sob stories of *Queen for a Day*.

Many of the same shows appear on both tables, as a testimony to their staying power—except for *You Bet Your Life, What's My Line?* and *Winner Take All*, the recent list contains the 40-year list. (*Win, Lose of Draw* resembles *Pantomime Quiz* so strongly as to be almost a latter-day clone.)

In addition, after the period covered by Table 6.2, *You Bet Your Life* gained a TV clone when Bill Cosby replaced Groucho (starting in fall 1992). And the show has its latter-day radio clone in *Whaddya Know?* featuring Michael Feldman's ad libs and the pairing of two contestants who do not know each other. The game show, born on radio, has come full circle.

3. Interactive and spectator formats-worldwide

To gain understanding of worldwide TV preferences, this section will use a more detailed typology than the previous section on U.S. game formats. One category, "mixed format," will be added to accommodate shows with game and non-game segments. Second, the interactive category will break out one prominent type of game that looms much larger in certain countries outside the United States: what Fiske calls "academic knowledge" quizzes (*Television* 269).

Table 6.2
Categories of U.S. Game Shows Based on Problem Type and Means of Solution, 1987

Category	Format	Shows
INTERACTIVE		
Alphabet puzzle	Solve word, phrase or name puzzles as more information emerges with each round of play	*Bumper Stumpers* *Chain Reaction* *Crosswits* *$1,000,000 Chance* *Scrabble* *Wheel of Fortune* *Concentration*
Buzzer Q and A	Supply correct response to a question before the competing player(s) do, or before clock runs out (*=specialist; others = common knowledge)	*Fandango* *High Rollers* *Jeopardy!** *Play the Percentages* *Press Your Luck* *Sale of the Century*
Q and A	Supply correct response to an open-ended or multiple-choice question (each player in turn)	*Celebrity Hot Potato* *Double Dare* *Hollywood Squares* *Jackpot* *Strike It Rich* *Tic, Tac, Dough*
Player's gamble	Pick one of two or three possible choices, based on little or no data	*Anything for Money* *Let's Make a Deal*
Coorientation	Intuit how other(s) will (have) respond(ed) to a Q or set of choices	*Family Feud* *Newlywed Game*
High/ low	Give a numerical answer close to target number, without going too high	*Card Sharks* *Price Is Right*
Clue giving	By actions, words or pictures, make partner(s) give the correct response	*Password* *$25,000 Pyramid* *Win, Lose or Draw*
SPECTATOR		
Voyeur	Audience listens to players describing details of personal lives	*Love Connection* *Dating Game*
Stunt	Players act like perfomers as audience watches physical (often amusing) exhibitions	*Truth/Consequences*

Not only do Brazil's programs include variety segments such as singing and dancing mixed in with games; they also include many different game show segments (see Ch. 9). Some of the game segments are interactive and some are spectator-oriented, but trying to categorize each one individually would violate the local network's choice of airing a single program. Moreover, some last just a few minutes and would not be parallel with other countries' shows or with this study's exclusion rule of screening out shows less than 15 minutes long. Finally, the segments do not remain constant from show to show. Thus we count Brazil's *Silvio Santos Show*, the Philippines' *Lunch! Bulaga* and Chile's *Sabado Gigante* as one show, just as Brazilians, Chileans, and Filipinos do.

Beginning with the radio version of *The Quiz Kids* in 1940, certain game/quiz shows have emphasized mental prowess. These shows that set mind over greed still trouble some critics, such as Himmelstein, who complained that "knowledge was equated with memorization of facts and rapid recall under pressure" (273). Nevertheless, a system that airs or a people who watch these knowledge shows are sending a message: television *should* emphasize mind over greed. If a country can afford to air only a few game shows, do knowledge quizzes make up a high proportion?

Finally, because not all of the coding forms had enough information to accurately judge format, the unclear category had to be added. As Table 6.3 shows, 12.4 percent of shows fell into the "not known" category.

In sum, the following categories were used:

1. Interactive game—a game the average person can play in real time by solving problems or answering questions some or

Table 6.3
TV Game/Quiz Shows in 50 Countries
Mode of Play, Autumn 1990

Region	# of Shows	Inter-Active (%)	Spectator (%)	Know-ledge (%)	Mixed (%)	Not Known (%)
1. N. Europe	32	62.5	18.8	3.1	0.0	15.6
2. W. Europe	70	60.0	15.7	5.7	12.9	5.7
3. E. Europe	9	44.4	0.0	22.2	11.1	22.2
4. Nr./Mid E	9	44.4	0.0	55.6	0.0	0.0
5. Africa	16	31.3	0.0	56.3	6.3	6.3
6. S/SE Asia	16	50.0	18.8	6.3	25.0	0.0
7. E. Asia	45	60.0	17.8	18.8	4.4	0.0
8. Pacific	8	75.0	12.5	0.0	12.5	0.0
9. Lat. Am.	14	7.1	21.4	0.0	64.3	7.1
10. No. Am.	41	70.7	4.8	9.8	7.3	7.3
Totals	260	56.1	13.1	11.1	13.5	6.1

most of the time. Subcategories include general knowledge Q&A word puzzles, and guessing games (higher/lower prices or cards).

2. Spectator game—a game in which the viewer can identify with the player but can't actually play along. Included are games of physical prowess, obstacle courses and narrative games (*Dating Game, Love Connection*) .

3. Knowledge quiz—like interactive games, but meant to showcase speed and high-level knowledge for the ability group that is playing. (Adults could answer kids' questions, but other kids might not.) High school and college quiz bowls, as well as *Mastermind* and *Des Chiffres et des Lettres*, are included.

4. Mixed game—includes elements of 1) and 2) above, or includes non-game segments, or both.

5. Unclear—unable to determine from coding form.

Table 6.3 shows that 56.1 percent of TV games are interactive, but only 13.1 percent are spectator. The knowledge game, a special form of interactive games, represents 11.1 percent of the total. The mixed category represents 13.5 percent.

Table 6.3 further shows that Northern/Western Europe, the Pacific (Australia/New Zealand) and North America group together, liking the same kind of games: interactive. In this preference, East Asia joins the Western bloc. By contrast, Latins avoid play-along formats in favor of spectator and mixed games.

In only Africa (56.3 percent) and the Near/Middle East (55.6 percent), knowledge games constitute the most popular game format. Since interactive, spectator, and mixed games will be discussed elsewhere, knowledge shows in Africa and the Middle East deserve some mention here.

Saudi Arabia's *Information Bank* dates from an earlier time than most of the shows in this study. It is included here because of its true uniqueness. An all-male audience in traditional dress cheers on an all-male group of players, also in traditional dress, each of whom sits at a computer. For certain questions, computers are used for questions and answers. Other questions are verbal, some even in English. Still others require math skills. The quizmaster, a well-known professor, explains answers as if giving a lecture demonstration to a large advanced class. The graphics are modern but clearly indigenous.

Tunisia's *Jeu d'Afrique* has, for Westerners, low production values. The pace moves maddeningly slowly, as young student players answer questions, without buzzer pressure at a leisurely pace, about the nations of Africa. The spinning device used to choose the focus countries in

Africa looks a bit crudely made to Western eyes. Despite the French name, players and hosts use Arabic exclusively.

In sub-Saharan Africa, even more than in North Africa, knowledge shows emerge as the dominant format. Most of the programs are student quiz contests rather than adult *Mastermind* clones. In Kenya, all three of the shows studied are of this type. Ghana's two knowledge shows are *Best Brain* and *Kacici Kacici*. In the Ivory Coast, *Les Genies en Herbe* (*Budding Geniuses*) has been adopted from a French format.

Israel has a subject-specific quiz for young people, *Olympia Science Quiz*. Turkey's *Bir Kelim, Bir Islen* and Cameroon's *Cherchez le Mot* resembles France's adult brain-teasing *Des Chiffres et des Lettres* (see Ch. 8). A production company attempted to transfer England's adult brain-teasing *Mastermind* to the United States, but unsuccessfully (see Appendix).

A mirror opposite of sub-Saharan Africa, Latin America shows no knowledge shows at all. Japan, a nation obsessed with education, has one nationally aired student quiz on NHK, *That's Perfect*. But many of its other shows have an educational "feel" (see Ch. 8); in fact, the highly rated *Takeshi and Itsumi's TV School* features a panel of celebrities at stylized student desks, a celebrity "teacher" and another celebrity wearing a typical military-style high school uniform.

The United States has various local but few nationally aired "quiz kid" shows; one, *Texaco Star Academic Challenge*, aired in 1990. U.S. academic shows lean towards entertaining educational *games* rather than educational *quizzes*. This approach may portend a change in other countries.

4. International format transfers

All the world loves interactive games. In large part, the world loves interactive games as much as it does BECAUSE U.S. viewers do. Popular formats, primarily from the United States, can do well in other settings if subtle adaptations take place.

FORMAT SOURCES. Table 6.4 shows that transfers account for about one-third (36.9 percent) of all TV game shows. Again Northern/ Western Europe, the Pacific (Australia/New Zealand) and North America show a similar preference pattern. The first three regions take two-thirds or more of their games as transfers, most of them from the United States. North America, the game source, does not show up as a recipient of game transfers on Table 6.4, but the formats are nonetheless shared. (The United States accounts for 34 of the 41 games listed for North America). All other regions take about one-third or fewer of their games from elsewhere, preferring homegrown formats.

Other than *Wheel of Fortune* and *Jeopardy*, which are licensed by King World International, most U.S. shows produced overseas are licensed by Fremantle (e.g., *The Price Is Right*, *Dating Game*, *Blockbusters*, *Family Feud*, and *The $25,000 Pyramid*).

Some shows, of course, have been copied in format but not formally licensed. Japan's *100 People Polled Quiz*, for example, has the same set and format as *Family Feud*, but was not officially licensed. Furthermore, some countries (e.g., Japan, France and Italy) in addition to the United States spin off versions of local productions in other countries.

These cross-national transfers are all in addition to domestic shows widely seen outside the home country via

Table 6.4
TV Game/Quiz Shows in 50 Countries
Format Transfers, Autumn 1990

Region	# of Shows	Transfers (%)
1. Europe	32	62.5
2. W. Europe	70	68.6
3. Europe	9	33.3
4. Nr./Mid E	9	55.6
5. Africa	16	12.5
6. S/SE Asia	16	31.3
7. Asia	45	4.4
8. Pacific	8	100.0
9. Lat. Am.	14	14.3
10. No. Am.	41	7.3
Totals	260	36.9

satellite, taped shows that run in other countries (e.g., France's *Des Chiffres et des Lettres* runs in its France-produced version in Tunisia and Canada) and cross-border capturing of TV signals. Chile's *Sabado Gigante*, a unique cross-border show (see Ch. 10), runs via satellite throughout Latin America.

The last column of Appendix 2 notes whether a show has an original or transferred format. Appendix 2 shows *Wheel of Fortune* to be currently the most appealing show; at this writing, it was running in 25 countries outside the United States, with reruns in about 10 more. *The Price Is Right* runs in eight; *The Dating Game* in eight; *Family Feud* in five; and *Jeopardy* in five.

Appendix 2 also shows that certain games have more limited appeal. The high skills required of the numbers and letters manipulations of *Des Chiffres et des Lettres*, which has run for 20 years in France, have succeeded in Turkey,

Cameroon, and Belgium, with taped reruns in Canada. This show involves a great deal of dead silence as players try to make the longest word from given letters.

Game shows featuring nudity run in Germany, Turkey, Japan, and Spain, as spinoffs from or reruns of the Italian original, *Colpo Grosso*. Anyone with access to a satellite service that carries RTL+ can see Germany's strip-tease game *Tutti Frutti*. In Israel, ratings systems that track individual homes became a matter of some controversy because so many sets tune into *Tutti Fruitti* via RTL+.

Japan emerges as a significant game show source. Appendix 2 shows that Taiwan took over the format of *Takeshi's Castle*, a physical game that resembles *American Gladiators* but is tame enough for nonprofessional athletes. In addition, not included on Appendix 2 is the show *Waku Waku Dohbutsu Lando* (*Exciting Animal Land*), which featured questions based on video clips of animals filmed on location; it was adapted by about 15 countries in Asia and elsewhere. In the United States, it was called *Animal Crackups*. However, none of the countries sampled happened to run the clones when the data were taken for 1990-91. Moreover, Japanese travelogue and dating shows have been adopted in Taiwan and Korea, although not in 1990.

Appendix 2 shows that France also exports formats to some extent, notably *Les Genies en Herbe*, that runs in Canada and Ivory Coast. England received the popular show *Wetten Das* from Germany, which ran as *You Bet*. The English radio quiz shows *My Word* and *My Music* run on U.S. radio, but the U.K. show *Mastermind*, which was to run in the United States, did not air after all. (The author tried out for this show in California in 1989, but it did not survive the development process. See Appendix 1.)

VARIATION AND CONVERGENCE. The adaptation of transferred formats takes many forms (other than changing the language and the inclusion of questions related specifically to a target audience):

* lower prize values—approach taken by *The Price Is Right* in the Netherlands (Ferry 28).
* increase questions' difficulty—approach taken by *The Price Is Right* in France (Ferry 26).
* change length (time)—the British *Blind Date*, for example, runs one hour, but airs only once a week.
* change name of show—the various incarnations of *Family Feud* are shown in Appendix 2. *Hollywood Squares* becomes *VIP* in Spain; *The Newlywed Game* becomes *Between Husband and Wife* in Italy.
* add celebrities—Australia favors this approach, airing celebrity versions of both *Family Feud* and *Wheel of Fortune*.
* make show a segment—in France, a *Dating Game* segment constitutes part of *Tournez Manege*, while Nickelodeon games become part of a long Saturday children's show on the BBC in England.
* change the set—Spain's *Price Is Right* proved successful after it subdued the brash U.S. stage set.
* put show in prime time (once/week)—the non-prime time placement of U.S. shows resulted from the quiz show scandals of the 1950s. Because other nations escaped that stigma, game shows often have prime time slots in the schedule (e.g., *Wheel of Fortune* in France).

Geertz, quoted earlier, refers to anthropology's "deepest theoretical dilemma: how is such [cultural] variation to be squared with the biological unity of the human species?" (23). To paraphrase Geertz, neither total unity nor total variability prevails (23).

Entertainment programming shows us that cultural preferences follow patterns. On the one hand, no game show format or style has touched audiences universally. For example, *Wheel of Fortune*'s 25 markets represent only 14 percent of the world's national TV systems.

On the other hand, people naturally form cultural groups that do not coincide with political borders (see Ch. 10). The array of shows in this study helps us understand that certain concepts—not just specific shows—have worldwide appeal.

* matchmaking/dating—six countries of the 50 in the study run licensed versions of *The Dating Game*, with the UK and New Zealand versions adding a date rehash segment that resembles *The Love Connection*. In addition, Japan, Taiwan, China, and Korea had matchmaking programs that differed from the *Dating Game* format (three unseen women or men being interviewed by a potential date). Taiwan's *We Love the Matchmaker* introduces the families of a couple that the producers of the show have matched up; it resembles a Japanese show from the 1970s, *Punch-de Date-o*. Taiwan's *Sparks Fly* puts ten college women and ten men together for a round of relay races and other feats—and lets them pair up at the show's end; it resembles but proceeds at a slower pace than Japan's *Red Whale Tribe*.
* studying—as noted in the previous section, *Les Genies en Herbe*, a young people's quiz, runs in French-speaking countries. The *College Bowl*, which ran from 1953 to 1970, was licensed in Australia, New Zealand, and England, where it ran 28 seasons as *University Challenge*. In addition, many countries have student

quiz programs that look much like the College Bowl, but are independently produced: Belgium, Korea, Ghana, Kenya, and Saudi Arabia (see KQ notations in Appendix 2).

* shopping—*The Price Is Right*, which runs in at least eight countries beside the United States, is not alone in its simulation of the buyer's experience. *Wheel of Fortune* includes a shopping segment, as the winner of each round spends his or her earnings for consumer goods.
* family ties—the name changes of the six *Family Feud* versions that run outside the United States can be instructive. As Talbot explains, the Hatfield-McCoy feud means little to an overseas audience. Thus the show has run as *Family Fortunes* (UK), *Golden Family* (France), *Dear Parents* (Italy), and *We Asked 100 People Quiz* (Japan). The Japanese unlicensed version interestingly emphasizes the consensus nature of the *questions* in its title, even though two family teams compete in the game.

We can set these mostly similar shows against some that simply would not make the transition elsewhere. The subject-specificity would prevent some shows from traveling abroad. For example, U.S. shows dealing with black culture (the Black Entertainment Network's *Family Figures*), football (ESPN's *NFL Triva Game*), or country music (the Nashville Network's *Fandango*) would not survive in Japan. Conversely, some shows, such as Japan's *Ultra Quiz*, which tests the physical and mental endurance of players and punishes losers unmercifully, would not survive the transition to any other culture.

Chapter 7

THE PARTICIPANTS

"Jungle Gardenia." Remember? It was a ladies' perfume. The inimitable Bob Barker, host of the NBC daytime hit *Truth or Consequences*, awarded a bottle of the stuff to each and every loser. And oh, were there losers! Thousands and thousands of them. (Meisler 7)

1. Players

Take 30 game shows a day in the United States alone, with an average of four contestants each; that's 120 winners and losers appearing each day, or 600 a week. Since game shows take no summer vacations, that's 31,200 people a year. If only a quarter that number of players appear on shows in each one of the 50 nations in this study, that's 382,200 contestants outside the United States. Many bottles of Jungle Gardenia. Or Jungle Aftershave.

CIVILIANS. Talk to the people next to you at a meeting or standing in line; it will not take many conversations to unearth a game show story. This author once spoke to a class of about 50 college students in Taipei; two had appeared on a game show. Of a university communications faculty of less than 100, one had appeared on *Jeopardy!* and another had appeared on a quiz show in India.

For each civilian who claims his 15 minutes of fame on a

game show (see Appendix 1b), at least 20 others have stories to tell about trying out unsuccessfully (Schiffres 59) (see Appendix 1a). For *Jeopardy!*, the odds are 35 to 1 against getting on the air, or 1,000 to 1 for advancing to the Tournament of Champions (Meisler 23). A U.S. publication, *TV Game Show Magazine,* has been started to give TV hopefuls the numbers and names they need to try to make it into the spotlight.

For those who do make it, small-town newspapers turn them into local heroes (e.g., Linstrom). Contestants themselves have something to write about (e.g., Fermaglich). Friends and relatives have something to talk about. Duncan, while researching a story on Brazil's phenomenal game show hostess, Xuxa, quickly encountered someone "who couldn't wait to show an inquirer pictures of her little girl on stage with Xuxa" (14).

Fleeting TV fame has its negative side as well. U.S. winners must pay taxes whether they win cash or merchandise, although they may simply decline a prize that they do not want (no substitutes permitted). One *Tic Tac Dough* winner, Kit Salisbury, had a giant game show sale to convert his $160,000 worth of golf clubs, stoves, rowing machines, talking lamps, Doritos, cough syrup, and other items into cash (Graham 104).

The thousands of losers who walk out with only Jungle Gardenia cannot simply fade away. Their moment of defeat will turn up on VCRs at parties and reunions for years to come. In 1988, Kerry Ketchum, the biggest winner in *Password*s history, experienced the ultimate defeat. He was arrested for credit card fraud after bank officials recognized him on the show (*Game's over*). Most other winners or losers can get another chance on another show—for a maximum of three appearances.

Answer: fame and fortune. Question: What makes 15,000 people a year try out for *Jeopardy!*? Or stand in line for hours on the slim chance of getting called to "come on down" to compete on *The Price Is Right*? And for one man on *Wheel of Fortune*, his $49,633 paled in comparison to the chance to meet Vanna White (Waters 68). Children react even more strongly; a little girl sobbed uncontrollably when Brazil's Xuxa picked her out of the audience and gave her a hug.

No one has ever polled game show contestants in various countries to compare motivations. Nor does anyone have even basic demographic data about them, due to the need to watch and code each show in various nations over a selected time period. Only one study looked at contestants on U.S. game shows (Cooper-Chen). It found that more women (55.4 percent) than men appeared; blacks (12.5 percent of players) were fairly represented, but Hispanics (only 1.4 percent) and people over 60 (2 percent) were seriously under represented when compared to the U.S. population. (See Ch. 6, section 2.)

An alert viewer cannot help but gain impressions while watching game shows from here and there. In Peru, where most contestants look European, a person with obvious native (Indian) ancestry stands out. In Brazil, where contestants are often chosen from audiences for brief appearances, each show has some mixed-race (but few dark-skinned black) players; however, the proportion does not equal that of Brazil's population at large (43 percent black or mixed race).

In the Muslim world, all contestants on Saudi Arabian game shows are male. However, Tunisia, Egypt, Turkey, and

Lebanon seem to have nearly equal proportions of male and female players.

The former Soviet Union tried a show called *Let's Go, Boys* that failed, while a companion show, *Let's Go, Girls*, proved to be a gigantic success. Hosted by Alexander Malyakov in the 1970s and 1980s, it featured women demonstrating or answering questions about career skills, household skills, and cultural knowledge. One episode focused on vacuuming and ballroom dancing skills. Although the prizes were mere sets of dishes, the women players earned celebrity status and numerous marriage proposals.

The "ban" against older players seems universal. Sometimes the format favors youthful players, such as the grueling, obstacle-course games popular in many nations: *100 Battles, 100 Victories* (Taiwan); *Falling Bridge*, *Olympia* and *Passa ou Repassa* (Brazil); *Trans-America Ultra Quzi* (Japan); *Lucky Studio* (Korea); and *Double Dare* (United States). On advertising-supported systems, "unwritten rules" work against older players no matter what the format: according to Fabe, "The shows and their sponsors are looking to appeal to people with buying power, the housewives between the ages of 18 and 49; not *you*, I'm afraid" if you're over 60 (7).

An exception is Korea's *Century Quiz*. Three players from each generation receive a starting score equal to their combined ages; thus the older the grandmother or grandfather, the higher the starting score.

In Yaounde, Cameroon, player selection for *Cherchez le Mot* takes place on Mondays. From about 15 candidates, two will eventually appear on the 8 p.m. Wednesday word game. Teachers (who fear losing publicly) and women are under-represented as players; students, office workers, and residents of Yaounde—especially members of the Yaounde Scrabble Club—are well represented. Those who win at least ten matches can appear in the tournament, gaining a shot at a trip to Paris and other prizes ("Cherchez").

CELEBRITIES. In the 1990-91 season, most games carried on without celebrity players either exclusively or in tandem with civilians. In most countries, to paraphrase Shakespeare, playing the game's the thing. However, in others, audiences like to see celebrities "playing themselves"—especially in England, Germany, Australia, and Japan.

Table 7.1 shows that East Asian audiences prefer to see *gliteratti* rather than "plain folks" as players/panelists; in only that region, a majority (62.2 percent) of shows features celebrities. Just as the United States dominates the North American region, Japan dominates East Asia, accounting for 32 of the region's 45 shows; thus East Asia largely reflects Japanese tastes. In 1992, only six of Japan's 32 shows had civilian players (see Ch. 9).

The British like clever, witty performers for whom the game provides a comedy showcase. *My Word* and *My Music*, which U.S. audiences used to hear over National Public Radio, featured Dennis Norden, Anne Scott-James, and Frank Muir. In 1990-91, Muir was "a household name—and a household face—because of his enormously popular TV appearances in a verbally inventive panel game, *Call My Bluff*" (Andreae). In *Have I Got News For You*, which calls itself a "topical comedy quiz show," two teams of celebrities face off. The Appendix 2 U.S. listing on HA!, the comedy channel, for *Whose Line Is It Anyway?* is a taped 1988 rerun of the British show that was still going strong in

Table 7.1
TV Game/Quiz Shows in 50 Countries
Celebrities, Autumn 1990

Region	# of Shows	Celebrities (%)
1. N. Europe	32	15.6
2. W. Europe	70	14.7
3. E. Europe	9	0.0
4. Nr./Mid E	9	0.0
5. Africa	16	5.6
6. S/SE Asia	16	18.8
7. E. Asia	45	62.2
8. Pacific	8	33.3
9. Lat. Am.	14	33.3
10. No. Am.	41	6.8
Totals	260	19.0

the 1990s. Four comedians compete for points via ad lib performances (except that MC Clive Anderson gives "10 points to everyone"). In Round 2, for example, comedians must portray an accident investigation in the style of Japanese Noh drama and Gilbert and Sullivan. A fourth British show featuring celebrities is Bruce Forsyth's *Generation Game.*

U.K. celebrities need not be entertainers to appear on game shows. *Quizbowl*, a sports quiz in the 1991-92 season (thus not listed in Appendix 2), featured writers from The Guardian and Independent newspapers. Finally, as in Japan, quiz specials appear from time to time, such as a December 1991 show pitting celebrities against scientists in predictions about the year 1992.

In Germany, according to Donald Browne, TV quizzes "are one of the great German national pastimes" (*Com-*

paring 21). German audiences like two U.S. imports that no longer run in the United States. *Die Pyramid* pairs celebrities with civilians who try to guess target words. *Dingsda*, which ran in the United States as *Child's Play*, has celebrities trying to guess a word that children have been asked to define; if the key word is "brain," children on videotape may be shown talking about "something squishy with a lot of tubes."

The popular homegrown German show *Wetten Das*, which airs about four times a year, features civilians with odd abilities: naming a person's hometown after hearing him or her say just a few sentences; balancing a Volkswagen on wineglasses; lighting 1,000 matches in 30 seconds. The celebrity bets whether or not the civilian can perform the feat as claimed. ITV in Britain has adopted the show as *You Bet*.

Australia favors celebrity versions of U.S. imports. In 1990-91, three such shows aired: *Celebrity Family Feud*, *Celebrity Wheel of Fortune*, and *Sale of the Century*. Harris calls the latter "a hardy perennial" that has remained high in the ratings ever since it began in 1980. In 1990, three former politicians won prizes on the show: Gough Whitlam, former prime minister, got a set of saucepans; David Lange, ex-prime minister of New Zealand, a lawn mower; and former party leader Don Chipp, a set of luggage.

But the celebrity trophy goes to Japan. Of the nation's game shows that ran in 1992, 80 percent featured celebrities, most of them in prime time. Chapter 9 describes them in detail.

Tojun Oh, producer of *Let's Go! the World*, credits his highly rated show, which began on October 6, 1981, with switching game shows from civilians to celebrity players. "In the old days, quiz show participants were almost all ordinary people," he wrote to the author. "The purpose of this show is the *process* of guessing the solution to a mystery. Thus the interchange between the MC and the panelists becomes a show in itself. Ordinary people's conversation is not so interesting." Once the celebrity approach succeeded, other Japanese shows began using them. Stars on these "talk quizzes" are impulsive, irreverent, and unreserved, unlike most shy Japanese citizens.

Two shows especially deserve mention for their creative use of celebrities. Egypt's *Dawry ep Negoum* (*Stars Tournament*) appears every year during Ramadan, the month of daytime fasting. As many as ten men and ten women, most of them film stars, answer questions or engage in physical games. No prizes are awarded—just prestige, since during the evening hours families gather to eat after fasting and enjoy watching television.

The French-language *Les Detecteurs de Mensonge* on CBCF in Montreal, Canada, features three celebrities on each show. Each one makes three amusing/outrageous statements, such as "I danced with Superman." The other two ask questions and try to ferret out the lie ("mensonge"). The celebrities' personalties and poise keep things moving, while the format requires no fancy sets, no prizes, and almost no budget. Each segment lasts just six or seven minutes, so the pace is brisk. With the game's simple rules and well-dictioned speaking, the show presents a painless way for students at any school with a satellite dish to practice French.

2. Umpires: hosts and assistants

A. "It's not acting, it's not singing, it's not dancing. It's moving things along, being a pointer." (Graham, *Come* 78)
Q. What is a game show host?

That's how Dick van Dyke described his stint as a host of the game show *Mother's Day* in 1958-59, before he found work in Broadway musicals and on TV comedies. Van Dyke's definition could also fit a game show assistant. But despite some similarities, the two umpire jobs have one great difference: hosts speak; assistants remain silent. And then there is that gender matter.

HOSTS. A facetious answer to the question above comes from Tom Kennedy (*Name That Tune*, *You Don't Say*): "Game show hosts are tall guys with Shinola on the hair and pearly white teeth" (Graham, *Come* 69). In fact, for Christmas 1987, Galoob toys put out a plastic doll with shiny black hair, big teeth, money in one hand, and a mike in the other—Mr. Game Show (69).

In the United States, that stereotyped doll's characteristics reflect the truth. Of some 400 U.S. game shows, many of which ran for years, only five white women and five black men have ever been hosts (see Ch. 8). If we remove cable shows, the numbers decline even more.

The demographics do not hold for most of the rest of the world, however. Nor does the single host-single announcer pattern dominate in domestically produced shows. Yet one universal is clear: the host's role as a constant in communicating with the home viewers. According to Mendelsohn, radio and television's "importantly unique aspect" is the pleasure of parasocial interaction:

> television and radio afford an intimacy and degree of privatization that allows performers to simulate informal, face-to-face, friendly conversations with their unseen mass audiences. This same intimacy...allows audiences to react to them as if some sort of real social interaction was taking place—although, of course, all this occurs in the audience's imagination. (129)

We can draw firmer conclusions about hosts than about contestants, since hosts do not change from week to week. What patterns can we find? Demographics prove the easiest aspects to analyze, as hosting "styles" may vary from person to person. We can first take a wide view, looking at regional patterns.

As Table 7.2 shows, East Asia practices equal opportunity in game show hosting, having a woman as host or cohost on 51 percent of its shows. Not obvious from Table 7.2 is the fact that most Japanese shows have female *co*hosts. Latin America, by contrast, tends to have female *hosts*, not just cohosts; nearly half of Latin games have women in charge. Again, Northern/Western Europe, the Pacific (Australia/New Zealand) and North America share a trait—this time in common with the Near/Middle East—of no or few female game show hosts.

Generally, all around the world, black women do not serve as game show hosts. Only in sub-Saharan Africa do we find a few; in Cameroon, West Africa, host both *Mister Word* (Endale Lottin) and *Cherchez le Mot* (Sylvie Nguiamba) are hosted by females.

In Western countries, women's rare hosting appearances have a strong association with dating shows. Arlene Francis, probably the first woman to host a network TV game show (in 1949 on Dumont), began the pattern of

Table 7.2
TV Game/Quiz Shows in 50 Countries
Female Hosts/Cohosts, Autumn 1990

Region	# of Shows	Female Hosts/ Cohosts (%)
1. N. Europe	32	15.6
2. W. Europe	70	12.8
3. E. Europe	9	11.1
4. Nr./Mid E	9	11.1
5. Africa	16	25.0
6. S/SE Asia	16	18.8
7. E. Asia	45	51.1
8. Pacific	8	0.0
9. Lat. Am.	14	42.9
10. No. Am.	41	0.0
Totals	260	20.0

woman-as-matchmaker with her show *Blind Date*. In more recent times, licensed versions of *The Dating Game* have provided women with hosting jobs in England, Sweden, Finland, and France. Ironically, the show's home, the United States, had a female host only briefly—Elaine Joyce, in 1986.

In Europe, the Low Countries provide the best variety of hosting opportunities (1990-91 season) for women: Luxembourg with *Atoukado* on Sundays; the Netherlands with *Wie Ben Ik?* on Tuesdays and *Op Goed Geluk* on Fridays; and Belgium with *Ingrid, Ingrid*, a sports quiz that includes identifying a mystery guest in the studio, on Mondays. All the weekday games air in prime time.

Of the Western countries that have many game shows, Germany, Australia, and the United States have the worst equal-opportunity record. The numbers and status of ethnic and racial minorities vary from country to country (blacks in the United States differ from Turkish guest workers and first-generation Vietnamese in Germany); thus the best cross-national comparison involves women.

Still, the numbers game can be misleading. The fact that Italy has a genetically deviant, large-breasted woman as co-host on the X-rated *Colpo Grosso* does not represent a milestone of progress, but rather business as usual. The co-host had made her debut on the show as a contestant and had wowed the audience with her striptease.

In the West, where a single-host pattern prevails, women hosted 15.6 percent of shows in Northern Europe, 12.8 percent in Western Europe and none in North America. Unfortunately, what's good for American business—the lively trade in of U.S. game shows—exports U.S. stereotypes of women's roles. For example, all letter turners on the 25 versions of *Wheel of Fortune* are female and most hosts are male—just as in the show's parent U.S. version.

Homegrown formats shake free of preconceived patterns more easily than imported formats. In Asia, the co-host (or even triple host) pattern dominates game shows, almost always a male/ female team. U.S. network news broadcasts resemble game shows in their one-man, top-dog schema. But Asian newscasts often have male and female anchors, as do their game shows.

For whatever reasons, the Philippines, Thailand, Taiwan, Korea, and especially Japan all have male/female hosting teams. Two of Taiwan's shows have a dating theme (*We Love the Matchmaker* and *Sparks Fly*), but the other Asian shows run the gamut from academic quizzes to messy stunt competitions to word games to travelogues. And the dating show, *Red Whale Tribe,* in Japan defies stereotypes by featuring a two-man comedy team as host. (See Ch. 9 for details on Japan's and Taiwan's games.)

Another non-Western pattern, the long-format, variety-plus-game program, usually creates a need for several hosts—sometimes including women. The long shows, usually airing on weekends, prevail in Latin countries. In Peru, *Triki Trak*, a five-hour Sunday show in Peru, has a female co-host, as does the daily show *Fantastico*. However, both hosts of Brazil's 10.5-hour Sunday extravaganza the *Silvio Santos Program* are males, as is Don Francisco, host for more than 20 years of Chile's 3.5-hour *Sabado Gigante*.

Mexico's *El Hora del Gane*, no longer running, featured Kippy Casado as one of its hosts. Now Casado has her own radio game/variety show, broadcast live Mondays and Thursdays from the Teatro del Pueblo, Monterrey. Other Latin women who host TV shows include Patricia Panini of Mexico's *Familia Millionaria* and Peru's Gisela of the daily *Alo, Gisela* show.

Finally, some surprises stand out from Appendix 2. Turkey's *Hangisi* is a rare example of a female-hosted show in a Moslem country. Brazil's Xuxa and Anjelica (*Club de Crianca*) are rare examples of women hosting children's game shows. One might think that if women host dating shows, they would also host children's shows, but they do not. The PBS and Nickelodeon programs all have male hosts. But in 1992, breaking precedent, Nickelodeon installed a black male, Phil Moore, as host of its new *Arcade* game program. By 1993, the new game *Caesars Challenge*, taped in Las Vegas, also featured a black male host (and male assistant).

ASSISTANTS. *Ms.* Maxene Fabe devotes three paragraphs to the subject of assistants—all three of them about "*the* quintessential game show assistant," Roxanne, a U.S. TV phenomenon in the 1950s (39). *Mr.* Jefferson Graham, on the other hand, devotes 19 pages to that "sexy, silent fantasy object" (134).

U.S. shows have seen few washing machine fondlers who did not conform to a stereotype just as unshakable as *Mr. Game Show*. A toy *Miss Game Show* would have white skin, a shapely body, tall stature and a lovely face—in short, a Barbie doll. An exception occurred when, in 1983, Reg Grundy, an Australian game show producer, brought a revised version of *Sale of the Century* to NBC that included male models (*Sale* had previously run on NBC 1969-73; Grundy then revamped it for Australian viewers, where it has run since 1980).

The ultimate stereotyped assistants appear on *Colpo Grosso*, which started in Italy and has since been licensed in Germany, Spain, and Brazil (with reruns in Japan and Turkey). The show has eight assistants, the "Cin cin girls," who do much more than point to prizes. One game has a player guessing if a tattoo does or does not appear on the assistant's breast; to award points, there's only one way to prove if the player guessed right. Furthermore, interlude segments feature the Cin-cins doing strip teases.

Quite a far cry from Vanna White, the best-known game show assistant in U.S. TV history. In September 1992, she turned letters as usual on a taping segment without realizing until the audience went wild that the phrase spelled "Vanna's pregnant." (That incident and White's subsequent miscarriage made headlines in the United States.)

The worldwide diversity in the role of assistants parallels that of hosts. If a show has been exported, the "package" looks fairly similar around the world, partly because form follows function. In other words, versions of *Wheel of Fortune* have not substituted three assistants, who after all would trip over each other turning one or two letters per round. Neither have they substituted a mechanical letter turner for the Vanna White role, which viewers in all countries no doubt have come to expect. Similarly, *The Price Is Right* has a number of assistants to demonstrate showcase prizes in all the countries that have adopted the show.

Since U.S. exports go mainly to Western nations (including Australia), because of pre-existing cultural and business relations, the entertainment norms get reinforced. Thus most European shows, even the homegrown ones, have a host-plus-assistant(s) pattern.

Asian programs that have multiple hosts do not really need assistants. At the other extreme, some Latin long-format variety/game shows have assistants who dance and energize the audience—as many as eight per show. *Fantastico* and *Triki Trak* (Peru), *Xou da Xuxa* and *Club de Crianca* (Brazil) and *Sabado Gigante* (Chile and Mexico) all have bevies of female dancer/ assistants.

Fabe, in discussing the dearth of female game show hosts, laments that "alas, most women, for cultural reasons, have been cast in the role of the sexy assistant who slinks across the stage to giggle or wink" (37). Asia has broken that stereotype. But nowhere in Asia do we find older women as hosts. The silver-haired Bob Barker does not have a female counterpart anywhere.

3. Fans: audiences and ratings

Except for a loyal fan who dutifully tapes every episode of *Wheel of Fortune*, the author and her husband would have missed their brief appearance within the "o" of the superimposed words *Wheel of Fortune*. (At the August 1989 taping we attended, we learned that "our" episode would air in October, but we did not realize that the camera had caught us in its pan.) Seeing the show again did not seem important, but each episode *was* important to our friend, a real estate agent in her mid-50s.

Game show fans remain elusive, except for their presence in a barrel of postcards to be picked for a prize or as Nielsen numbers. Neither Fabe (1979) nor Graham (1988) devote any pages to fans. But legions of them do exist.

This author finds hesitation, then a few sheepish grins and half-raised hands, when she talks about game shows and asks if anyone watches them. As *Super Password*'s host, Bert Convey, tells it this way:

> People always come up to me and say, "You know, Bert, I don't watch daytime TV, but I was home with the flu and really enjoyed *Password*." Well, there must be twenty million people out there with the flu. (Graham 7)

Nielsen measures TV audiences in the United States and overseas, where services are tailored to local markets. Major services include Audits of Great Britain (AGB), which operates in Europe, Asia, and Australia; GFK in Germany; Secodip in France; Dentsu Advertising in Japan; and IBOPE in Brazil (Poltrack 427).

Units of measure include the rating and the share. The rating is the percentage of all possible viewers who are watching a particular TV program at a particular time. Considering all people who are watching at a given time (Homes Using Television, or HUT), the share is the percentage who are watching a particular program. The Nielsen NTI is based on the number of viewers who turn to a program during the average minute. Ratings take on more importance in advertising-supported TV systems and less in government-supported systems.

THE UNITED STATES. In the mid-1980s, game shows were riding high in Nielsen syndication ratings (called Cassandras). Ratings for November 1986 (released in January 1987) showed four game shows in the top 15 syndicated programs:

1)	*Wheel of Fortune*	19.3 rating
2)	*Jeopardy!*	12.3 rating
4)	*New Newlywed Game*	8.9 rating
14)	*Hollywood Squares*	7.2 rating

The Cassandras also revealed age and gender differences in viewing patterns: among the top five shows watched by women 25-54 were *Wheel of Fortune, Jeopardy!* and *New Newlywed Game*; by men 25-54, the only game show was *Wheel of Fortune*; and by teenagers, the top five were all comedies.

When network and syndicated shows are considered together, *Wheel of Fortune* has by far the greatest household audience, based on ratings by Arbitron (a U.S.-only service) for 1986:

1)	*Wheel of Fortune*	23.6 million	NBC & syndicated
2)	*Jeopardy!*	12.9 million	syndicated
3)	*Newlywed Game*	8.7 million	syndicated
4)	*Price Is Right*	6.2 million	CBS

5) *Hollywood Squares*	5.5 million		syndicated
6) *Card Sharks*	5.3 million	CBS	
7) *Dating Game*	4.2 million		syndicated
8) *Scrabble*	3.9 million	NBC	
9) *$25,000 Pyramid*	3.7 million	CBS	
10) *Love Connection*	3.4 million		syndicated

In local prime time, game shows often compete directly with local or network news. For example, ABC's New York City affiliate moved *Jeopardy!* into competition with the CBS and NBC evening news—with disastrous ratings results for both Brokaw and Rather. Similarly, *Wheel*, the top show in its time slot in 87 percent of the 198 stations that carry it, killed competing news shows, according to *60 Minutes* (1986).

Five years later, for the week ending February 17, 1991, games had slipped somewhat, but *Wheel* and *Jeopardy* held firmly to the top two syndication slots:

1. *Wheel of Fortune*	14.9 rating
2. *Jeopardy!*	13.5 rating
3. *Wheel of Fortune* weekend	8.5 rating

Table 7.3 shows the tremendous popularity of game shows among women, especially among women aged 55 and over. Men like to watch daytime (weekend) sports (3.4 percent of total audience), while women prefer daytime game/quiz shows (3.1 percent of the total audience). As Chapter 4 argues, women like interactive mind games, while men like spectator physical games. Breaking down the female audience, women over 55 have the largest game/quiz preference of any group (5.5 percent). Older women and older men, by way of comparison, both prefer the nightly news to either daytime sports or daytime games.

Table 7.3
Popularity of U.S. Program Types, Men vs. Women
February 6-12, 1989

	Quiz/Audience Participation Weekday 6 am-4 pm		Nightly News 6-7 pm		Sports 6 am-4 pm Weekend	
HOUSEHOLD	4.3%		11.3%		4.6%	
TOT. WOMEN	3.1%		8.3%		2.4%	
Teens		0.8%		2.1%		1.4%
25-54		2.1%		5.8%		2.0%
55+		5.5%		15.0%		3.4%
TOT. MEN	1.9%		6.9%		3.4%	
Teens		0.8%		3.3%		2.4%
25-54		1.2%		4.8%		3.1%
55+		3.6%		13.6%		4.4%

Notes: teens = ages 12-17
% = percent of audience
Source: Nielsen

OTHER COUNTRIES. Unlike the United States, game shows elsewhere do not carry the taint of quiz scandals and thus often run in prime time, where they can pull in enough viewers to vault them into a nation's top ten programs—not just the top syndicated programs. Japan, Germany, the United Kingdom, Spain, and Brazil all have game show blockbusters.

Other countries' viewers may go gaga over games, but only unbiased ratings can offer proof. Unfortunately, ratings may not exist or this researcher could not get ratings for game shows in the Arab world or sub-Saharan Africa, where systems tend to be government-run.

Anecdotal evidence can fill some gaps. In Cameroon, for example, not all viewers are literate or can understand

Table 7.4
Top Five Game Shows in Selected Countries, 1991

Country/ Program	Source	Network	Time	Rating
UNITED KINGDOM				
Blind Date	LWT	ITV	Sat. 6:45	29.0
Strike it Lucky	Thames	ITV	Mon. 8:30	25.0
Family Fortunes	Talbot/ Central	ITV	Fri. 7:00	24.0
Krypton Factor	Granada	ITV	Mon. 7:00	23.0
You Bet	LWT	ITV	Fri. 8:00	22.0
NETHERLANDS				
Ron's Honeymoon Quiz	JE Ent.	RTL-4	Thu. 8:30	19 0
Who Am I?	John de Mol	RTL-4	Fri. 8:30	16.0
Soundmix Show	JE Ent.	RTL-4	no data	15.1
Lingo	IDTV/VARA	Ned.2	Tu. Sat 8:00	15.0
Hit Bingo	Joop Ende/P&G	RTL-4	Tu. 8:30	14.0
FRANCE				
Wheel of Fortune	Unilever	TF-l	6 days 7:20	22.9
Family Feud	T/Fremantle	TF-1	6 days 6:30	19.3
Price Is Right	T/Fremantle	TF-l	7 days 12:30	18.4
Fort Boyard	Antenne-2	A-2	Fri. 8:45	13.0
Dating Game	T/Fremantle	TF-1	W'kdays 7:05	12.1
ITALY				
Tele Mike	Finivest	Can.5	Thu. 8:40	7.8
Wheel of Fortune	Unilever	Can.5	6 days 7:00	7.6
Hollywood Squares	T/Fremantle	Can.5	6 days 6:00	6.5
We Loved Each Other So Much	Fininvest	Can.5	6 days 8:00	4.9
SPAIN				
Uno Dos Tres	Prointel	TVE-l	Fri. 9:00	24.0
Newlywed Game	T/Fremantle	Tele 5	6 days 7:30	24.4
Price Is Right	T/Fremantle	TVE-l	Mon. 9:00	19.3
Primi Juego	IVE	IVE-l	? 10:15	18.7
Don't Laugh, It's Worse	Music	TVE-1	5 days,2:30	14.0
AUSTRALIA				
The Main Event	LeisTime/Jnston	7 Net	Sun. 7:30	21.4
Wheel of Fortune	Grundy	7 Net	5 days, 5:00	20.6
Sale of the Century	Grundy	9 Net	5 days, 7:00	19.5
Family Feud	Grundy	7 Net	5 days, 4:30	16.9
Celebrity Wheel of Fortune	Grundy	7 Net	Sat. 8:00	15.8

Source: *Variety* Jan. 27, 1992

French, the language of CRTV's *Cherchez le Mot*. Those who understand explain the game's unfolding to those watching with them who cannot understand ("Cherchez..." 7).

The competitive European market makes ratings available to the general public. In January 1992, *Variety* surveyed game shows in Europe and Australia and provided ratings for the top five shows in each of six countries. (See Table 7.4.) Taiwan and Japan likewise must provide TV advertisers with reliable audience figures so media buyers know where to place their messages.

a. *Europe.* The United Kingdom loves game shows the most, judging from the over-20 ratings that the top five shows garnered in 1991. And the Brits do not mind imports. Productions may be local, as noted on Table 7.4 (e.g., London Weekend Television, Thames Television), but formats come from the United States, except for *You Bet* (German) and *Krypton Factor* (source unknown). Ten years earlier, Britons' tastes differed. The BBC's brainy *Mastermind* ranked as the sixth most popular show overall—not just the sixth most popular game show. Two other games—*Give Us A Clue* and *Play Your Cards Right*—also ranked in the nation's Top Ten.

The Netherlands "has perhaps the most voracious appetite for games in Europe," which by and large they originate themselves—"better-paced, snappier and more entertaining" than imports (Fuller 38). Besides the five on Table 7.4, the country's tiny population (14.7 million) supports 15 more shows. A different time period and different method yields different ratings. Expanding the list to ten for 1991 yields these shows (all of which run on RTL4):

		Rating
Ron's Honeymoon Quiz	JE Entertainment	17.1
The Soundmix Show	JE Entertainment	15.1
Who Am I?	Van OOyen/J de Mol	13.7
Second Youth Show	JE Entertainment	13.6
Hit Bingo	Procter & Gamble	12.4
Mini Playback Show	JE Entertainment	11.3
Wheel of Fortune	Unilever	9.8
Love at First Sight	Action Time	9.1
64,000 Guilder Question	Fremantle	7.0

Others include *Lingo*, *Black Out*, *Boggle*, *Fort Boyard*, *Does He or Does He Not? Triviant*, *The Surprise Show*, *The 100,000 Guilder Show*, and *Love Letters*.

France fell in love with *Wheel of Fortune* in 1987 and has remained steadfastly faithful to the show. *Wheel* had a 20.2 rating in June 1988, then did even better with a 22.9 rating for 1991. Table 7.5 gives more detailed age and gender data for 10 French shows. As in the United States, older persons—especially women—love games the most. Except for a children's show, games tend to have more than half of their viewers aged 50 and over (*Trivial Pursuit* appeals to both young and old). Just as significantly, every game appeals more to women than to men.

Italy has no games in double digits, but the genre performs steadily. The highest rating goes to *Tele Mike*, which features seasoned host Mike Buongiorno, who had his first quiz show in the 1950s (Clark).

Germany has seen spectacular ratings successes, often for shows that air infrequently. *Wetten Das* (*Make a Bet*), which is seen about four times a year, "regularly wins the top slot in the country's TV ratings, sometimes drawing as many as 50 percent of German households" (Revzin 1).

Table 7.5
Game Shows in France
Audience Sex and Age, 1989

Network/ Showtime		% tot. audience	% male	% fem.	% viewers aged 50+
TF-1					
11:30	*Jeopardy*	2.3	1.6	3.0	50.2
noon	*Dating Game*	7.3	6.3	8.3	59.3
12:30	*Price Is Right*	12.7	11.6	13.7	53.7
7:30	*Wheel of Fortune*	14.2*	na	na	59.0
A-2					
noon	*Newlywed Game*	4.9	4.0	5.8	50.1
12:30	*Trivial Pursuit*	5.9	4.7	6.9	37.8
6:40	*Chiffres/Lettres*	5.3	4.6	5.9	79.1
7:30	*Win, Lose, Draw*	5.9	5.3	6.5	43.5
LA 5					
5:30	*Road to Adventure*	1.1	0.8	1.4	11.2

*For June 1989; all other figures refer to September 4 - November 30, 1989.
Source: Mediamat

Flitterabend, which airs once a month (the game involves newlyweds), hit number 1 in the ratings in November 1991. Another love-theme show, *Love at First Sight*, which airs twice a month, has an average 37 percent share. *Die Pyramide*, which airs 15 weeks out of 52, gets about 20 percent. A clone of the Dutch *Love Letters* attracted 6.19 million viewers in its debut.

Spain's games do well against all shows. Of the 20 or so running in 1992, most air in prime time. Both U.S. transfers and Latin variety/game formats (*Uno, Dos, Tres*) do well.

When *Wheel of Fortune* (16.7) plays opposite a *Newlywed Game* clone, *Su Media Naranja* (an impressive 24.4), the love theme wins.

The only Eastern European ratings available to this study come from Poland, for its sole 1990 quiz, *The Big Game*. That show receives an annual average of 16 percent of general Polish viewers, 37 percent of whom rate it as "very good." (*Wheel* arrived in Poland in 1992.)

b. *Latin America.* Mexico's ratings are hard to get and somewhat suspect (Rota). The U.S.-based ratings for Univision (Spanish-language network) show that two-thirds to three-fourths of Hispanic homes watch Hispanic television. However, Univision officials believe that ratings consistently undercount Hispanic viewers (Feuer 83). In any case, *Sabado Gigante*, a Chilean show hosted by Don Francisco since 1962, made its debut on Univision in 1986. In three months, it became the number 1 show in Miami. As of spring 1988, about 34 percent of Hispanic households were watching it—and sometimes more than half the households.

Brazil has a sophisticated market research system, the Brazilian Statistical Public Opinion Research Institute (IBOPE), founded in 1942 and headquartered in Rio. According to Kottak (23), IBOPE has developed this scale of social classes:

Upper (A) & upper middle (B1)	6% of audience
Middle middle (B2) & lower middle (B3)	34% of audience
Working (C)	34% of audience
Abject poverty (D)	25% of audience
Total	100%

Globo, the world's fourth-largest network, generally outpulls the other networks, making Globo's children's game/variety shows *Xuxa* and *Millandro* the top shows in their daily morning time slots. The exception is Sunday, when SBT's *Silvio Santos Program* does better than Globo's *Domingo do Faustao*, a competing game/variety show.

In Peru, games routinely trounce the competition. Peru has three long-format game/variety weekend shows, as do many Latin countries. On Saturday, *Sabado Gigante* and *Trampolina a la Fama* stay about equal with 20 percent ratings, while the competing shows can manage only single digits. On Sunday, no other program comes close to ratings of the three-hour *Triki Trak* game/variety show. The daily *Gisela* and *Fantastico* shows both soundly kill the competition in their time slots.

c. *Asia/Pacific.* The world's largest TV audience, that of mainland China, has 600 million TV viewers. But "scientific and systematic study of Chinese audiences" is sadly lacking (Lau 161). The first national survey was done in 1987, but no regular national followup surveys track audience likes and dislikes. The 1987 Beijing audience survey and the 1983 Zhejiang Province survey did not include "game shows" as a program category.

Across the Taiwan Strait from mainland China, the Republic of China's games have a different viewing pattern from those in the West; rather than older viewers, especially women, all four of Taiwan's programs feature young contestants and appeal to male and female young viewers (Peng). Like the Latin countries, Sunday has active, long-format (but only to a maximum of 90 minutes) competition shows head to head. Both *100 Battles* and *Sparks Fly* have similarly respectable ratings, over 20 percent. The other

Table 7.6
Game Shows in Peru
Audience Ratings, Autumn 1990

Triki Trak Sun., 3-6 p.m. Canal 4

3:00	17.0 rating
3:30	18.5
4:00	20.4
4:30	20.1
5:00	20.1
5:30	18.2

Alo, Gisela M-F, 12:30-2 p.m. Canal 5

	M	T	W	TH	F
12:30	12.4	10.0	8.6	13.1	15.9
1:00	13.9	11.4	11.3	15.5	16.0
1:30	14.2	12.6	11.6	15.8	15.4

Fantastico M-F, 8-9 p.m. Canal 5

	M	T	W	TH	F
8:00	18.2	18.1	18.9	19.0	19.2
8:30	19.1	19.2	19.5	20.7	20.5

Sat:	*Sabado Gigante* Canal 9	*Trampolina a la Fama* Canal 5
4:30	17.2	—
5:00	21.1	21.3
5:30	22.4	21.3
6:00	21.7	23.5
6:30	22.0	23.8
7:00	20.4	26.5
7:30	19.8	26.0

Note: ratings refer to September 16-22, 1990.
Source: Mediamat

Table 7.7
Game Shows in Taiwan
Household Viewing, Autumn 1990

Unlucky Strike M-F, 6:30-7 p.m. Taiwan TV

M	T	W	Th	F
24.3	25.0	23.3	23.8	23.5

We Love the Matchmaker Sat., 5-6 p.m. Taiwan TV

5:00	15.8
5:30	15.1

Sun.	*100 Battles, 100 Victories* China TV Service	*Sparks Fly 50* China TV
12:30	26.3	23.5
1:00	27.5	22.5
1:30	25.7	

Note: Figures represent November 12-18, 1990.

show (Taiwan has three networks) does not do quite as well. The other weekend show, a dating format, draws ratings lower than its competing programs. The only daily show, *Unlucky Strike*, splits the early evening (6:30-7 p.m.) audience about evenly with its competition. Taiwanese viewers have a healthy but not voracious appetite for game shows.

Japan's viewers cannot get enough game shows, it seems. In 1984, six game/quiz programs hit the top 15 list in Japan, making this genre the single most popular in the nation. In 1992, only two games landed in the top 20 evening shows: *Let's Go! the World* (number 5) and *Takeshi and Itsumi's Heisei Educational Foundation* (number 19). Tojun Oh, producer of *Let's Go! the World*, wrote to the author that the formerly top-rated *Trans-America Ultra Quiz*, created in 1977 but now "an outmoded concept," has dropped drastically in the ratings. (See Table 7.8.)

Australia's love for games has one matchmaker: Reg Grundy. His top four of 1992's top five games only begin to tell the story, as Grundy has been producing and adopting games since the 1960s. One of his games has even gone back to the United States: an Australianized *Sale of the Century*. (See Table 7.4.)

Table 7.8
Game Shows in Japan
Audience Ratings, Autumn 1992

Show	Network	Day	Time	Share
Let's Go! the World	Fuji	Tu.	9-10 p.m	20.8
Takeshi and Itsumi's Heisi Educational Foundation	Fuji	Sat.	7-8 p.m.	18.7
World Professionals Quiz	Nippon	Wed.	8-9 p.m.	17.8
Tunnels Red Whale Tribe	Fuji	Sat.	11-11:30	17.8

Note: ratings refer to December 14-20, 1992.

Chapter 8

TV GAMES IN THE UNITED STATES

American popular culture, for better or worse, good or bad, is omnipresent. ...it can also be used as a showcase for the study of other popular cultures. (R. Browne, *Against* 76)

The United States—especially, Los Angeles—is the game show capital and prime game show exporter of the world.

The United States, which broadcast game shows earlier than almost any other nation, may have helped other countries with commercial systems to avoid the monumental mistakes made during the quiz show scandals of the 1950s. These scandals, whereby contestants were coached on how to perform (including when to lose), taught us that "advertisers control this medium" (Gerard). Thus game shows played a key role in U.S. television history. To understand the scandals' context and consequences, we must begin with the first mass mediated quiz shows.

1. The first 40 years: stunts, scandals, syndies

Radio game shows entertained U.S. audiences for more than a quarter century, beginning in 1924 when a news quiz sponsored by *Time* magazine went on the air. But the question-and-PRIZE format of the genre as we know it today, featuring non-celebrity players, dates back to 1936 and the radio hit *Uncle Jim's Question Bee*. But just ten years later, the days of the radio quiz were numbered. The war had interrupted its development, but by 1946, 6,000 of those new contraptions called televisions were in use.

The true beginning of television as an entertainment medium and the TV game show came in 1948, the first season offering viewers four full network schedules. From a modest 142,000 TV sets in use in 1947, U.S. consumers had 977,000 sets in operation in 1948. Fabe lists ten new TV games in 1947, all in local markets or on the doomed Dumont network (300-01). Then just a year later, in fall 1948, 25 new local and national TV games made their debuts.

Game show fever continued unabated. In 1949, in addition to an incredible 48 new TV games, eight of radio's best quizzes were simulcast: *Winner Take All*, *Break the Bank*, *Stop the Music*, *Juvenile Jury*, *Life Begins at Eighty*, *What's My Name? Quiz Kids*, and *Twenty Questions*. A show that had met success on KTLA Los Angeles, Mike Stokey's *Pantomime Quiz*, went network on CBS in 1949 and succeeded nationally as well.

Like *Pantomime Quiz*, after 1949, many popular game shows featured celebrities as either hosts, guests, or panelists—shows such as *What's My Line?* (1950), *You Bet Your Life* (1950), *I've Got a Secret* (1952), and *Do You Trust Your Wife?* (1956). In others, civilians "performed" as entertainers, by demonstrating physical prowess (*Break the Bank*, 1947; *Beat the Clock*, 1949), putting themselves in ridiculous situations (*Truth or Consequences*, 1950), or telling heart-rending stories (*Strike It Rich*, 1950; *Queen for a Day*, 1956).

The networks ran these spectator shows during television's early years because in 1949 the Federal

Communications Commission proposed a ban on giveaway quiz programs. However, in April 1954, the Supreme Court ruled against the proposal, declining to define giveaway shows as lotteries. Soon shows offering substantial prizes for civilian contestants emerged as hits on daytime television; *To Tell the Truth*, *Tic-Tac-Dough* and *The Price Is Right*, for example, all made their debuts in 1956. These shows tested not only the on-stage players, but incidentally at-home viewers as well; like *Uncle Jim's Question Bee*, viewers could play along. However, prime-time shows relied on entertainment value rather than interactivity to attract viewers.

The era of big-money, prime-time quiz programs began in June 1955 with CBS's *The $64,000 Question* and ended in 1959 with a Congressional probe of charges that they were rigged. Since the viewer could not play along by answering esoteric questions, the civilian contestant was still an entertainer—much more like a show-biz professional than viewers realized. Isolation booths, bank vaults, and affidavits emphasized the security of the big-money questions and honesty of the proceedings—all of which was an illusion.

Albert Freedman, the producer of *Twenty-One*, justified the fixing of quiz shows as a process similar to creating an exciting dramatic plot, arguing that "quiz shows, as entertainment, were a breath of fresh air" (Castleman and Podrazik 135). Charles van Doren told the House Legislative Oversight Committee in 1959 that *Twenty-One* aimed "to be as entertaining as possible" (Fabe 208).

Popular contestants were allowed to continue winning, while certain others were coached as to how and when to lose, in order to milk each episode for maximum excitement and tension. In 1957, the uncoached Dr. Joyce Brothers, a psychologist, beat the ratings-driven, advertiser-controlled system: the sponsor of *The $64,000 Question* (Revlon) had marked her for a fall, but she correctly answered the questions meant "to do her in" (Fabe 209). Yet in another sense, Brothers was part and parcel of the system. Playing to the show's entertainment formula of expertise-against-type, she boned up on a non-academic subject that had relatively few statistics to memorize: boxing. She won $134,000 for a topic she cared little about.

After the quiz show scandals, game shows fell into disrepute. From an impressive 31 new network TV games in 1953 and 28 in 1958, only three made their debuts in 1960—all during daytime, and now pointedly called game shows. Numbers of new shows crept up steadily year by year in the early 1960s, including some classics: *Password* (1962), *Let's Make a Deal* (1963), *Jeopardy* (1964), *The Dating Game* (1965), *The Newlywed Game* (1966), and *Hollywood Squares* (1966).

But tastes and political concerns soon changed, such that no new shows became hits in 1967, 1968, and 1969. Indeed, in 1969 the networks bought no new shows, forcing producers to sell locally, station by station. Not until 1972 did CBS and ABC take a chance on "new" games—and then only revivals (*Password* and *The Price Is Right*).

Besides revivals, other trends of the 1970s included gambling, sex, and coorientation. Graham calls *Gambit* (1972) "TV's first pure gambling show" (41). Producer Merrill Heatter followed it in 1974 with *High Rollers*. Gambling as a motif remains popular in the 1990s. Coorientation proved so successful that two 1970s' shows relying on that formula (second-guessing another person's or persons' responses) stand out as the first game shows to finish in first place in daytime ratings: *The Match Game* and *Family Feud.*

As originated by *The Newlywed Game* (1966), many 1970s' formats combined coorientation and sexual double-entendre. *Hot Seat* required a wife to judge a husband's answers; *Three's a Crowd* pitted a wife's against secretary's knowledge of a man; *Tattletales* gave prizes if a couple's answers matched; *The Better Sex* required players to predict opposite-sex team members' answers; and *Mindreaders* had team-mates predict the completion of personal statements.

By the end of the 1970s, "audiences has grown tired of the bawdy shows. Tradition came back in" (Graham 44). The 1980s also saw the rush to syndication by game shows, for two reasons. First, the burgeoning number of independent stations, hungry for programs with proven track records, found that syndicated game shows cost less than network reruns. Second, the Federal Communications Commission decided in 1970 to give local stations one hour of prime time per night (7-8 p.m.), hoping that stations would use the time for public affairs programs, high-quality children's programs, or other original shows. But instead most stations purchased light entertainment from syndicators for the 4-8 p.m. period.

Comedy remained the king of syndication until November 1983, when the Nielsen ratings for syndicated programs (Cassandras) put a game show (*Family Feud*) in first place. Game shows have held the top spot ever since. (See Ch. 7.)

The 40-year history of TV game/quiz shows in the United States, from 1948 to 1988, saw the decline of passive "performance" shows and the rise of interactive formats. Celebrities—famous people appearing on game shows as well as famous people created BY game shows—have lost their appeal as the game has ascended. The contemporary game show, freed from the pressure of prime time, bears out these trends.

2. U.S. television: games for the 1990s

The year that *Newsweek* put *Wheel of Fortune*'s Vanna White on its cover (February 9, 1987) and *Nightline* devoted one program to TV game shows (March 6, 1987) was a good one; in 1987, 31 shows were available to viewers in central Ohio (Cooper-Chen). But things would get even better.

Tables 8.1, 8.2, and 8.3 show an astounding 36 formats available in 1988, 35 in 1990, and then a sharp decline to 22 in 1992. Jarvis opines that we "may be witnessing the slow death of that great American institution, the game show" (5). However, Fabe observed the same cyclical game show decline in 1960 (after the quiz show scandals) and in 1970-71 (during the Vietnam/Woodstock era). After each transition period, game show fever returned.

STAYING POWER. Five shows have survived throughout the 1988-92 period, each of them occupying a unique niche. Solid formats have made these shows age like old wine rather than turn sour like vinegar. Indeed, each made its debut before 1988, making their longevity even more impressive. They are:

Price Is Right network 1956-64, 1972-
Jeopardy 1964-75; 1978-79; syndicated, 1984-
Family Feud network, 1976-85; 1988- (and syndicated)
Wheel of Fortune network, 1975- ; syndicated, 1983-
Double Dare 1986- , Nickelodeon children's cable channel

Table 8.1
Game Shows on U.S. Television
Autumn 1988

	ABC	CBS	NBC	CABLE	PBS/ FOX/IND
Sat.					
11:30-noon				*Double Dare*/ Nickelodeon	
7 pm-7:30	*Wheel of Fortune*+				
7:30-8	*Jeopardy*+				
Sun.		NONE			
Mon.-Fri.					
8 am-8:30					*Fun House*/ Fox
9-9:30				*Fandango*/ Nashville#	
9:30-10		*Sweethearts*	*Scrabble*		
10-10:30		*Family Feud*	*Sale of the Century*		
10:30-11		*Card Sharks*	*Concentration*		
11-11:30		*Price Is Right*	*Wheel of Fortune**		
11:30-noon			*Win, Lose or Draw**		
noon-12:30			*Super Password*	*Remote Control*/ MTV *Let's Make A Deal*/USA	*Love Connection* Fox#
12:30-1 pm				*Play the Percentages*/USA	*Lingo*/ Ch. 30 *Dating Game*/Fox

	ABC	CBS	NBC	CABLE	PBS/ FOX
1 - 1:30				*Hot Potato/* USA	*Relatively Speaking/* Fox
1:30- 2				*Chain Reaction/* USA	
2 - 2:30				*Bumper Stumpers/* USA	
2:30- 3				*Jackpot/* USA	
3 - 3:30				*Press Your Luck/* USA	
3:30- 4				*Tic, Tac, Dough/* USA	
4 - 4:30			*Double Dare+*	*High Rollers/* USA	
4:30- 5	*Win, Lose or Draw+*		*Finders Keepers+*		
5:30- 6					*Square 1* TV/PBS
6:30- 7					*Gong Show/* Ch. 30
7 - 7:30	*Wheel of Fortune+*	*Wheel of Fortune+*			
7:30- 8	*Jeopardy+*	*Jeopardy+*	*Family Feud+*	*NFL Trivia Game/* ESPN *Double Dare/* Nickelodeon	
11:30- midnight					*Newlywed Game/* Fox

Network affiliates are located in Ohio and West Virginia.
Data for this chart based on week of October 1-7.
*network version +syndicated version
#repeats on same channel later on same day (repeats not listed).
NOTE: all shows on the USA Network are repeats from past years.

Table 8.2
Game Shows on U.S. Television
Autumn 1990

	ABC	CBS	NBC	CABLE	PBS/ FOX
Sat.					
11 am-11:30				*Think Fast*/ Nik	
11:30-noon				*Double Dare*/ Nik	
1 pm-1:30				*Family Figures*/ BET	
7:30-8 pm					*Texaco Star Academic Chmp*
10:30-11 pm				*Whose Line Is It Anyway?*/HA!	
11:30-midnite		*Jeopardy*			
Sun.					
6pm-6:30				*Double Dare*/ Nik	
7 pm-7:30		*Wheel of Fortune*+			
Mon. Fri.					
10-10:30	*Quiz Kids Challenge*	*Family Feud*			
10:30-11	*Trump Card*	*Wheel of Fortune*			
11-11:30		*Price Is Right*	*To Tell the Truth*		
noon-12:30				*Remote Control*/MTV	

Note: BET = Black Entertainment Television; TLC = The Learning Channel; TNN = The Nashville Network; Nik = Nickelodeon

	ABC	CBS	NBC	CABLE	PBS/ FOX
12:30- 1 pm				*Top Card*/TNN *Name that Tune*/ USA	
1 pm- 1:30				*Supermkt Sweep*/ Life *Bumper Stumpers*/ USA	
1:30- 2 pm				*Hot Potato*/USA *Chain Reaction*/USA	
2 pm- 2:30					
2:30- 3 -				*Wipeout*/USA	
3 pm- 3:30				*Hollywood Squares*/USA	
3:30- 4				*$25,000 Pyramid*/ USA	
4 - 4:30				*Press Your Luck*/USA	
4:30- 5				*High Rollers*/USA *Teen Win, Lose or Draw*/Disney	
5:30- 6				*Square 1* TV/PBS	
6:30- 7				*Make the Grade*/Nik *Clash*/HA!	
7 - 7:30		*Wheel of Fortune*+	*Challengers*		
7:30- 8		*Jeopardy*+	*Tic, Tac, Dough*	*Quiz Me* (TU ONLY)/ *TLC* (Athens)	
midnite- 12:30				*Turn It Up*/ MTV	
1:35- 2:05am	*Love Connection*				

*network version +syndicated version
#repeats on same channel later on same day (repeats not listed).
NOTE: all shows on the USA Network are repeats from past years.
Data for this chart based on week of October 7-13.
Network affiliates in Columbus, Ohio; PBS in Athens, Ohio.

Table 8.3
Game Shows on U.S. Television
Autumn 1992

	ABC	CBS	NBC	CABLE	PBS
Sat.					
9:30-10 am				*Fun & Games*/ Learning Channel	
5 pm-5:30				*Family Dbl Dare*/ Nickelodeon	
5:30-				*Arcade*/ Nik	
7 pm-7:30		*Wheel of Fortune*+			
7:30-8		*Cash Explosion*			
Sun.					
5:30-6 pm				*Arcade*/ Nik	
Mon. -Fri.					
11-11:30		*Price Is Right*			
1 pm-1:30				*Supermarket Sweep*/Life#	
1:30-2				*Shop 'til You Drop*/Life	
3:30-4				*Top Card*/ Nashville	
4-4:30				*$25,0000 Pyramid*/USA	
4:30-5				*Press Your Luck*/USA	
5-5:30				*Arcade*/ Nik	
5:30-6					*Where in World Is Carmen Sandiego?*

	ABC	CBS	NBC	CABLE	PBS
6 - 6:30				*What Would You Do?*	*Square 1* TV
7 - 7:30		*Jeopardy!+*			
7:30- 8		*Wheel of Fortune+*			
Midnite				*Studs*/ WTTE	

The following shows run daily M-F on network affiliates outside Columbus (available on cable):

10 am	*Family Feud Challenge*
11:30	*Classic Concentration*
7:30 pm	*You Bet Your Life*
	Family Feud
1 am	*Perfect Score*
1:30 am	*The Personals*

*network version +syndicated version
#repeats on same channel later on same day (repeats not listed).
NOTE: all shows on the USA Network are repeats from past years.

Double Dare has some interactive questions, but its fame rests on its physically uninhibited stunts and messy obstacle course replete with greased slides, green gelatin, and mounds of mashed potatoes. Switching the adult players on a *Beat the Clock* format to youngsters, Nickelodeon created a merchandising miracle, including T-shirts, a home game, and a road show. Ratings in its time slot increased more than 250 percent after *Double Dare*'s introduction (Granville VI-8).

Each of the other survivors, all interactive, taps a different skill type and knowledge level. *Jeopardy!* draws on book-learned facts that “hover tantalizingly around the fringes of your useful knowledge...all you needed was a few more seconds, right?" (Meisler 8). *Wheel* proceeds more slowly, so that "without straining their craniums, the 'folks back home' can stay comfortably ahead of the action" (Meisler 12); furthermore, *Wheel* deftly fills television's need for at least one word game. The remaining two shows draw on common-sense knowledge. *The Price Is Right* showcases shopping skills and feeds some Americans' fascination with consumer products. *Family Feud* tests coorientation skills—figuring out how others would react—and has the universal appeal of a family reunion.

EMERGING TRENDS. A number of characteristics in the 1988-92 transition period may point to future programming. Some are unique to the U.S. scene, with its extensive cable saturation, and some bring the United States closer to trends in other countries.

* The children's market. Games represent a low-budget answer to television's long-criticized reliance on (and falling ratings of) what Peggy Charen of Action for Children's Television calls "toy-based cartoons" (Waters, "Much" 73). Recently games have provided flesh-and-blood alternatives, both educational and commercial, to 2-D robots. (Brazil, by contrast, combines cartoons and live games in one show.) PBS introduced *Where in the World Is Carmen Sandiego?* to teach geography in 1991 and consistently uses game segments within *Square 1 TV* to teach math. (See Ch. 10.)

  The commercial cable channel Nickelodeon, buoyed by the success of *Double Dare*, has aired a number of other kids' game shows. *What Would You Do?* hosted by DD's Marc Summers, brings kids and parents together for sloppy pie-in-the-face games. Like *Arcade*, it is produced at Nickelodeon's new facility near Disneyworld. *Finders Keepers*, no longer running, let players trash a stage-set house during a wild treasure hunt. (It resembled Lorimar's syndicated *Fun House*, which took place in a three-story playhouse.) *Think Fast*, likewise no longer running, featured a *Jeopardy*-type game board and relied on mental skills.

Other games, such as CBS's *I'm Telling*, were more controversial. Three sets of brothers and sisters replaced the three couples of *The Newlywed Game*, but the object remained the same: reveal personal secrets about your opposite number. Neither *The Newlywed Game*—"the worst piece of sleaze on television"—or its children's clone are still running (Merrill 40).

* Under-35 market. Ratings have shown that game shows appeal to older viewers (see Ch. 7). Three "mating/dating/hating games" of the early 1990s are bidding to capture a younger audience (Jarvis 5). The euphemism "make whoopee" has been replaced by the phrase "have sex." The curtain gimmick of *The Dating Game* has given way to sets that resemble cocktail lounges, where the hip, glib singles get to look each other over.

"Studs" involves two bachelors who date three women and then try to match their quotes with the right person. *The Personals* scans ads to find three potentially perfect matches for the main player. A typical Q & A runs like this: What makes you a great lover? I can make a pretzel with my body. (Viewers may call a 900 number to leave a message, at $2.95 per minute, for any of the four contestants.) *Score 1* features host Jeff Marder, who was a matchmaker/host on 1991's *Night Moves*. Three friends pick someone for the main player's blind date, which they rate at the end of the show as a "perfect score" or not.

* Cable-specific content. The narrowcasting of cable makes special-subject game shows inevitable. Country music, sports, rock music, black culture, and children's culture each have their own games: *Top Card* (The Nashville Network), *NFL Trivia Game* (ESPN), *Remote Control* (MTV), *Family Figures* (Black Entertainment Network) and various children's shows (Nickelodeon). Lifetime carries *Shop til You Drop* and *Supermarket Sweep*, which seem more suited for cable's shopping channels—so producers may already be working on *The Cholesterol Game*.
* Talky-host showcases. Hosts on U.S. game shows usually assume a facilitator role. The host may contribute, but seldom IS, the show's main appeal. (In Brazil, the opposite holds true; see below.) However, currently one TV and one radio game show hark back to the Groucho Marx model. Michael Feldman's ad lib banter on American Public Radio's irreverent *Whaddya Know* (1986-) manages to pull studio and phone-in players together to work as teams. Bill Cosby's easy-going style bears little relation to Groucho's, but his show has taken everything else from the original—including the floppy bird and old show's name: *You Bet Your Life*. Reviews said the secret word was "vapid" (Moore).
* Demise of gambling motifs. As of this 1993 writing, the cards, casinos, and games of chance have left the air. (The wheel on *Wheel of Fortune* determines winnings, but plays no role in solving the puzzle.) In 1990, *Trump Card*, made a brief splash. Whether Garry Trudeau's acid cartoon putdown in *Doonesbury* had anything to do with the demise is unclear.
* Lack of innovation. Other games that went nowhere include Michael Reagan and *Lingo*, a word game that made its debut in 1988; Dick Clark and *Challengers*, cosponsored by *Newsweek;* and *Monopoly*, from King World, based on the board game. Not counting the swinging singles "talk games," Jarvis complains

that "America hasn't invented a hot new [interactive] game in years." A leap back into prime time might revitalize the game scene, but since 1959, no games except summer replacements have broken the 8 p.m. barrier.

* Unequal opportunity. No women hold the rank of host on commercial television at this writing, whereas in the late 1980s, both Elaine Joyce (*The Dating Game*) and Vicky Lawrence (*Win, Lose or Draw*) had the top slots. At PBS, women sometimes host the game segments of *Square 1 TV*. But on *Carmen Sandiego*, the Chief, a black woman, sits on the sidelines in her office, while a young, white male serves as active host. Its role as a breakthrough is debatable, but a sexy female voice serves as announcer on *The Personals*.

  Bill Cosby's debut in fall 1992 was a breakthrough. No black has hosted a network or syndicated game show (except on BET) since Nipsey Russell served briefly on *Your Number's Up* (January-April 1986). Cable has been more progressive. A young black man, Phil Moore, began hosting *Arcade* on Nickelodeon earlier in 1992. At this writing, in 1993, the new show *Caesar's Challenge*, telecast from Las Vegas, has a black male host.

3. Game shows as dramas, comedies, and parodies

Game shows have served as a context for a few U.S. TV plots. Lucile Ball used the device so long ago that her TV persona in *I Love Lucy* appeared on a *radio* quiz show called *Females Are Fabulous* to try to earn $1,000. Much later, in the *Cagney and Lacey* episode of November 16, 1987, the two detectives went under cover as contestants on a show resembling *Let's Make a Deal* to solve a crime.

The comedy *Mama's Family* of October 12, 1990, featured Vicki Lawrence (Mama) as a winning contestant on

Jeopardy, with a guest appearance by Alex Trebek. In another guest shot, this time on *Cheers*, Trebek saw Cliff the mailman pile up winnings on a *Jeopardy!* episode that featured categories like "Shoes mailmen can wear with white socks."

But game shows lend themselves better to another type of comedy: parody. Often *Sesame Street* has used the device to get points across, such as its *Squeal of Fortune* takeoff, which featured a pig being rolled inside a wheel until it squealed (Cerf).

In the 1970s, an era of "wilder and wilder game shows", audiences seemed ready to accept anything (Graham, *Come* 41). After Chuck Barris created a parody talent show, *The Gong Show* (1976), and a parody beauty pageant, *The $1.98 Beauty Show* (1978), his partner Chris Bearde created the syndicated *Cheap Show* (1978), a celebrity panel/stunt show. Comedian emcee Dick Martin and panelists such as Truman Capote and Jill St. John watched players get wet and slimy, after which Oscar the Wonder Rodent determined their prizes. The *Cheap Show* is no longer with us.

However, the NBC comedy program *Saturday Night Live* has consistently aired game show parodies, including nearly 20 such segments 1987-92 (see Table 8.4). Game shows are the single TV genre to spawn so many different SNL parodies. The venerable talk show has inspired only a few (*The Pat Stevens Show*, *Coffee Talk*, *Sprockets* from Germany and *Wayne's World*, the bit that became a movie). These one-note variations build loyalty week after week with an anchor character or characters that audiences get to know. But game shows are so instantly comprehensible that each SNL creation is unique and makes one point.

The game show concept is so ingrained in the U.S. psyche that SNL audience members can naturally suspend disbelief and imagine themselves as game show audience members. They then can easily accept a twist on the game. The sound of Don Pardo, a real game show voice (live on the original *Price Is Right* and in the 1970s on the taped program *Jeopardy*), helps the audience accept the premise. Pardo had worked on SNL since the show began in 1975.

GAME SHOW PARODIES. Table 8.5 (top) shows eight of the SNL segments, which run for about five minutes each, parodying characteristics of game shows themselves. Both *You Bet Your Finger* and *Eternity* have fun with the physical stunts used as penalties best represented by the 1950s game show *Truth or Consequences.* Exaggeration results in bloody amputations (of fingers or, in the case of *Eternity,* limbs), medieval tortures, and worse for a wrong answer. The winners (those still alive) on *Eternity* beg to forego the privilege of a return visit as defending champion. The winners on the previous week's *You Bet Your Finger* are shown waving stumpy hands as they enjoy their prize vacations. However, most parodies, like most contemporary game shows, deal with mental rather than physical formats.

Love Werks looks simple (a bachelor chooses one of four bachelorettes, none of whom he can see), but it is actually a complex triple parody. The segment takes off from *Sprockets*, an earlier-created SNL parody of a German talk show, while lampooning German personality archetypes and culture. At the same time, it pokes fun at *The Dating Game*'s premise, the shadow between the imagined and the real (the bachelor may wrongly imagine a heavy woman to match with a jolly personality, or a svelte model to match a sophisticated voice). Here bachelor Wolfgang chooses "Susan," only to find out that "she" is really a male cross-dresser.

Sabra Price Is Right supposedly originates on Israeli television. Its premise is, Move the merchandise; tell the customer anything, just so you sell, sell, sell. No ethnic stereotype is sacred with SNL writers, Israeli and Jewish mercantilism being no exception. The prize roster resembles the *Wheel of Fortune* shopping spree wherein players are forced to spend "earnings" in a showcase of items they probably do not want or need.

Table 8.4
Saturday Night Live Game Show Parodies
1987-92

Show	Date	Format	Parody Object
Bob Swerski's Quiz Masters	1/92	*Jeopardy*	Fanatic, couch potato sports fans
Comedy Killers	/92	*Jeopardy*	What isn't funny in comedy
Common Knowledge	1/88	generic	Failed high schools; dumb 17-year-olds
Community College Bowl	/92	*College Quiz Bowl*	Failed jr. colleges; dumb 19-year-olds
*Die Squaren Ost Berliner**	10/89	*Hollywood Squares*	E. Europe politics; rush to head West
Dysfunctional Family Feud	10/91	*Family Feud*	Family relations—cruelty, dominance
Bensonhurst Dating Game	/92?	*Dating Game*	Racial taboos—personal relations

Show	Date	Format	Parody Object
Stand Up and Win	?	*Jeopardy*	Stand-up comedians' hackneyed delivery
Whose Ass Should I Kiss?	11/91	generic	Businessmen's rules: flattery, hypocrisy
Game Challengers	11/90	generic	Political correctness, righteousness
Jew/Not a Jew	10/88	generic	Whispered ethnic gossip; not PC
*Love Werks** (German)	2/92	*Dating Game*	Game show fantasy vs. bitter reality
Sabra Price Is Right(Israeli)*	5/92	*Price Is Right*	Game shows' unwanted prizes-real garbage
Eternity	1/90	*Truth or Conse-quences*	Game show penalties so bru-tal, no winner
Game Breakers I	/87	generic	Game show host who can't dismiss player
Game Breakers II	12/90	generic	Game show host who's blatantly partial
Who's Dumber?	11/89	generic	Game show players who AREN'T geniuses
You Bet Your Finger	/87?	*Truth or Conse-quences*	Game show losers who smile through pain
Sucker Punch	12/91	generic	Game show penalties

*Overseas show (also parodies ethnic stereotypes of nation).

Five other shows poke fun at the game genre without mimicking a specific show. *Game Breakers I* and *II* portray traits that the perfect host should NOT have, but probably do; can flesh-and-blood hosts really view all contestants as created equal? Version I has the host, who feels sorry for a defeated contestant, following her offstage and taking her out to dinner as the remaining players wonder what happened. Version II takes advantage of guest Susan Lucci, who appears as her *All My Children* persona Erica Kane. Contestant Kane, flirting shamelessly, dominates the other shy player on a game show that turns into a soap opera; it ends with the wedding of Kane and the host, with Don Pardo's voice conducting the ceremony.

Dialogue includes these exchanges:

Host: Now, I'm sure you are familiar with the game.

Erica: Oh, yes, Jack. I watch every day. I watch you. I hope you won't think I'm too forward in saying this, but I just have to tell you, you have such a commanding presence.

Margaret: [gives correct answer]

Erica: I hate to be a problem; I really do. But I pressed my buzzer too late. Could we do it again.

Host: (to himself) What's happening to me? Am I losing all sense of fairness? I'm a game show host. I've got to be impartial.

Who's Dumber? focuses not on game show hosts, but on contestants. It turns the *Jeopardy* concept of player-as-encyclopedia on its ear by making stupidity the sine qua non of winning. This segment pokes its finger not only at quiz kids, but also at the "common knowledge" questions on such shows as *The Price Is Right* and *Family Feud.* If the players cannot answer such questions, the smarter home viewers know how to answer the question, *Who's Dumber?*

The segment includes the following dialogue:

Host: Now remember, these are questions Woody and Victoria picked out three months ago. So they have had plenty of time to do research. OK. What year was the War of 1812?

Woody: Could you repeat the question?...

SOCIAL/POLITICAL COMMENTARY. In a sense, all SNL game show parodies poke fun at the genre, with their overdone, flashy sets and hosts who deliver the fatal words "I'm sorry!" with a lilt in their voices and a toothy smile. But many SNL parodies carry another, more prominent message.

Table 8.5 shows that 11 comic segments make a social or political comment. Topics range from schools that produce ignorant students to over-zealous sports fans to the mysteries of comedy itself. Even politically correct attitudes towards minorities and ethnicity may well get sliced to bits by SNL's sharp blade. For example, *Game Challengers* ridicules self-righteous native Americans (they capture Don Pardo and force him to read a statement), but also callous Caucasians (the show's host offers a tribal chief's bones as a bonus prize).

Seven of the segments mimic specific shows, with three of those using a *Jeopardy* format. The simple category board and Q&A format permit an emphasis on verbal

Figure 8.5
Message and Format of SNL Game Show Parodies
1987-92

OBJECT OF PARODY	FORMAT Specific game show	Generic game show
Game show genre	*Love Werks* *Sabra Price Is Right* *You Bet Your Finger*	*Game Breakers I & II* *Who's Dumber?* *Eternity* *Sucker Punch*
Social political phenomenon	*Bensonhurst Dating Game* *Bob Swerski's Quiz Masters* *Comedy Killers* *Community College Bowl* *Die Squaren Ost Berliner* *Dysfunctional Family Feud* *Stand Up and Win*	*Common Knowledge* *Game Challengers* *Jew/Not a Jew* *Whose Ass Should I Kiss?*

humor—in the dialogue, the questions, and even the names of the categories. For example, *Bob Swerski's Quiz Masters* has a category titled "The Bears" for which every answer is "The Bears." Like *Love Werks*, this segment puts a game show twist on an SNL-created show broadcast from Chicago, *The Super Fans*.

The other three represent brilliant marriages of form and content. *Dysfunctional Family Feud* takes the whispered group consultations on the real *Family Feud* and turns them into a Freudian case study. Sample dialogue includes:

Host: Name something families would say to a recent college graduate.

[Suggested answers "We love you" and "Congratulations" are not on the board. The #1 dysfunctional answer on the board is "Get out."]

The *Community College Bowl* turns a typical Duke vs. Baylor matchup on the *GE College Quiz Bowl* into a professor's worst nightmare by pitting Belt Parkway against Jasper County. Dialogue includes:

Host: Who were our enemies during World War II?

[Both teams remain quiet, chewing gum, looking at their nails.]

Die Squaren Ost Berliner (aired October 1989) needles the unpopular East German government and socialist system. Before the Berlin Wall fell in December 1989, Hungary opened its borders to West Germany in September, enabling East Germans to escape to the West from Hungary via Czechoslovakia. The nine-box *Hollywood Squares* set with its missing celebrities—some of whom leave during the segment with packed suitcases—shows strikingly the rush toward defection. Viewers seemed to react with wry smiles rather than guffaws to this "overseas" show with dialogue in (fractured) "German." (Female player gives occupation as "Ich bin ein homemacher.")

The author has not encountered game shows parodies in any other country except Canada, although many have strong game show traditions. A show on Canada's Much Music channel, *Test Pattern* (see Appendix 2), takes the wheel motif one step farther by positioning the contestants themselves in the wheel. In another segment, instead of hand buzzers, players who know an answer must hit themselves in the head to make their hat-buzzers ring. For the "Pablo's Hands" segment, they must identify smelly substances into which Pablo has plunged his hands.

Besides the games, a culture must enjoy parody to accept as many segments as SNL has created. The United States seems to stand nearly alone in loving its games and loving to laugh at them as well.

Chapter 9

SEVEN COUNTRIES' GAME SHOWS

Quiz shows look at first to be cut from the same cloth, but closer examination reveals that monetary prizes are nonexistent on Soviet TV, modest in the Netherlands.... participants engage in "zany" stunts that their opposite numbers in the United States might be ashamed to undertake. (D. Browne, *Comparing* 387)

These seven case studies will let us take a vertical look at entertainment television. Ideally, we would have enough resources and book pages to profile all 50 nations in this study. Instead, we chose these seven culturally and geographically diverse TV systems to study in depth, though not pretending that they represent the entire world.

1. Great Britain (England)

With a population of about 56.65 million, England has about 19 million licensed TV sets. Although Scotland, Northern Ireland and Wales receive basically the same TV programs as England, the information for this section comes from TV viewing in and listings for the London area.

Game shows never seem to go out of style in England, hugging the late afternoon and early prime time (daily and weekend) spots—but with a difference: a specific game show slot (e.g., Fridays at 7:30 p.m. on ITV) may rotate as many as three or four separate games. The direct broadcast

Sky Channel, ITV, Channel 4, and the noncommerical BBC1 and BBC2 all run games (the Independent TV network incudes 15 privately owned regional channels, while Channel 4 broadcasts nationwide).

In 1992, game shows "are certainly booming," according to Malcolm Quigley, head of production for Action Time (Coopman 37). Action Time, a game show specialist, joins established producers/licensers Reg Grundy and Talbot/Fremantle in the healthy English scene, where games account for about 2.5 percent of broadcast time (Hardy 37). Action Time has reached beyond the ground systems, selling *One False Move* and *Love at First Sight* to Sky One, a satellite channel.

Table 9.1
Game Shows on British Television
Autumn 1992

Take Your Pick	ITV Mon. 8 pm	reincarnation from 1960s
*Strike It Lucky**	ITV Mon. 8 pm	version of U.S. *Strike It Rich*
*Wheel of Fortune**	ITV Mon. 8 pm	transfer from U.S.
You Bet	ITV Fri. 7:30	transfer from Germany
*$64,000 Question**	ITV Fri. 7:30	transfer from U.S.
*Family Fortunes**	ITV Fri. 7:30	version of U.S. *Family Feud*
*Blind Date**	ITV Sat. 7 pm	version of U.S. *Dating Game*
One to Win	BBC Sat. 5:30	U.K. original
Big Break	BBC Sat. 6:40	U.K. original
Bullseye	ITV Sun. 5:40	U.K. original
*Keynotes**	ITV M-F, 9:25	version of U.S. *Name that Tune*
*Blockbusters**	ITV M-F, 5:10	transfer from U.S.

*survived from 1990

Seven of the 1990 shows listed on Appendix 2 have survived until 1992 (*). Indeed, *Blind Date* has been around since the mid-1980s. It represents a combination of *Dating Game*, wherein the date is arranged, and *Love Connection*, whereby a returning couple rehashes their date. Neither show runs in 1992 in the Columbus, Ohio, area, having been replaced by the more explicit (and usually late-at-night) *Personals*, *Score One* and *Studs*. Yet "in Great Britain, the land of the double-entendre—nudge, nudge, wink, wink—innuendo rules" (Ferry 28), at least for the 1992 season. Hostess Cilla Black's good vibes style has helped the show hit the nation's top ten TV shows list (see Ch. 7).

A show that held a place in England something like *Des Chiffres et des Lettres* in France, *Masterteam*, seems to have disappeared from the BBC. This elimination championship program made *Jeopardy*'s Tournament of Champions look like adult day care. Fast-talking host Angela Ripon would begin her barrage of esoteric questions with the ominous phrase, "And your time starts NOW." Then followed a heart-stopping minute of questions that a team of geniuses had to answer instantly or make a quick decision to "pass" (Sample question about horse racing: Name the two fences jumped only once in the grand national; answer: 15 and 16). The Lifetime channel began production of a U.S. version (see Appendix 1), but it chose instead to run what may be the worst game show ever, the exuberant *Supermarket Sweep*.

Other unusual shows from the past included *Through the Keyhole* (from the mid-1980s), which showed videos of a star's home, after which players had to guess the name of the star. In *Talkabout* (see Appendix 2), couples tried to reveal ten hidden words by talking fast and furiously on a subject (for the topic of dandruff, the hidden words might include "dry," "flaky," "itchy" and "white"). *Countdown* (mid 1980s, Channel 4) resembled the French *Des Chiffres et des Lettres*, requiring players to manipulate randomly chosen numbers and letters; at the end, players had ten seconds for the Conundrum Round (unscramble "bodelust" to make "doubtless").

Everybody's Equal (see Appendix 2) started off with about 200 players who answer multiple-choice questions with control boxes. It does not take long to eliminate all but ten players, who then assemble on stage for harder questions. The format resembles Japan's *Ultra Quiz*, but on a smaller scale (*Ultra* starts with a football field of players).

Also like Japan, the British have enjoyed travel-theme shows—studio-bound, however, rather than featuring on-location questions. *Runway* (mid-1980s ITV) gave players vacation trips as prizes for travel-related questions. *Where in the World* (see Appendix 2) combined *Family Feud*'s family teams with a travel questions/travel prize format. *Worldwise* (ITV mid 1980s) billed itself as another "travel quiz."

As in Australia, Nickelodeon has sold to the British formats for a BBC Saturday morning children's time block, 9 a.m.-noon. Another long-running show on the commercial ITV network, *Blockbusters*, appeals to teenagers. Players aged 16 to 18 try to forge blocks on a honeycomb-patterned game board filled with letters. If a player picks "P," the question might read, "What 'P' must enter the goal to score?" (answer: "puck"). The U.S. show no longer runs in its home of origin, but it also targets teenagers in Israel (see Appendix 2).

In 1993, regulations limiting the size of prizes will be eliminated. With lessons learned from the United States, presumably no scandals will touch big-money games. According to TV host Jeremy Beadle, "There is something very Presbyterian in our culture which makes people think it's almost evil to get something for nothing" (Ferry 28). Taken to its extreme, this Puritanism sees that the winner of *Mastermind*, after 22 weeks of the world's most difficult lightning rounds, receives only a modest wooden plaque.

2. France

France's population of 55.81 million owns 29.3 million TV sets and supports five networks: TF-1, formerly public but now private; Antenne 2, public; France Regions 3, public; M6 Metropole TV, private commercial; and Canal Plus, a private subscription system. La Cinq, a private commercial channel, went out of business in 1992.

In the mid-1980s, the French government brought to its TF-1 network a new management team with a mission: boost TF-1's ratings so the network could be sold. In January 1987, the team wisely launched a licensed version of *Wheel of Fortune* in access prime time. The show shot to number one in the ratings, breaking all viewing records and greatly easing the network's sale (Ferry 26-27).

Wheel changed French television. In early 1987, it stood out as "the only show with this [American] kind of speed and dynamism" (Pfeffer 29). Its phenomenal success brought more U.S. shows, including more games (*The Price Is Right* made its debut on December 13, 1987).

Appendix 2 shows that by 1990, TF-1 had tried to build on *Wheel*'s fabulous success by adding six more games, all but one of them (*Intervilles*) U.S. clones. The public network A2 had one new clone (*Newlywed Game*) and one silver classic, *Des Chiffres et des Lettres*, still popular in 1992 after more than 25 years on the air.

Despite 15 minutes of dead silence on each show as players ponder their solutions, the show in 1989 had higher ratings than *Jeopardy* or *Trivial Pursuit* (see Ch. 7). Like *Scrabble*, half of the game involves making the longest possible word from nine randomly selected letters. Then come the "chiffres" ("numbers"). Hostess Benedicte triggers a machine to select a three-digit number as the target; then six others are chosen as the means to the target (add, subtract, multiply or divide them to arrive at the three-digit number).

This unlikely hit, representing television at its most interactive, has become a way of life for many fans. *Des Chiffres et des Lettres* circulates on tape throughout the French-speaking world (see the listings in Appendix 2 for Tunisia and Canada). France has legions of Chiffres Clubs of fans who watch the daily show together, play along, and sometimes do better than those in the studio. In July, ever since 1985, the Cup of Clubs final tournament match has been shown live, broadcast around the world from the Palais des Congres d'Antibes Juan-les-Pins (Rips 77). In 1986, the national finals drew an audience of some 16 million. Only the grand champion—none of the weekly winners— receives any prizes.

What explains the phenomenon? Rips cites France's long tradition of scholastic testing, as well as "what the French consider their most prized talent: the ability to think and speak as quickly and as glibly as possible" (77). It meshes perfectly with how the French think TV shows should be.

In theory, asserts Pfeffer, "French culture, even popular culture, is profoundly intellectual" (24). But in practice the French prefer fast-paced, dynamic U.S.-style TV shows. In the words of *Wheel*'s French producer, "It's good to be intellectual; it's better to entertain" (Pfeffer 30). France could offer no more poignant proof of its telemediated ambivalence than the juxtaposition of two game shows, *Des Chiffres* and *Wheel*.

From January to June 1987, the lively, U.S.-born *Wheel* aired opposite the slow, uniquely French *Des Chiffres*. Within four weeks, *Wheel* had passed *Des Chiffres* in the ratings. By May 1987, *Wheel* had ten million viewers; *Des Chiffres*, eight million.

Chiffres and the hour-long *Fort Boyard*, which runs once a week in prime time, represent rare local products. By 1992, France had added even more games to its TV schedules, bringing the total to about 12 games, mostly U.S. clones running in stripped slots (Monday through Friday for 30 minutes). *Fort* players must overcome obstacles in order to gather enough keys to enter a treasure room.

France's game production companies form a tight, closed "mafia," according to Mandraud and Martinat (14). EC Television has the rights to *Wheel* and produces *Jeopardy*. In turn, Tele France Productions produces *Wheel* for EC; it was founded in 1987 by Marc Gurnaud, then aged 33. Gurnaud previously worked with Jacques Antoine, whose JAC created *Fort Boyard*. JAC is "France's leading game show maker" (Williams 40).

JAC, which employs 70 full-time and 500 part-time workers, has sold the *Fort Boyard* concept to Germany, Sweden, the Netherlands, Belgium, and Britain's Channel 4 (where it runs under the title *The Crystal Maze*). Antoine, who started in radio with a mechanic's license, had a brief partnership with Jean-Claude Buchez, who has since created a company called Projeux (For Games).

Standing apart from the French mafia, Australia's master gamesman Reg Grundy has only one show running in France, *Questions pour un champion*, FR3's sole game (see Appendix 2). Grundy, who has sold about 80 games around the world, has found France a difficult market.

The French game boomlet that began in the late 1980s has already had some hint of scandal. In April 1988, FR3 had to cancel *Le Sphynx*, a Jacques Antoine production, after only two weeks on the air when travel agencies offered contestants free trips. Then in mid-1988, an Association of Cheated Contestants—380 couples who had appeared on *L'Arche d'Or*—complained that the company A-2 had hired to dispense the winners' gifts had failed to do so. Finally, France Sponsoring Publicity, founded in February 1989 to handle advertisements within games, had so many complaints against it that a court order stopped it from doing business as of June 1989. At the slightest hint of dishonesty, say Mandraud and Martinat, the game show phenomenoncan "break into pieces" like a mirror (4).

3. Tunisia

Located across the Mediterranean from Italy, Tunisia has a population of about nine million. TV sets number about 650,000. The government-operated system,

Radiodiffusion Television Tunisienne, has an Arabic-language network and a French-language network.

Countries embracing Islam do not have the range of game shows found elsewhere because Islam forbids gambling, eliminating roulette wheels and decks of cards as motifs. Religious and social customs are not compatible with dating shows, according to a producer who had such an idea rejected (Belghith).

Thus Q&A formats stand out as the main acceptable subgenre. But even if a Q&A show succeeds, state policies can intervene. "The more popular the show, the sooner it is taken off the air," states Rached Belghith, a producer since the late 1960s. Authorities do not want viewers to overdose on one show and ignore the rest of the state's offerings. Furthermore, when top personnel change at RTT, new authorities want to start with a clean slate of their own offerings.

Tunisia has since the late l960s produced a number of game and game/variety shows. Belghith himself created three: *Avec le Peuple*, a one-hour show that went on location to various towns, included informal game segments whereby people answered simple questions. A more formal Q&A show, *La Grille Malicieuse* (*Mischievous Crossword*), which ran for a year, got so many letters (15,000) that a special staff had to be hired to deal with them.

Another Belghith production from the mid-1980s, *Si Vous Permettez*, resembled an Italian show called *Domenica*, which used to run 1-8 p.m. on Sundays. Like Brazil's long-format Sunday shows, *Domenica* included songs, interviews and other segments besides games—all held together by the personality of a charismatic host. (Most Tunisians can receive TV shows from Italy without any special equipment;

indeed, Tunisian newspapers all print the schedules of RAI Uno, Italy's premier channel.) The popular Tunisian long-format show featured Nejib Khattab as its host, but eventually it was cancelled (Adhoum).

Another creator/producer, Bechir El Fekih, has three game shows to his credit: *Afrique, Notre Continent*; *Fi Youm, Fi Chahr, Fi Sanaa* (*In a Month, In a Day, In a Year*); and *Mondio*. Since 1975, El Fekih has had one passion: a "war against boredom" waged through the creation of educational and cultural games.

"Everybody mocked me at first...People refused everything [of mine] that was new, especially what was Tunisian, whereas others tapped the market effortlessly by pirating games known worldwide" ("Le Savior" 1990).

Mondio, El Fekih's most recent geography game, had a predecessor that ran in 1988: *Jeux d'Afrique*, which despite its name ran on the Arabic network. College-age players picked numbers corresponding to a spot on a game board, which had a total of 12 wheels. The MC, a woman, spun the wheel to determine the question. A teacher/judge added additional information to the contestant's answer as a kind of booster lesson. To Western eyes, the pace seems snail-like, as the camera follows the hostess' every step on her numerous walks back and forth across the stage. But the amount of information conveyed in 40 minutes is impressive (Mount Kilimanjaro? It's in Tanzania.)

Tunisia, like many countries (see Ch. 6), has a tradition of school challenge quiz shows. *Baina al-Maahid* (*Between the High Schools*) ran on Sundays for many years on RTT (the Arabic network). Play began within cities, with semi final and final competitions taking place in May in Tunis.

Winning school teams went to RTT studios for the televised final matches. The quiz teams included five members each, both male and female, but the entire match included a talent competition as well. Schools brought lively cheering sections that the camera often showed (Adhoum).

A popular French-language show (listed on Appendix 2 under W. Europe/France) is *Des Chiffres et des Lettres*, which Tunisians can see as part of A2's offerings.

4. Nigeria

Based on an essay by Bitrus Gwanma written for this book

Nigeria has 42 television stations, all of them formerly state-run; in 1992 the Nigerian Broadcasting Commission began privatization by licensing 14 investor-owned stations. Cable service is now available around Lagos. The television stations were divided equally among the federal government, represented by the Nigerian Television Authority, and the 21 state governments, represented by radio and television corporations.

None of the game shows discussed below is televised or produced nationally. Aided by repeater stations, some local programs, for example those of NTA Kaduna, NTA Ibadan, and NTA Lagos (headquarters), can be seen by audiences stretching beyond the immediate catchment areas. But no locally produced game shows are marketed through national syndication. Nigeria does not show imported games from Europe or the United States—not even from other Third World countries.

No Nigerian games have celebrity players—not even for guest appearances on behalf of charities. Some stations do have a radio show like *What's My Line*, whereby audience members try to identify important personalities hidden from them by asking questions. (No blindfolds needed as in the 1950s U.S. televised version.)

The games to be discussed below do not reflect all shows on every Nigerian television station. They are those that stand out in the author's mind and thus represent the most memorable formats, both past and present. They fall into two categories: student Q&A quizzes and general-interest games.

STUDENT QUIZZES. *Test on the Testaments* was a quiz designed to test high school students on their knowledge of the Bible. Each show had three contestants, with the champion returning each week to face new opponents until he was defeated. It was shown in the 1960s on the then NTS (Nigerian Television Service) Lagos. That station is now NTA (Nigerian Television Authority).

Fastest and Best used to be shown on NTA Ibadan. Three contestants competed to answer the most questions at the end of the hour-long program. Questions were asked on a variety of topics and the person who raised his hand got a chance to respond to each question.

On Plateau Television is *Right Answer*. Contestants are asked to choose, from a set of choices, the response that best answers a question.

Schools Challenge, another quiz show, has high schools competing with each other on a variety of general knowledge questions. Most TV stations in Nigeria have programs with this format.

GENERAL-INTEREST GAMES. *Take a Trip* was a quiz show begun in the 1960s on NTS Lagos and later NTA Lagos. Two contestants begin to respond to questions on a variety of subjects at two opposite ends of the board. A correct response would cause an individual to advance or 1ose squares. The individual with an incorrect answer does not make any advances. At the end, the individual who has completed his squares gets a prize and returns the following week to face a new contestant. Four consecutive wins qualify a person for a six-day air trip to any holiday resort in the country (formerly any holiday resort in Europe).

A variation of this game is *Family Quiz*, begun in the 1970s on NBC Lagos, now NTA. Two couples are tested on a variety of topics with the winning couple leaving the half-hour show with a prize. Two new couples are introduced the following week.

Plateau Television has a quiz with the same title, *Family Quiz*. The difference is that the families are not asked to take risks by requesting chance cards. The game resembles *Trivial Pursuit*.

Word Game is shown on Plateau Television. Letters are jumbled and contestants are asked to form words from the letters. NTA Lagos had a variation of this game in the 1970s, with contestants asked to fill in missing letters. The viewing audience was shown the correct words, while the contestants struggled to provide correct answers.

On NTA Ibadan is *Tokotaya*, designed for Yoruba audiences. It takes the format of the *Newlywed Game* on American television. However, the families do not have to be newly married couples. NTA Kaduna has its English equivalent.

A Hausa show, *Kacici Kacici*, pits Hausa viewers against each other on a variety of general knowledge questions. One can watch this show on most television stations in the north of Nigeria. The languages of Nigeria are English (official), Hausa (spoken by 21 percent of the 115 million population), Yoruba (20 percent), and Iho (17 percent).

A show that resembles *Win, Lose or Draw* was shown on NTA Kaduna. Members of the audience are invited to interpret messages conveyed to them through nonverbal cues by carefully selected individuals.

5. Taiwan

The Republic of China on Taiwan, population about 20.28 million, was established in 1911 on the mainland and moved to the island of Taiwan (Formosa) when Mao Zedong created the People's Republic of China in 1949. Residents have 6.66 million TV sets in use. Three networks accept advertising but are directly or indirectly government-controlled: China TV, run by the Kuo Min Tang, Taiwan's ruling political party; China Television Service, run by the government; and Taiwan TV, privately run.

Many Taiwanese game formats come from Japan, both formally licensed and informally transferred. *100 Battles, 100 Victories*, an outdoors, physically demanding game, was called *Takeshi's Castle* in Japan; *Naughty Family* (no longer running in 1992), with its animal theme, was called *Waku, Waku Animal Land* in Japan; *Running Around the World*, with a travelling hostess (aired in the mid 1980s) was called *Let's Go! the World* in Japan. The ROC's two dating shows likewise have Japanese roots.

We Love the Matchmaker originally took one hour to arrange one match, whereas the Western format makes two on-the-spot matches in 30 minutes. In its original form, it strongly resembled a Japanese show of the mid-

Table 9.2
Game Shows on Taiwanese Television
Autumn 1992*

Time/Day	Network		
	China Television Service (CTS)	China TV (CTV)	Taiwan TV (TTV)
MONDAY-FRIDAY			
6 pm			*Chan pan Tsuji* (*Unlucky Strike*)
SATURDAY			
noon	*Hao-tsai Tou* (*Good Luck*)		
1 pm			
4 pm			*Wo Ai Hong Nyang* (*We Love the Matchmaker*)
10 pm	*Celebrity Travelogue*		
11 pm			
SUNDAY			
noon	*Bai Tsang, Bai Sheng* (*100 Battles, 100 Victories*) 12:20-2:10 pm		
1 pm		*Laiten* (*Sparks Fly*) 12:50-2 pm	
2 pm			

*Listings for November

1970s, *Punch-de Date-o* (*Push-button Date*), in that the producers arranged the match beforehand. In both countries, the couple could only hear about each other throughout the show, climaxing with their actually being able to get a look at each other; in both, a large neon heart decorated the set.

Sparks Fly, with its 14 or more players, resembles a freshman mixer that uses egg tosses, relay races, and other outdoor games to acquaint the males and females; it strongly resembles Japan's *Red Whale Tribe*. By 1992, its format had changed little, but locations were more imaginative than athletic fields (such as one of Taipei's night markets). But an unchanging format is unusual.

Many long-lived games in Taiwan change their formats so drastically that only the name remains. *Unlucky Strike*, for example, in 1986 used film clips from *That's Incredible* on which to base its questions; by 1989, it had live attractions, such as a tiger cub or a demonstration of kites. A test of manual dexterity used in 1986 was dropped in later incarnations, and the players shifted from college students to young celebrities. By 1992, *Unlucky Strike* was using a *Wheel of Fortune* format, loosely adapted. (This author appeared on the show in December 1989.)

The target audience for all games remains young people, whereas the three networks try to attract older viewers with costume telenovelas (limited to 40 weeks in length) and traditional Chinese operas. Older viewers would find appearing on a game show undignified. Independent producers create most game shows, which station coordinators keep on the air as long as ratings remain at about 20 percent (Peng).

Taiwanese law prevents giving away large amounts of money or naming products on the air (a panning shot gives viewers an idea of the type of prizes they may win). This author's prize for answering two simple questions on *Unlucky Strike* was some plastic sandals and chicken soup mix.

The formats of some shows—those that do not follow a single-focus theme—may seem confusing to Westerners. For example, *Everybody Gets Together*, which aired in 1986 on CTS, began with clues to help players guess the mystery celebrity; then a *Password*-type game took place; next a *Family Feud*-type game involved matching poll answers. A 1992 show called *Good Luck* began with a travelogue video and a traveling host asking panelists a question; next came a *Price Is Right*-like pricing game; and finally there was an endgame resembling *Supermarket Sweep*.

Many Taiwanese shows emphasize audience involvement. If players can not answer a question, the hosts throw it to the audience, picking someone with a raised hand to answer and win a prize. What resembles an audience warmup for U.S. games takes place on camera in Taiwan.

Hosts often work in male-female teams, as Ch. 7 noted. In the case of the longest-running game show, *Unlucky Strike*, the same male host has held his post since 1986, but the young female assistant has changed. The host works on other shows for the Taiwan TV network, as do most TV personalities in Taiwan, pulling double to triple duty.

6. Japan

In a well-known grammar book, a sentence that teaches the use of the word "doshite" ("why") reads:

"Why are there so many quiz programs on Japanese television?" Indeed, especially on weekends, the viewer confronts a dazzling array of games (called in Japan by the English word "quiz"): ten on Saturday and seven on Sunday in 1992 (see Table 9.3). Adding in the regular weekday shows gives a total of 31, making Japan in 1992 more quiz-crazy than even the United States, which has twice Japan's population. And that figure does not even count the many two-, three-, or four-hour quiz specials that dot the fall TV schedules.

In the 1960s and 1970s, song variety shows filled in around the costume and modern-dress dramas, documentaries, and sports programs in prime time. But in the late 1970s, this genre began to fade, replaced by more and more quiz programs. By 1988, 18 regular shows had hit the airwaves.

In 1992, eight 1980s' shows were still running: *Quiz Derby*, *Discovering the World's Mysteries* (TBS); *Attack 25* (Asahi); *Let's Go! the World* and *Young vs. Old Quiz* (Fuji); *Round-the-World Gourmet Quiz* and *Changing Locales Quiz* (TV Tokyo); and *World Professionals Quiz* (Nippon). Moreover, the *Trans-America Ultra Quiz* (Nippon), a regular/special, has continued not only from the 1980s, but from 1977; in 1992, it ran on four Thursdays from October 22 to November 12.

In Japan, according to Kato, "intellectual snobbery is almost nil...'conspicuous non-ownership of television'...is totally alien in Japanese society" (*Handbook* 315). The high ratings of prime-time game shows (Table 7.8) bear out this assertion. Japanese viewers have told the author that since testing is a way of life for the Japanese, they feel comfortable with the Q-and-A format. Indeed, one quiz, *Takeshi and Itsumi's Heisei Educational Foundation*, poses actual questions from high school entrance exams to its panel of celebrities, who sit at stylized school desks.

Also according to Kato, mass tourism developed in the mid-1700s, with the result that the "Japanese group tour of today is world famous, sometimes even notorious" (*Handbook* 306). A desire to break out of the studio (and the Japanese archipelago) characterizes quizzes in Japan as in no other country. In contrast to Western shows that aim for low costs and high profits, Japan's quizzes spare no expense as they compete in the fierce prime-time hours.

In 1992, *Discovering the World's Mysteries* (TBS), *World Professionals* (Nippon), *Let's Go! the World* (Fuji) and *Round-the-World Gourmet Quiz* (Tokyo) featured on-location scenes from exotic overseas destinations—or unusual Japanese sites, in the case of *Changing Locales Quiz* (Tokyo) and *Look Out for Doubt* (TBS). The shows present travelogue videos, into which a question is woven for a panel of celebrities to discuss. The answer is then shown by the on-location host or hostess.

After *Let's Go! the World* created its popular travel format in 1981, other shows followed suit. The shows succeeded because the insular Japanese "have a strong interest in the unusual customs and habits" of the world's peoples (Oh). If these shows bring the outside world into the TV studio, the peripatetic *Trans-America Ultra Quiz* brings the studio (hosts, contestants, desks with buzzers—everything) to the outside world. A grandiose mixture of luck, skill, physical endurance, and wanderlust, the *Trans-America Ultra Quiz* thinks big in every aspect of its conception and production.

It begins with thousands of contestants gathering in a sports stadium in Tokyo to answer "yes" or "no" questions by moving to designated sections of the playing field. Winnowed down to about 100 finalists, who must quickly pack their suitcases, more questions on a flight to California eliminate all but about 25 players. These continue their video trek from West to East as the eliminated 75 take the return flight back across the Pacific. Buzzers and player desks are set up in such improbable locations as an open field near Stone Mountain.

At each stop, more quick-fire questions eliminate players, who must perform exhausting, bizarre, and humiliating feats in the "batsu (loser's) game," like walking up 72 flights of stairs. According to long-time watchers, only young men end up as the final 12 or so star players. In the end, only two of them make it to Oz/Utopia/Shangri-la (read the Statue of Liberty, New York), one of whom emerges as the "ultra" champion. The show's ratings, once spectacular, have recently plummeted, since a trip to New York (within reach of any middle-class Japanese pocketbook) has lost its magic allure (Oh).

The elimination mode, which exactly duplicates the funnel-like Japanese education system, is used in two other civilian quizzes: *Genius Quiz* (TBS) for children (girls vs. boys) and *That's Perfect* (NHK) for college students. As in real life, from a large starting pool, each round of testing eliminates more players, until an elite group survives at game's end.

These three shows, plus four others, constitute Japan's only quizzes that feature civilian players. All 23 others feature celebrity panelists—drawn from a finite stable of

Table 9.3
Game Shows on Japanese Television
October 1992*

Time/Day	Network					
	NHK-G	ASAHI	FUJI	NIPPON	TBS	TOKYO
MONDAY-FRIDAY						
7 pm					*The*	
8 pm					*Move*	
SATURDAY						
5 pm					*Shingo Yamashiro's Information*	
6 pm					*Genius Quiz+*	
7 pm	*Suzy Q Number Game*		*Takeshi & Itsumi*	*Resemblance of Others*	*Quiz Derby*	
8 pm				*Magical Brain Powers*		
9 pm					*Discovering the World's Mysteries*	
10 pm						*Tamori's Music World*
11 pm			*Matchmaking Variety: Red Whale Tribe+*			

Time/Day	Network					
	NHK-G	ASAHI	FUJI	NIPPON	TBS	TOKYO
SUNDAY						
2 pm		*Attack 25+*				
7 pm	*That's Perfect+*	*Kyosen's English Hinto de Pinto*		*Teach Me! Galileo*	*Amateur Video Quiz*	
8 pm						
10 pm			*Cult Q+*			
11 pm						
MONDAY	none					
TUESDAY						
7 pm		*Seeking Men's & Women's Hearts*		*What's the Question?*		
9 pm			*Let's Go! The World*			
10 pm						
WEDNESDAY						
7 pm				*Interview Quiz*		
8 pm				*World Professionals Quiz*		
9 pm					*Gourmet Quiz*	
10 pm						

Time/Day		Network		
	FUJI	NIPPON	TBS	TOKYO
THURSDAY				
7 pm	*Young vs. Old Quiz*	*Trans America Ultra Quiz+*	*Look Out for Doubt*	
8 pm				*TV Champion+*
9 pm			*Info Variety*	
FRIDAY				
8 pm				*Changing Locales Quiz*
9 pm	*Family Present Quiz*			
10 pm				

*specials omitted
+civilian (non-celebrity) players

Note: NHK is a non-commercial, fee-based network with G (general) and E (educational) channels. NHK-E does not air quiz shows.

singers, comedians, and personalities (including a few Japanese-speaking Caucasians). (See Ch. 7.) They appear so regularly that they nearly compete against themselves, hopping from one neon-lit quiz set to another on different channels.

Because celebrity panelists dominate the Japanese quiz scene, prizes do not inject a rags-to-riches dramatic element as they do in Western shows such as *The Price Is Right* or *Let's Make a Deal.* Some celebrities capitalize on their inability to win, bantering, and joking with hosts and other celebrities in a style reminiscent of the quiz/talk show *What's My Line.*

Celebrities who do get the right answers receive dolls (or a variant such as a small globe) from a silent, miniskirted assistant. At the program's end, the "top show" (person with the most dolls) usually receives a giant stuffed doll. The tolerance of Japanese viewers for cuteness extends to the cartoon characters that bounce around on the high-tech video portions of many shows and the cartoon-character voices that often deliver the questions.

The seven non-celebrity shows include only one that poses general-knowledge questions, *Attack 25* (Asahi)—the lone Western-style example in the vast Japanese quiz universe. The others vary greatly in format. *Tunnels Red Whale Tribe* (Fuji) plays matchmaker to young adults in their 20s and early 30s. *Cult Q* (Fuji) features young-adult experts on topics as diverse as Pachinko (a pinball game), and Japan's Disneyworld. *TV Champion* (Tokyo) features civilians who demonstrate rather than just answer questions about their talents, from Chinese cooking to sweating.

This author will never forget a compelling/repelling 30 minutes she spent watching three men eat hot noodles in front of a gas stove as the camera focused on bottles filling up with their perspiration—ending as the curtain drew across so they could wring a few last drops of sweat from their drenched bathing suits.

But this spectator show, along with the matchmaking show noted above, constitute the only non-interactive games on Japanese television. These exceptions prove the rule: the culture decidedly prefers interactive formats (see Appendix 2). However, the information content rather than the mode of play characterizes Japan's quizzes. For example, the hostess of a travelogue show may walk through the streets of Rio de Janeiro imparting information as she points out sights. After five minutes or so, she shifts the viewer's attention slightly by pointing to a building, asking, rather than telling, "What is the purpose of this?" That nugget of information comes eventually (after the panelists state their guesses). And the stream of information starts again.

7. Brazil

A Brazilian entrepreneur launched the nation's first TV broadcasts in 1950. By the 1980s, Brazil's TV advertising budget ranked as the fourth largest in the world, after the United States, Japan and England (Dassin 404). According to cultural anthropologist Conrad Kottak, who studied television in Brazil 1983-87, "*The main purpose of commercial television is neither to entertain nor to enlighten, but to sell.* American and Brazilian television strive not to train proper citizens, but proper consumers" (23).

Television has given new meaning to the idea of "local culture" in Brazil, a diverse nation that embraces many hitherto isolated populations.

> It isn't North American culture but a new pan-Brazilian national culture that Brazilian TV is propagating.... The programs that attract this horde are made by Brazilians, for Brazilians. (Kottak 16)

When Brazilians and Americans sit down to view a TV game show, they bring diametrically opposite cultural norms. Americans focus on the "thrill of victory," while Brazilians focus on the "agony of defeat," asserts Kottak (84). Brazilian viewers love to laugh at contestants falling off a slippery bridge, while North Americans like to play along with interactive games and feel smart. (See Ch. 8.)

Nothing like *Jeopardy* exists in Brazil, despite its success in many European countries. "Shows like *Jeopardy* are alien to Brazilian TV," explains Kottak; "game show contestants play, act, sing or do tricks. They almost never display their intellect" (86). However, believes Kottak

> Brazilians go too far in the other direction.... Brazilian game shows...derive from and are much more similar to such older, lowbrow American game shows as *Let's Make a Deal*, *The Gong Show* and *Name That Tune*. (87)

Recently, however, a Brazilianized version of *Wheel of Fortune*, called *Roletrando Novelas* (*Wheel of Soaps*), has started to run daily on SBT. Despite *Wheel*'s North American origins, its Brazilian elements may ensure its success: it has superstar game show host Silvio Santos as its MC; it plays on the Brazilian passion for telenovelas (prime time soap operas) by asking viewers to send answers to simple soap-related questions; and it has simplified the rules (one need not buy vowels; a player just calls them out like any other letter). The "wonderfully soothing" *Wheel* may appeal to those viewers who have seen too many balloons burst by frantic players wearing bird-beak hats (Meisler 10).

As Table 9.4 shows, only *Roletrando* offers a set daily schedule, but Brazilians have their choice of many more hours of televised games. However, most of these games come sandwiched between singers, amateur talent contests, and (in the case of the three children's programs) cartoons. Sometimes the games-within-a-show last more than an hour and have a defined beginning and end, complete with credits and logo, but sometimes they are more fleeting—a three-minute game gives way to a four-minute song, which gives way, in turn, to two one-minute games. Moreover, even the named games may vary in time slot from week to week.

Brazilian viewers may know approximately when the "Passo ou Repassa" game-segment will come on *Programa Silvio Santos*, and when the amateur talent show airs. However, the TV schedule purposefully lists only *Programa Silvio Santos*—all 10.5 hours of it—or *Domingao do Faustao*, only 3.5 hours. The producers hope people will watch whatever airs while they wait for their favorite segment.

The *Faustao* show on Globo has a segment much like *I'm Telling* called "Bubballoo"; a *Hollywood Squares* celebrity segment; a *Sexland* segment in which men and women predict others' answers; and a number of games involving physical prowess, wherein players have to burst balloons by sitting in each other's laps and walk on swaying bridges while basketballs pelt them from all directions.

A typical *Programa Silvio Santos* might contain the following segments, generously interlaced with commercials:

noon	A young male host oversees the show's first segments. Games involve videos of animals, followed by questions asked of celebrity panelists.
1 pm	Popular singers perform.
1:15	"Nacoes Unidas" ("United Nations") Two costumed teams—Italy vs. Israel—compete in studio and outdoor games, most of them physical: crushing ("grapes") purple balloons, catapulting objects with a giant slingshot, answering questions about Elvis.
2:45	"Passa ou Repassa" ("Try and Try Again") Two teams of teenagers compete in a messy food fight and other contests involving pies in the face, spaghetti on the players' heads, and lots of balloons.
4:00	"Bau Mina de Ora" ("The Treasure Chest") Silvio Santos himself now takes over as MC. He chooses letters from home viewers who belong to a club and buy tickets, hoping theirs will be chosen.
4:15	"Quanto Valo Show" A studio game with board something like that used on *Concentration*, but without the rebus.
5:00	"Plim Plim Game" Three couples try to match the words that celebrities will use in completing simple statements (coorientation).
5:30	"Jugo do Signos" ("Game of Signs") As in *Let's Make a Deal*, players choose between money or the chance for a big prize. Santos interacts with the audience, asking "What should they do? This one?"
6:15	"The President's Week": news summary
6:30	Amateur talent show

7:00 "Porta de Esperanza" ("Door of Hope")
Like a *Queen for a Day*, before-and-after videos show wishes coming true for poor or deserving applicants.

8:00 "Topa Tudo por Dinheiro" ("Anything for Money"). Yet another game segment.

9:00 Musical variety

10:30 Santos ends show by getting dunked in a fish tank.

Brazil has a sophisticated market research system, the Brazilian Statistical Public Opinion Research Institute (IBOPE), founded in 1942 and headquartered in Rio.

Brazilians watch less television on weekdays (2.5 hours) than on Sundays (4.5 hours), when shops close up and everyone, including live-in maids, has a holiday. IBOPE data shows SBT higher in the ratings on Sunday than Globo, especially later in the day when Silvio Santos himself takes over MC duties from his assistant. When Santos ran for mayor of Sao Paulo, Brazilian law limited his on-air appearance time, which caused ratings to drop. The lost revenue convinced him to eschew politics and continue his TV career. Santos, who started his career as a poor street vendor, founded SBT as a network for lower-income viewers.

Another personality rose from poverty (and a stint as a nude model) to superstardom through the game/variety show route: blonde, blue-eyed Xuxa (pronounced SHOO-sha). *Xou da Xuxa*, a children's program, used to air 8 a.m. to 1 p.m. daily, Monday through Saturday. Now Xuxa, who has many irons in the fire (albums, movies, books, clothes, dolls), has received some help on weekdays from Sergio Mallandro, who comes on the air 8:30-9:30 a.m. Both shows include game segments for young children, alternating with songs, stories, cartoons, and other entertainment. Besides commercials, games themselves advertise products such as Coca-Cola, as teams in Coke T-shirts carry six-packs of Coke on skateboards. Action for Children's Television would not approve.

Xuxa, "the biggest star, Brazilian or foreign, in the country," counters her show's blatant commercialism by serving as a positive role model (Pickard 1). Taking her clout seriously, she includes parents as well as kids in her on-stage audience—a kind of cholera-fighting Madonna who praces around the stage in hot pants, yet maintains an image of sweetness. Globo stole Xuxa away from Manchete, where she had started a show in 1986.

Manchete now has a similar children's variety show, *Club de Crianca*, featuring game segments and a Xuxa clone named Anjelica. Blonde Anjelica, like Xuxa, has a group of young Paquitas (assistants) who dance tirelessly during the show's frenetic live portions. Her trademarks include a large mole on her left leg and a fondness for kissing the camera.

At the other extreme from children's game shows is the X-rated *Cocktail*, featuring topless assistants and contestants, a late-night show on SBT. The show originated in Italy, but it meshes perfectly with Brazil's tradition of topless beaches, revealing Carnival costumes and nude nightclub dancers. Brazil exemplifies the third, mature stage of TV's international interactions; after years of massive imports, followed by domestic program growth, the few imports represent appropriate programming—in the case of game shows, even locally produced.

Table 9.4

Game Shows on Brazilian Television, 1992

	Globo	Manchete	SBT
Sun.			
noon			*Programa*
1			
2			
3	*Domingao*		
4	*Do*		*Silvio*
5	*Faustao*		*Santos*
6	(game show		(game
7	portion =		show
8	c. 1 hour)		portion
9			= c. 4
10			hours)
Mon.-Fri.			
8	*Show Do* (games =		
9	*Mallandro* c. 20 min)		
10	*Xou Da*		
11	*Xuxa*		
noon	(games = 30-45 min)		
1			
2			
3			
4		*Clube De*	
5		*Crianca*	
6		(games =	*Roletrando*
7		10-15 min)	*Novelas*
Thurs.			
11			*Cocktail*
midnight			1 hour

Note: Game portions are estimates and may vary from week to week. TV Educativa, TV Bandeirantes, and Rede Om have no game shows.

Chapter 10

CONCLUSIONS: ENTERTAINING IDEAS

There is no such thing as "pure entertainment." All entertainment contains messages and values, whether intended or not. (Fischer and Melnik xiv)

To paraphrase Giamatti, this author believes that we can learn more about "the conditions and values of a society by contemplating how it chooses to play," in the form of its TV game shows, than by watching its TV news (13). The variety and ubiquity of game/quiz shows makes them an honest broker when we contemplate the world's TV cultures.

So, through studying 260 shows in 50 countries, what have we learned about cross-cultural similarities and differences? This chapter will attempt to draw some conclusions and sketch some future directions for the genre.

An overview of game types (Ch. 6) showed a preference in Africa and the Near/Middle East for knowledge quizzes rather than voyeuristic shows like *The Dating Game* or cash-oriented games like *The Price Is Right* predominate. *Quiz Kid* shows may indeed stress education as a value, but do they *educate?* So far only scattered efforts have begun to tap game shows' development potential. Much more could be done.

1. Playing for change: game shows as development communication

Most industry personnel disavow the persuasive, informative power of "mere entertainment," following instead Hollywood's own first principle for writers: "'If we want a message, we'll send for Western Union'" (Barnouw and Kirkland 103).

However, some producers consciously attend to such content, using entertainment's messages in a positive way. The enter-education movement began in the 1950s with Jamaican pro-development radio soap operas (Cambridge). The approach came to television in 1975 when the Televisa network of Mexico produced its first pro-development TV soap opera (Singhal and Rogers, *Populi* 40). By 1989, when producers and researchers met at the Enter-educate Conference in Los Angeles, the movement had its own first principle: "Use the universal appeal of entertainment to show how [people] can live safer, healthier, and happier lives."

The conference did not, however, deal with game shows. Nor did a number of recent research projects (Cambridge; McWilliams; Sanders and Hagamed; Singhal, "Entertainment..."; and Thomas). By slightly twisting the theme of the 1989 conference, we propose a revised first principle:

> Play and the world plays with you.
> Lecture and you lecture alone.

TELEVISION AS A TEACHER. Television is a kind, non-threatening teacher for children, explains David Connell, producer of *Square-One TV* and a past producer of *Sesame Street* and *The Electric Company* for the Children's

Television Workshop. "There is no test at the end of the show.... they watch [shows] for the entertainment value, then maybe a seed is planted" (Shaper 12). Moreover, TV shows can include ethnic group members, women, and children as role models. And tapes can be used over and over, then erased.

Bang and Fibiger see television as a better potential teacher than live lectures, audio tapes, radio, print media, or computers because television can offer voice, writing, color, still pictures, animation, and on-site depiction of events:

> None of the other media is able to handle all forms of representations. Television can take students to places where they are unlikely to go to, it can let them experience persons whom they are unlikely to meet, and it can bring them inside institutions where they are unlikely to come otherwise. (2)

Bang and Fibiger include not only broadcast TV programs but narrowcast services, prerecorded videocassettes, and videodiscs in their definition of television (3). The problem with TV broadcasts, admit Bang and Fibiger, is "no interactivity between the media and the student" (13). By the year 2000, 40 percent of U.S. households may have interactive technology. But judging from the failure of the Qube cable system experiment in Columbus, Ohio, others doubt if the audience "truly wants interactivity, or is willing to pay for it" (Waters, "Talking" 56). Educators can induce interactivity by use of computers and videodiscs, explain Bang and Fibiger (8-9). However, such pricey hardware has little meaning for Third World needs. Game shows broadcast over the air or on cassettes offer an interactive alternative requiring nothing but the human psyche, a technology that comes free with each healthy human.

Developmental games include carefully selected questions of substance and problem-solving tasks deemed appropriate for viewers' age and skill levels. Because they aim to increase knowledge rather than change attitudes and behavior, we can refer to TV games as "info-tainment," to distinguish them from developmental dramas and music, usually called "enter-education."

Singhal and Rogers, in a summary of lessons learned from enter-education efforts to promote family planning, state that "despite the successes, the entertainment-education strategy is much more effective in creating knowledge of an issue than in changing overt behavior regarding the issue" (*Populi* 45). Thus the *info-tainment* strategy, in the tried-and-proven guise of the TV game show, has excellent potential for educational development.

Granted, game show producers aim to increase ratings rather than viewers' knowledge. But who is to say how many "Wheel of Fortune" fans have unconsciously improved their spelling by solving hangman phrases? It's hard to watch *Wheel* and not join in. (Quick! What's J _ _ _ N _ L _ _ M S T _ D _ _ T ?).

ADVANTAGES OF GAME SHOWS. There are many reasons that media development specialists should consider producing educational game shows. Although some of the examples below rely on visuals, others can also be adapted to radio (where many quiz shows got their start). Game shows are:

Cheap because of simple sets, few paid performers, and the need for only limited creative staffing to create the skits or questions. Because they can bring in advertising revenue, the economic advantage can be even greater. For example, in 1986 *Wheel of Fortune* cost $7 million to produce, but brought in $120 million in revenues, a 17-to-1 ratio. Indeed, when contestants play for the sake of developmental change, they likewise play for change—not pennies, literally, but for small change when compared with production costs for other TV genres.

Indigenous, and thus meaningful to a local or regional population. In general, audience research "suggests that viewers prefer their own audiovisual programming over imported shows" (Artwick 22; see Ch. 3).

Popular, judging from ratings in various countries. (See Ch. 7.)

Varied in format, such that any culture can adapt a suitable vehicle. They can involve intense time pressure (contestants must buzz in quickly with answers) or proceed leisurely (as a solution to a puzzle gradually reveals itself). They can have varying proportions of luck and skill. They can have one winner and one loser, or teams of winners and losers, or one winner and numerous losers, or an unspecified number of winners who match some criterion. Prizes can be expensive or merely symbolic.

Varied in learning, either focused or multifaceted. If focused, they can emphasize literacy or vocabulary building (word games), math (number games), factual knowledge (questions in specific categories), or problem solving. They could even teach physical skills or encourage exercise with simple props in the manner of *Double Dare* or *Sabado Gigante*.

Apolitical/inoffensive, which gives them a run potentially long enough to have an impact and fewer problems getting funded. If produced for a commercial system, they do not usually elicit content-related boycotts, which makes them "advertiser friendly" (Walley and Magiera).

Imitatable, so that watching groups or classroom groups, once they get familiar with the format, can play and learn on their own. Indeed, many TV game shows developed from children's and parlor games of pre-TV days (e.g., charades, hangman and tic-tac-toe).

Integratable, in case hardware is available. *Wheel of Fortune*, *$100,000 Pyramid*, and *Jeopardy* computer software exists. A few full-production developmental TV episodes could be created to interest viewers in a certain game, followed by an unlimited array of one-on-one or small-group "copycat" games on software. A hand-held, play-along device, something like the *Jeopardy! Challenger*, which sells for $45 in the United States, could be developed for use with broadcast developmental shows. A lap-sized control unit that lets a viewer play against on-screen contestants as well as all other control-unit players sells for $450 (Malley 58).

Conventional. "To communicate invention one must start with the common ground of convention," points out Hinds (120). As an established genre, game shows have great potential to teach because "they create a frame through which audiences have learned to read meaning" (120).

REAL GAMES FOR REAL GAINS. The largest-scale developmental game show to date, called *Where in the World is Carmen Sandiego?* made its debut on PBS in fall

1991. Based on a computer game, it teaches geography by "deputizing" young contestants who search the world for Carmen by answering questions and putting together large, room-sized maps. Other info-tainment game shows are rare, but ideas abound in sometimes unlikely corners.

Geography games: In addition to the above PBS program, an educational program in Tunisia, *Jeux d'Afrique*, stresses regional geography. Inadvertently, commercial channels in England, Japan, and Taiwan teach geography in their travel-theme game shows. The British (ITV) daily morning program *Runway*, that ran in the late 1980s, featured questions about a destination that, if the contestant answered correctly, resulted in a trip to that destination. The Japanese once-a-week prime time show *Let's Go! the World* breaks out of the studio in a spectacular way. (See Ch. 9.) Similarly, Taiwan's *The World is Very Strange* used on-location questions. The technique could be adapted for use with prerecorded scenes, interrupted by questions, then restarted to provide the immediate feedback of an answer or lesson.

Vocabulary games: Television lends itself perfectly to word games that gradually reveal their answers as contestants and viewers stare at letters. *Wheel of Fortune* and the many countries to which it has been licensed attest to the adaptability of such games to any culture with an alphabetic writing system. As aficionados know, the concept can be used to teach the names of notable persons and the titles of artistic and literary works, not just catchphrases; a developmental version could show Seurat's *A Sunday Afternoon on the Island of La Grande Jatte* after a contestant solved the puzzle or briefly explain the importance of author Joseph Conrad.

Blockbusters, a U.S.-licensed show now running in England (ITV), Germany (ARD), Italy (Canale 5), and Israel, which features young players who try to form words in a honeycomb pattern, inadvertently builds vocabulary and improves spelling. Shows modeled on *Password* and *Pyramid*, which can increase one's vocabulary through use of synonyms and homonyms, do not rely on alphabetic script; the Japanese (NHK) version features a round of words beginning with the same Chinese character, a concept easily adaptable to literacy training. *Password* and *Pyramid* versions also run in Portugal, England, and Germany. The concept behind *Scrabble* and France's *Des Chiffres et des Lettres*, which require contestants to make words from randomly selected letters, could also be adapted for education.

Mathematics games: The numbers portion of *Des Chiffres et des Lettres*, like the letters portion, requires creative thinking rather than spitting back accumulated facts. Contestants must use six randomly selected numbers—through subtraction, addition, multiplication, or division—to arrive at a target three-digit number (also randomly selected). The process may seem irrelevant and unable to engage the imagination, but in fact the show has run in France for more than 20 years and has spawned at-home, play-along clubs. More French viewers watched the show's finals than watched a recent World Cup soccer match (Rips). Tapes of the show air on Canada's French-language network, and a British version called *Countdown* ran in the late 1980s.

The only info-tainment game shows specifically stressing math skills appear as segments almost every day on *Square 1 TV*, a production of the Children's Television Workshop, which has run on PBS since January 1988. Young "panelists" (and home viewers) give answers to math problems that the frenetic "host" poses, such as which two-dimensional representations can be folded to create boxes; then the "hostess" reinforces the right answer by actually folding the flat cutouts. Hoping to attract parents and older siblings as well as children, the producers inject intergenerational humor and parody. Interactivity is crucial, since "math is not a spectator sport" (Shaper). The game segments reappear, such as *Triple Play*, which features two *Wheel of Fortune* wheels. If they stop at 11 and 5, for example, a player can claim the 16 block or the 55 block on a honeycomb game board.

Social studies games. WPSX-TV, a PBS affiliate licensed to the Pennsylvania State University, created and aired 50 half-hour programs in 1988 to teach and create interest in the state's history. Three on-air panelists answered multiple-choice questions, each followed by an explanation and video images. *The Pennsylvania Game* also included clues to identify a mystery Pennsylvanian, likewise featuring a video essay. The show earned an 18 share (28,000 households) and "attained the goal of being entertaining" (Hinds 124).

General knowledge games: Many game shows rely on general knowledge as the means by which contestants gain points, but educators would find much of the content frivolous (e.g., facts about rock music on MTV's *Remote Control* or the names of products on the Lifetime network's *Supermarket Sweep*). Even "highbrow" general-knowledge shows like *Jeopardy!* or the BBC's *Mastermind*, can be criticized as orgies of isolated meaningless facts—an orgy that nevertheless has made *Jeopardy!* the second most popular syndicated program on U.S. television (February 1989 Nielsen ratings). By contrast, info-tainment shows, usually featuring teams of high school or college students, tend to be static—yet do succeed in India, China, Ghana, and other cultures. *GE's College Quiz Bowl* survived in a number of countries after leaving CBS-TV during the Vietnam War era.

Well-produced general-knowledge shows, such as Nickelodeon's *Make the Grade*, can both entertain and inform. Using a *Jeopardy!*-style game board with knowledge categories across, the levels are coded by grade level instead of dollar values. *The Challengers*, hosted by Dick Clark and produced in association with *Newsweek*, devoted some of its content to current events matters. A British show (ITV) that ran in the late 1980s, *Headliners*, used video clips from past years as a means of posing questions.

As one fan put it:

> Game shows will continue forever because you can fit anything you want into a game show...A game show has elements of any show in the world. It's got drama, it's got pathos, it's got comedy. It's got everything. (Malley 96)

If the fan had added education, he would have defined the developmental appeal of this genre that has everything. The manipulation of content does raise the spectre of mind control, an issue dealt with by Brown and Singhal. In the case of game shows, the content is so manifest that any hidden agenda would be difficult to put over. The future may even see the return to live TV game shows that can be linked to the audience by telephone, as does the U.S. parody game show on non-commercial radio, *Whaddya Know?* As in the early history of enter-education, radio may lead the way.

2. Cross-border games: gigantic proportions

McLuhan declared that "electrically contracted, the globe is no more than a village" (20). Yet the world's TV viewers do NOT share global tastes, preferring their own to someone else's game shows (see Ch. 3). However, technology has evolved to enable cross-border game show production when certain conditions obtain:

1) dissimilar countries seek an apolitical means to increase cooperation and understanding;
2) a distinct culture straddling two countries' border wants to overcome political separation; or
3) physically distant countries with a common language and culture want to share TV programs.

Jeux sans Frontieres, an example of situation 1), features teams from various European nations in physical competition. The author has seen *Games without Borders* in Yugoslavia in 1990. French and Italian TV listings featured the finals of the series prominently (the week of September 2, 1990), but it does not appear to run in every European nation. The competitors' athletic skills approach the semi-professional level of *American Gladiators* rather than the clutzy enthusiasm of *Double Dare* or *What Would You Do?*

French-speaking nations in Europe (e.g., Belgium and France)—as well as throughout the world—run a student quiz show called *Genies en Herbe* (*Budding Geniuses*). An international championship takes place in the summer, which in 1992 ran on the CBC's French station Sunday, August 2. Such cooperative games could bring together minority enclaves separated from their home population, such as Croatians and Croatian groups in Serbia, but few governments would feel secure enough to encourage such relations (situation 2).

The Arabic- and Spanish-speaking worlds best represent situation 3, since the French-speaking world encompasses vast cultural differences. This author has not found any Arab-world quiz shows (no games of chance nor games with prizes that smacked of gambling would be appropriate due to Islam's prohibition against gambling). However, a Spanish-language game show not only exists, but has made broadcasting history.

Sabado Gigante (*Gigantic Saturday*), a long-format weekend game/variety program with a charismatic host, "is the first TV show produced in Spanish that has been successfully broadcast to the entire continent" (Silva 56). Viewers in 18 countries including the United States can tune in to the weekly program, which airs on the East Coast 7-10:30 p.m. (e.g., in New York City on Channel 41, WXTV) on the Univision network.

Joe del Cueto, Univision's vice-president for sales, divides U.S. Spanish-language television "into two eras—before and after 'Sabado Gigante.' ...That's how important it is" (Silva 56). Univision, based in Miami, sells an international edition of the game/variety show without commercials. Using *Sabado* as a springboard, eventually Univision hopes to create a stable of affiliates by providing a whole slate of programs for which local staffs would sell local commercials. This Spanish-language network, which Hallmark Cards bought in 1988 for $600 million, would work like ABC, CBS, and NBC, except it would be international.

Even the production has international dimensions. Identical stage sets have been built in Miami and Santiago, Chile, home base of the show's host Don Francisco. When

Francisco introduces a segment that actually takes place in Miami, the Chilean studio audience sees it on a screen. Francisco, whose real name is Mario Kreutzberger, ranks as "the most popular television emcee in the Americas" (Silva 56).

The program interweaves interactive games, spectator games, talk, variety acts, short documentary films, comedy skits, and numerous commercials; Francisco's personality provides the glue to make the combination work. A typical half hour includes two six-minute game segments. For example, on September 19, 1992, civilian contestants played a hangman-like word game, permitting the winner to proceed to another word game. Later, two teams engaged in a "talking contest," at the end of which audience applause decided which team had won.

Fast-talking Francisco descends into the audience to talk with those attending the show. Commercials form part of the show itself; the stage set and games themselves feature product names, and the audience joins in singing the praises of Downey. Female assistants help deliver live, on-stage commercials. In addition, local ads appear, such as for the New York lottery in the WXTV (Patterson, NJ) version.

The phenomenal Francisco, who started *Sabado* in Chile in 1962, is the subject of a sociological analysis, *Asi, Asi se Mueve Don Francisco* (Altamirano). Is Francisco a saint, an idol, and a man of the people as his fans claim? Or is he authoritarian, tiresome, uncultured, and gross as his critics claim? As for the show, is it authoritarian or democratic; participatory or manipulative; culturally important or merely commercial? The total "admiration/subordination of the public to a star" as powerful as Francisco may be cause for concern (179).

Altamirano sees the variety format as part of a long tradition of popular entertainment that survived despite criticism from the church and the arbiters of good taste (27). Popular television harks back to Moliere in the 17th century and to music halls and live variety theaters in the 19th century.

Games include "La Gran Opportunidad," "Mister Chile," and "Los Dobles." The games portions have three objectives: promoting products and brand names (e.g., a game board may have a product's name emblazoned on it); audience involvement, which produces certain psychological effects; and entertainment. They even have a kind of dramatic structure, including suspense, conflict, anxiety and catharsis (Altamirano 154-55).

The culminating dramatic moment comes when Don Francisco "succeeds in pulling out tears of gratitude from those favored"—that is, the prize winners; the paternalistic Francisco manipulates, even abuses, the grateful contestants for purely commercial reasons. On the positive side, some of the games promote democracy and an aura of equality of opportunity (Altamirano 160). Francisco asks the studio audience about who should get what prizes, while the viewer at home participates by expressing an opinion vicariously. But is this real democracy or only fictional escapist entertainment?

More worrisome may be the show's commercialism, which includes 12 or more minutes of commercials per hour, plus in-show merchandising (40 percent of the show's income) (Castellon). Still, most Chilean families spend at least part of Saturday watching the show together, as families have for the past 30 years (Castellon).

Table 10.1
TV Game/Quiz Shows in 50 Countries
Scheduling, Autumn 1990

		TIME PLACEMENT				TIME DURATION			
Region	# of Shows	Weekend Prime/ Daytime (%) 1)	Weekday Prime (%) 2)	Weekday Strip (%) 3)	Not Known (%)	15-45 Min. (%)	46-59 Min. (%)	Over 60 Min. (%)	Not Known (%)
1. N. Europe	32	15.6	28.1	34.4	21.9	75.0	3.1	3.1	18.8
2. W. Europe	70	21.4	28.6	34.3	15.7	65.7	15.7	4.3	14.3
3. E. Europe	9	33.3	33.3	0.0	33.3	0.0	33.3	11.1	55.6
4. Nr./Mid E	9	33.3	22.2	11.1	33.3	77.8	11.1	0.0	11.1
5. Africa	16	43.8	31.2	0.0	25.0	93.8	6.2	0.0	0.0
6. S/SE Asia	16	50.0	31.1	6.3	12.5	50.0	25.0	12.5	12.5
7. E. Asia	45	53.3	44.4	2.2	0.0	35.6	51.1	11.1	2.2
8. Pacific	8	25.0	12.5	50.0	12.5	75.0	0.0	0.0	25.0
9. Lat. Am.	14	42.8	21.4	35.7	0.0	0.0	35.7	64.3	0.0
10. No. Am.	41	14.6	17.1	60.9	7.3	92.7	2.4	2.4	2.4
Totals	260	30.4	28.8	27.7	13.1	61.5	19.2	8.5	10.8

1) Shows airing on Saturday and Sunday.

2) Shows airing on one or more days, 7-11 pm; includes late prime shows airing after 11 pm once a week as well as early prime shows airing at 6 pm once a week.

3) Shows airing on two or more days 7 am-7 pm.

Note: Data for Japan and Brazil from 1992.

3. Cultural continents

This study of 260 game shows in 50 countries confirms the "triumph" of culture over technology (Kato, *Essays* 6). Writing in another context, Geertz refers to anthropology's "deepest theoretical dilemma: how is such [cultural] variation to be squared with the biological unity of the human species?" (23). The game show genre, which has spawned both the world's most-watched format (*Wheel of Fortune*) and the world's first truly international TV show (*Sabado Gigante*), can shed light on that dilemma. To paraphrase Geertz, neither total unity nor total variability prevails (23).

Entertainment programming shows us that cultural preferences follow patterns. We cannot see these cultural continents—groupings of people that do not coincide with political borders—when we look comparatively at TV news shows, as many authors have done (Dupagne 1991).

A close look at format and mode-of-play, adulation accorded celebrities and gender roles (Ch. 7) can reveal differences and similarities of game shows. We can get further insights by studying scheduling decisions made by TV programmers around the world. Table 10.1 shows that the weekday "strip" schedule familiar to U.S. viewers is favored as well in Northern/Western Europe and in the Pacific (Australia/New Zealand). However, in Europe, audiences in addition like their games in prime time. East Asia differs markedly, virtually ignoring the daytime strip approach in favor of weekend and prime time viewing. Almost everywhere, viewers prefer shorter rather than longer (more than 60 minutes) programs. However, Latin tastes differ; in that region alone, long shows prevail (indeed, Brazil's *Silvio Santos Show* runs 10.5 hours every Sunday).

GLOBAL VILLAGE/NATIONAL TOWNS: TWO MYTHS. McLuhan's 1964 image of unity has not come to pass. Judging from TV game show content, no format or style has touched audiences universally. *Wheel of Fortune*'s 25 markets represent a small percent of the world's national TV systems. Countries from China to Germany and France to Japan air dating shows, but modes of matching couples in a TV game are as diverse as these nations' cuisines. A number of nations air "educational" student-contestant quizzes, but anyone who sees *Where In the World Is Carmen Sandiego?* (PBS-United States) and *That's Perfect* (NHK-Japan) will find comparisons odious. Furthermore, many countries have opted NOT to run such shows (e.g., the Philippines, Taiwan, Germany, Brazil, Mexico and Egypt).

On the other hand, the United Nations' 180 members do not each represent disparate, atomized national towns, even though TV news studies overemphasize national uniqueness. TV news often reflects national political control or national issues (laws, currency rates, weather, border problems). TV news studies (e.g., Straubhaar et al.) can tell us about within-border interests, while entertainment studies can speak about cross-border interests.

CULTURAL CONTINENTS. Specific shows like *Wheel of Fortune* and *Sadabo Gigante* can cross borders. Furthermore, certain approaches to TV entertainment cross international borders. Besides the four "game worlds" described below, we could point to a fifth, because many less-developed nations have yet to produce enough game shows for a pattern to emerge. (See Fig. 10.1.)

The East Asia Model. Since Japan stands as the world's foremost game/quiz producer, with 31 such shows running in fall 1992, this model applies most specifically to Japan. However, Taiwan and Korea fit the model to some extent, both with their own shows and with formats imported from Japan. The following characteristics apply:

* interactivity (home audiences can play along)
* emphasis on content and information rather than mode of play
* deemphasis on expensive prizes and huge cash amounts to be won
* celebrity players (from a finite stable) rather than civilians
* activist hosts (direct the action, give opinions, evoke laughter)
* women as co-hosts but also as silent assistants
* high cost, high technology, out-of-studio production values
* prime-time, once-a-week scheduling (weekdays and weekends)
* high tolerance for sentimentality
* moderate pacing (most shows do not use a buzzer)
* game-only formats (no variety acts intervene)
* length: 30 to 60 minutes (except for longer specials)

The Western Model. Almost every trait of the East Asian model finds its mirror opposite in the Western model—except that they both share a love for interactive games. The group includes the United States, Canada, all of Western Europe, Australia, and some other states. Turkey, for example, has games more like the West than like the Arab Muslim world, so its audiences have voted with their channel changers for a place in this Western model:

* interactivity
* emphasis on mode of play (game moves in stages;

the winner tackles a special endgame after regular rounds)

* emphasis on expensive prizes and huge amounts of cash to be won
* civilian players rather than celebrities
* facilitator hosts (move game along, explain rules, ask the questions, announce commercial breaks)
* women as silent assistants, not as hosts
* low-budget, high-profit, studio-bound
* strip scheduling (five days a week, same time slot)
* low tolerance for sentimentality
* quick pacing (use of buzzer and rewards for quick responses)
* length: 30 minutes (rarely 60 minutes; no specials)

The Latin Model. Brazil is the prime example of this nearly language-unified model (considering Spanish and Portuguese somewhat mutually intelligible, and Spanish as one language of the Philippines). But Chile, home base of *Sabado Gigante*, Mexico, and Peru admirably fit as well. Outside of geographic Latin America, the Philippines, and probably other nations not in this study share many of the traits below:

* spectator formats
* emphasis on mode of play (physical games)
* emphasis on expensive prizes and huge amounts of cash to be won
* civilian players
* dominant hosts (show rests on host's personality)
* women sometimes hosts and always as wiggling assistants
* weekend scheduling
* high-cost, high production values, in and out of studio
* frenetic, physically fast pacing
* high tolerance for sentimentality

* mixed formats: games alternate with variety performances
* length: one to ten hours

The Equatorial Model. Table 6.3 shows a decided lack of current popularity for "knowledge" quizzes—those that showcase above-average mental skills. However, as Appendix 2 shows, a certain handful of countries actually favor this type of show, whether featuring adults or children (often representing their schools). The group includes Jamaica, Ivory Coast, Ghana, Cameroon, Kenya, Morocco, Tunisia, Nigeria, Saudi Arabia, United Arab Emirates, and India. These countries, which cluster around the equator, typically have state-run broadcast systems that try to use television for developmental aims and try to control its commercialization. Their games share these characteristics:

* emphasis on education through knowledge quizzes
* low production values (simple sets and format)
* large proportion of teams of young people representing their schools
* deemphasis on expensive consumer-good prizes

In fall 1993, India, for example, had three national programs that all stations have to carry via Doordarshan, the network operated by the Ministry of Information and Broadcasting. Two—*Quiz Forum* and *Sports Quiz*—involve a large audience and free-for-all questions, while *Quest Science Quiz* requires three-member student teams to explain the results of experiments.

In the past, the late Rajiv Gandhi promoted two national TV quizzes. *Discover India Quiz* encouraged citizens to travel in their own country; questions, to which anyone

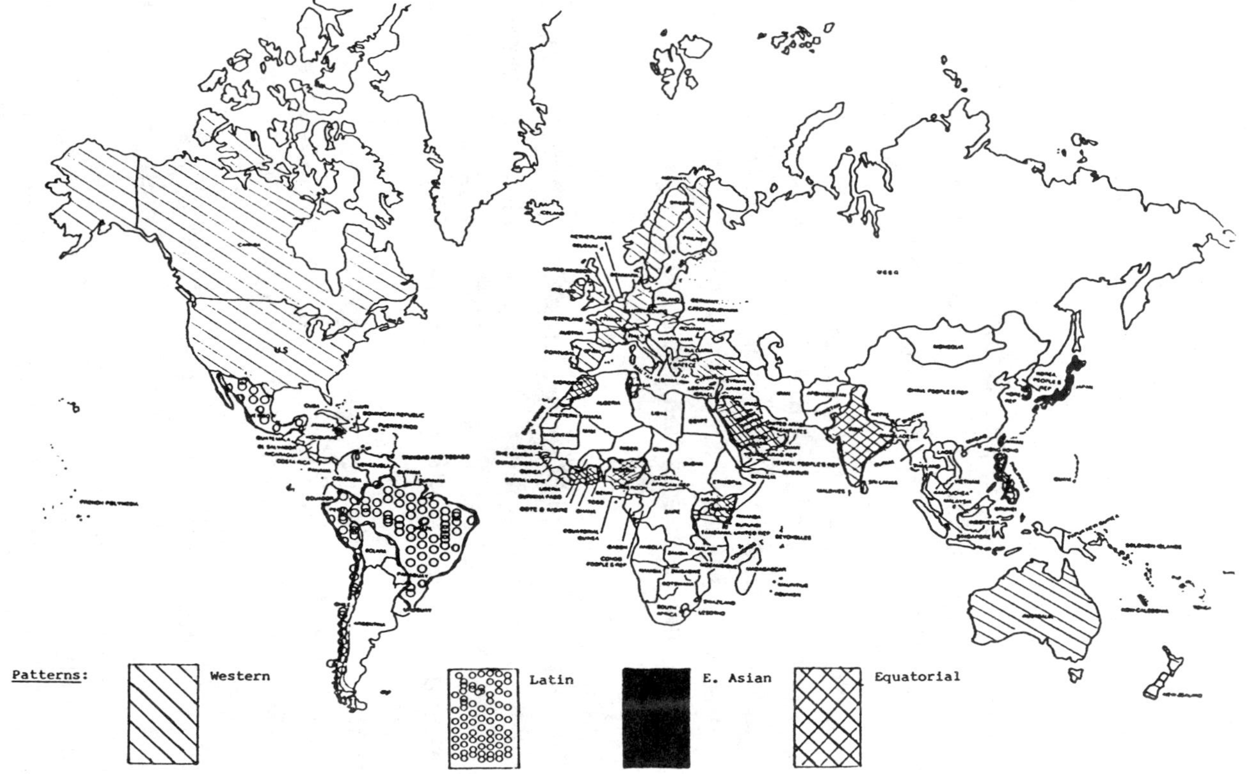

Figure 10.1. Cultural Continents: cross-border similarities in TV game shows.

could respond, were printed in newspapers. The *Nehru Centennial Quiz* of 1989 commemorated the 100th birthday of Rajiv Gandhi's own grandfather. Before national TV service began in 1982, the *Bounvita Quiz* on radio, hosted by Amin Sayani, gave high school teams a nationwide audience. To promote regional cooperation, the *SAARC Quiz*, acronym for the South Asian Association for Regional Cooperation, featured questions on Nepal, Bangladesh, Pakistan, and other nearby nations.

Thirty years ago, McLuhan's pronouncement that "electrically contracted, the world is no more than a village" represented not a description, but a prediction (20). Now that television has arrived in virtually all countries, we can revise its accuracy to wit: "Electrically connected, pre-existing cultural continents can coalesce."

4. The future

Two particular game types can speak volumes about a culture's current social mores: dating shows and striptease games. In the future, we can track social change as audience tastes and comfort levels regarding courtship and nudity evolve.

Noting the rate of acceptance and locus of *Tutti Frutti* could make for an entertainment diffusion study of which Everett Rogers could be proud (Singhal and Rogers, *India's*). This show, which features both civilian and professional female strippers, began in Italy as *Colpo Grosso*. It then conquered Germany and subsequently Spain. Brazil and Turkey followed soon after. Although cable penetration in Japan is very low, some viewers in Japan can see the Italian-language *Colpo Grosso* early Wednesday morning (2:15 a.m.) on one cable network.

In the future, satellites may make control by individual countries of "offensive" shows impossible. Today most of Europe, including Eastern Europe, can watch the strip show's German version via RTL satellite. "I don't understand much German," a Polish man told this author, "but for this show, who need words? It helps me relax. Life here is difficult. We need to relax."

By contrast, dating shows from another culture may hold little interest for audiences even if they could view them easily by satellite. Asia and the West have their own distinctive matchmaking shows, none of which could successfully transfer between regions. However, the subtle variations within the two regional cultures hold almost as much interest as their overriding similarities.

Both Taiwan (*Sparks Fly*) and Japan (*Red Whale Tribe*) have mixer shows for young people in their 20s. At the end of each, women stand passively as the young men ask for dates; women have the power only to accept or reject, not to choose. But not all Asian shows duplicate this format exactly. Korea once had a show that matched farmers with women from cities and towns. China's *Let's Meet Tonight* often features groups of singles from specific factories and unions.

Taiwan's *We Love the Matchmaker* has evolved dramatically from a control-from-above format in the mid 1980s (producers arranged the match beforehand and ended the show with a dramatic meeting of the young man and woman). By 1992, three men and three women participated actively in a mutual choice process. The parallels with Taiwan's evolving political freedom make for intriguing speculation.

The change of U.S. dating shows from the innuendo of *The Dating Game* to more explicit cocktail-lounge conversation has not occurred in other countries. *Dating Game* clones were running in various Western nations even after the show had disappeared in its home nation.

Finally, technology can allow cultural continents to share not only program formats, but actual content. *Sabado Gigante* (*Gigantic Saturday*), profiled above, is the first but probably not the last successful cross-border game show. Thus the future will probably see more multi-nation game show hosts or hostesses like Don Francisco. Such powerful celebrity status worried Altamirano, who had an uncanny prescience about the power of TV personalities (179). Indeed a game show host could grow up to be president.

In November 1989, game show host Silvio Santos appeared tied for the lead with Fernando Collor de Mello in Brazil's presidential race ("Brazilian TV"). Santos had to quit the race on a technicality, leaving Collor to go on to victory. Considering the trauma of Collor's 1992 impeachment due to corruption, a game show host might not have been such a bad choice.

Appendix 1

CONTESTANTS' DIARIES

A. LOS ANGELES TRYOUTS, 1989

Sunday, August 27

Arrived in Los Angeles from Columbus, Ohio; bought LA *Times* and turned immediately to classifieds, Category 1270, "TV Contestants." During this late summer time period, only a few shows advertised for contestants: *Win, Lose or Draw*, *Family Feud*, *Classic Concentration,* and three shows being newly deveoped: *Mastermind*, *Divorce Wars* and a third divorce game that required "all 3 of you"—you, your ex and your new spouse. My ex, whom I had not seen for three years, was not along on the trip; nor were four other members of my family, so that eliminated two shows.

Monday, August 28

Considered going to *The Price Is Right*, where contestants are told to "come on down" from the audience (I had ordered "first-come, first-served" tickets to the taping in advance). Decided not to, since that project would take all day with little chance of being chosen. I was told to arrive in line at 7 a.m. for the 2:15 p.m. taping and at 10 a.m. for the 6:15 p.m. taping. (Tapings are held Monday, Tuesday and Wednesday.) Began instead to make phone calls for tryout appointments. Repeated calls to *Divorce Wars* brought response from an answering machine only. Got appointments for *Win, Lose or Draw*, *Classic Concentration,* and *Mastermind.*

Tuesday, August 29

1:45 p.m.

7800 Beverly Blvd. (CBS studios). My husband and I are

directed to a room with plastic chairs and snack machines. I ask others if they are waiting for *Win, Lose or Draw.* "I watch shows I think I can be on," one young woman tells me. Phyllis, who is from Scottsdale, AZ, was on *Name That Tune* in 1977 and won $2,000.

2:15 p.m.

The 25 (10 males, 15 females) of us with appointments are summoned to follow Tim Heritage, the show's assistant contestant coordinator, who says people watch game shows because they "have nothing better to do." Tim says someone like Phyllis can appear on this show, but *Wheel of Fortune* is much stricter about repeat contestants. We ride an elevator up to the testing room and take our seats. "ENERGY, GUESSING, DRAWING" reads a sign in the testing room. The contestant coordinator gives us some drawing hints (symbols for "in" and "out"; an ear symbol to indicate "sounds like") and guessing hints, using the phrase "Put your money where your mouth is." He then calls groups of three names from the sheet we have signed.

"I watched the show for the first time when I was sick," says one young woman in her brief introduction. "We play the game at training seminars, using the name of finishes, products, and competitors' names as phrases," says a furniture salesman. "I have a friend cover up the title on the screen so I can play along," says another young woman. Most are young Californians. The first person to go to the drawing board in my group of three draws an arm, prompting us to guess—energetically, of course—"Neil Armstrong," but the right answer is "Louis Armstrong." My own phrase, "back seat driver," prompts an analytical approach. I break the phrase apart and draw a person with an arrow at his back and another person sitting on a chair. As I start to draw a steering wheel, my minute has run out. I should have drawn a car, a driver, and a stick figure in the back seat. I look back at my effort before the coordinator flips to a clean sheet and see an ungodly mess. "Now comes the hard part," says the coordinator. From 25 hopefuls, he chooses a black woman (who had earlier been on *Love Connection*), a white woman, and two white males. By fall of 1990, *Win, Lose or Draw* is off the air.

3:15 p.m.

As we descend to the waiting room, the 3:30 p.m. tryout group is already gathering. As my husband and I pass a booth, we see that audience tickets for *Wheel of Fortune* are available for the next taping. We're among the first people to line up.

4:40 p.m.

The studio warmup begins. "Our contestants play off the energy of the audience," says announcer Charlie O'Donnell. "You are important." Three shows have been taped today, making a total of 53 in the past ten days. The show about to take place will air October 25, he tells us. All of a sudden, there is Vanna White, coming out to meet us. She introduces us to the contestants.

4:53 p.m.

Taping starts. Round 1, with the phrase "Dr. Seuss," ends in five minutes, after which taping stops and a curtain is pulled across the game board. The time to reset the board takes about as long as a commercial will take when viewers see the show, so that one day's show takes about 30 minutes, barring mishaps.

5 p.m.

Assistants uncover the reset game board, stage right, in view of the contestants, who stand above the wheel, center stage. Charlie O'Donnell, unseen by cameras, sits stage left. With her back to us stands the crew woman who tends the used letter board (an aid to contestants so they don't waste a turn). About 20 staff and crew hold up signs, work the cameras, and perform other jobs. Round 2, "Watergate tapes," takes 5 minutes. Round 3, "Killing me with kindness," takes 4 minutes. Round 4, "Hit the sack," which one contestant solves incorrectly as "Hit the ball," takes 3 minutes. Round 4, "County fair," takes 2 minutes. The bonus round, "Eskimo pie," takes 1 minute.

5:28 p.m.

While the winning contestant and Vanna White change outfits, Charlie O'Donnell asks the audience members to come on stage and tell a joke. I volunteer and ask, "How many psychiatrists does it take to change a lightbulb? One, but the lightbulb has to really want to change." O'Donnell gives me a "cheap *Wheel of Fortune* hat." Most of the other joke tellers are kids. There is no change of audience between this and the next taping.

5:46 p.m.

New contestants, two young men, come out to meet the audience.

5:50 p.m.

Taping of the second show begins. The champion wins a car.

6:26 p.m.

The taping ends.

6:30 p.m.

We are out of the studio and on our way to dinner.

<u>Wednesday, August 30</u>

We take the day off and visit Universal Studios.

<u>Thursday, August 31</u>

1:15 p.m.

5757 Wilshire Blvd., suite 206. For *Classic Concentration*, I fill out an application form in a nearly empty room with the words "Mark Goodson" painted in black boldly on a yellow wall. A young employee with a clipboard asks another person filling out an application some questions, which I realize have nothing to do with *Concentration*. "Where do people leave their umbrellas?" he says. The applicant has become one of the 100 people who form the percentages for responses that *Family Feud* contestants try to match.

1:30 p.m.

Assistant Bev Morrison takes me into the tryout room and snaps a Polaroid for my file. Contestant coordinator Jerry Modine explains to the 25 or so hopefuls that we need to take a test because "*Concentration* requires some degree of skill, unlike, say, *Card Sharks*." Expecting and fearing a memory test, I am surprised that we will take instead a rebus test. Modine explains a few rebus symbols, such as "2+2=4," which stands for "some" ("sum"), and a picture of an awl, which stands for "all."

1:45-1:55 p.m.

We must write the solutions for 20 partly uncovered rebus puzzles, such as would be visible part way through a real *Concentration* match with about half the squares' clues uncovered. Passing score is 8.

2 p.m.

I talk to a college student who has dropped out "temporarily" and looking for work and adventures. The sheets are quickly graded, eliminating all but eight of us. Four of those who made the cut introduce themselves briefly and play a mock game. "Keep talking as you're deciding what squares to match," advises Modine. "And you might mention the prizes so as to keep the prize division happy."

2:20 p.m.

I participate in mock game #2, along with two people on callbacks whom the producers wanted to see again. In my introduction, I tell Modine that I am writing a book on game shows. But I make the terrible blunder of not knowing what the symbol "take" means (if you match that word, you can take your opponent's prize). "I can tell that you watch the show every day," says Modine. I see my chance for stardom evaporate. (As it turned out, about two weeks later, I did get my acceptance letter.)

2:40 p.m.

After the mock game, Modine explains that we may get a letter putting us in the "go" file. If we get a phone call, we must clear three days on our schedules, since we can be on as many as five shows. California residents get one week's notice; out-of-state residents get one month's notice—"but don't cancel your cruise. We'll understand if you really can't come." If you're out of state and coming to LA, you should call even if we haven't called you. Seven women and seven men are called up for the six shows done on each taping day (Wednesday, Thursday, and Friday of every other week; *Family Feud* tapes Thursday, Friday, and Saturday on alternate weeks). The rules for this and all game shows are listed in the show's "bible," a legacy of the scandal era. For example, what does one do when a contestant says, "I want 22—no, 5—no, 7." The "bible" makes for a "structured, not loose, show," Modine says.

3 p.m.

We leave the building.

4 p.m.

3330 Cahuenga Blvd. W., Suite 306. I arrive at MAC III Productions, a subsidiary of a Scottish company, to find 13 men and two other women lined up in the hall. Associate producer Charlie Rader soon ushers us into the firm's offices. The Lifetime cable channel will give out about $500 a day in prize money, with a grand prize in Week 13 of $25,000. The show, although based on the British program of the same name, will not use teams as the original does. "How many of you have taken the *Jeopardy* test?" he asks. Four people raise their hands. Later someone tells me that this *Mastermind* test is much harder. Although the show also requires specialized knowledge, Rader explains that the screening starts with a general-knowledge test that has been given to 300 people.

4:30 p.m.

In eight minutes, we must answer 30 questions, including:

1) Who composed the *Clock* symphony?
2) Who created the cartoon *Peanuts*?
3) What structure uses girders?
4) What does ZIP mean?
5) Who established the idea that planets revolve around the sun?
6) Who invented the geodesic dome?
7) Who teamed with Betty Comden?
8) What is the name of the medical symbol with a snake?
9) What detective was in *The Pink Panther*?
10) What has been the motto of the United States since 1956?

1 1) What profession uses the term "clerestory"?
1 2) In what ballet by Khachaturian is the "Sabre Dance"?
1 3) Who used the slogan H20 Au in l964?

While a "highly sophisticated system" (an assistant with a pencil) grades our tests, we go over the answers. (The answers to those above are: 1) Haydn; 2) Charles Schultz; 3) bridges; 4) Zone Improvement Plan; 5) Copernicus; 6) Buckminster Fuller; 7) Adolph Green; 8) caduceus; 9) Inspector Cloiseau; 1 0) "In God We Trust"; 11) architecture; 12) *Gayne Suite*; and 13) Goldwater.) Only three people are asked to stay, me not among them.

5 p.m.

While leaving the building, I talk to a schoolteacher who had won $26,000 in prizes on *Classic Concentration*. After getting her letter of acceptance but not a phone call, she kept calling and writing. Her persistence paid off.

Midnight

We take the red-eye special back to Columbus, Ohio.

B. REMOTELY CONTROLLABLE: AN MTV EXPERIENCE

Interview by Andrew Russ
for Games in the Global Village

Meet Gary Sisto. He's a graduate of American University in Washington, D.C., who majored in philosophy and enjoys playing the guitar. Sisto appeared on Music TV's *Remote Control* show December 23, 1987. He now works for a management consulting firm, but he still enjoys talking about his experience.

So why did he do it? "I had never really had a spot on TV, and I wanted to see what the whole experience would be like and maybe win some prizes. It was an ego thing," Sisto said. "[I could] get away from school for a couple days.... It was a blast."

He didn't go to the show; it came to him. Sisto was a resident advisor for 48 male freshman dormitory residents when MTV announced they were coming to campus in early November 1987 to audition potential contestants for a new game show.

"I recruited about four of them to try and get on the show, and they had a tryout in the student center, and they all went up and flopped and at the same time I was like 'Well, it would be great to be on TV' and they were looking for kind of like, you know, wild people, and at this time I had the long hair and used to wear this, like, rock and roll clothes and all that...So I tried out," Sisto said, recalling his decision to journey into television land.

The 100 or more hopefuls assembled in the room of the A.U. student center. They were given a short test of trivia and then each person got up and said something about themselves in 20 seconds.

"I told them my name and where I was from, and I did it really silly—very strict." Sisto stressed the last word with a funny voice, sort of a New Jersey redneck accent. "I knew I had to be silly; one guy pulled his pants down...but he didn't make it."

They picked 30 people for the next round, a simulation of the show before an audience at a local tavern. Sisto described those two minutes on stage: "They see how you react and how you play along. There was this pretty good-looking girl who became my partner for the thing, and we got a point, and we got up and hugged one another, you know, just kidding around, and all the people watching. It was a big goof."

The MTV people took Polaroid shots of all the second-round aspirants, and after a 20-minute break they announced the seven finalists.

About two weeks later, the MTV people called Sisto and set a date for recording. On December 6, the day before the taping, Sisto and two friends drove up to New York and stayed "in Spanish Harlem with somebody I never met before."

Sisto and his friends got up early, met two more friends who came up separately, and walked around the city before going to the studio at 11 a.m. "It was right in Manhattan; it was right by

Broadway," Sisto said. He signed in and "they said 'you really don't have to come back until 12:30,' so we went down the street and had some drinks."

Sisto's friends went to the audience area in the studio. But "they sent me to this one room upstairs, it was like an administrative area. ...[They] shoot seven shows, and they don't tell you which show you're going to be on until ten minutes before it goes on." There were 24 people there, including three alternates in case there was a no-show. While they are filming one show, "they're trying to figure out which combinations they're going to put on next."

Sisto's show was at the end of the session, so he spent most of the time waiting. "I had no idea what to expect on this show; never saw it. And we were just playing Monopoly up there and charades, and we weren't allowed to leave the studio, so we just hung out and bullshitted with these people from all over the East Coast."

He described the other contestants. "Most of them had a different attitude—they were all pretty excited. It was such a treat to be on TV. And they wanted prizes. A lot of them were like the kind of people who wanted the spotlight; they would do anything to get the spotlight; they would kill their friend to get the spotlight. I thought a lot of them were obnoxious. I didn't like most of them; there were maybe five I thought were cool people."

Then the next set of contestants would be announced. "It was like 'Oh yeah, you're on the show, and you go on in 10 minutes,' and it's like 'holy shit.'

"And you see [the contestants] come back like an hour later and they have a prize or whatever, and they weren't allowed to say anything about what it's like," Sisto said. Sisto waited nearly seven hours in that room.

"Then they said my name, and I was relieved that I didn't have to go back without being on the show. There was like three other people that knew they weren't going to be on, and they were all bummed. One guy came all the way down from Maine or someplace."

So Sisto went on the show. "I was a little nervous when I got out there; it was all professional with the lights and the camera men and the audience and all my friends were cheering, but once the cameras went on and the MC came out it was like 'Aw, this is cool,' and I had a good time."

The show works like this: the three players sit in recliners in the MC's basement and answer questions about TV trivia.

"You're holding this fake remote control in one hand, and you're pointing it at this large TV and changing the channel. You have to say which one you want, and in the other hand you got your buzzer. And it's a little uncomfortable at first," Sisto remarked.

The different channels are the different categories of questions. If you have the remote control, you get to choose the category. The question is then read, and the first person to press his buzzer gets to answer. If he is correct, he gets some points and control of the remote.

Some of the channels are joke channels; when you pick one, say the shopping network, you lose some points and have to watch a silly short sketch.

"And sometimes you get a snack break, and food falls on your head," Sisto recalled; "that's how I won. You have the remote control at that time; they had three refrigerators, and you had to pick which refrigerator the CDs were in."

Sisto won a collection of ten CDs, but still hasn't acquired a CD player. He warns prospective game show contestants that "not all prizes are user-friendly."

"The prizes weren't that great," Sisto commented.

The other contestants got more questions correct. "I'm trying to be honest here. I was in the middle and there were two girls. One was this really ditzy blonde, and they were both—I mean I'm not chauvinist or anything—but they were both stupid. But they knew TV. They just grew up watching every fucking show. But they didn't know any hard questions; they knew the obvious ones like 'Name all the Partridge Family.' Now I don't know all that and I don't care to."

So after the first 20 minutes, Sisto was losing. "I was winning for awhile, and I just kept goofing off."

Since he was losing, Sisto was the first to be taken off the show. "Your chair ejects through the wall, and these guys in ape suits hit you on the head.

"Actually, I got taken off the show first, but I won more prizes than the other two contestants on my episode."

He didn't get out of the studio until after 8:30, and his two friends drove him back to D.C. that night.

The show was broadcast on December 23, when most students were home for break. "It was a great night—half the people who saw it didn't know I was on it." He became a minor celebrity on campus, and Sisto enjoyed the extra attention.

He even left a small legacy on the program-the word "strict." As he puts it, "It was New Jersey slang, Monmouth County. There was a certain community of people who understood the whole thing—it's just a silly slang, and we got the MC kind of saying it. He really liked it. He said something to me, and I said, 'You know, Ken, you're really strict,' and he lost it. It's a really catchy word. In fact, the next show that was taped, which I saw when I was home, there was a question about something Jewish, and the guy answered the question, and the MC was like 'Yes, very strict rabbinical.' It was really funny."

Appendix 2

CHARACTERISTICS OF GAME SHOWS IN 50 COUNTRIES AUTUMN 1990*

*Schedule for a typical week reconstructed as far as possible, using various sources; year is noted if 1990 data not available. Does not include Armed Forces TV programs (e.g., in Korea) or satellite services whereby one country's games may be seen in numerous other countries (e.g., Germany's *Tutti Frutti* is seen across Europe and as far away as Israel).

Type:

IG = interactive game (home viewers can play along)
SF = spectator format (home viewers watch players perform)
KQ = knowledge quiz (quiz tests above-average intellects)
MX = mixed (game segments appear with variety acts, or IG and SF game types are mixed, or both)
UN = unclear (available data not sufficient to judge type)

Host: person who controls action, directs players.

M = male
F = female

Transfer: format has been formally licensed (T) or informally adapted (T?) from a game created in another country; if not identifiable as a transfer, format assumed to be original (O). (Home name) included if known. [Translation] included when meaning not obvious.

Note: most but not all transferred formats originated in the United States.

Title/ Type	Day(s)	Time/min.	Host	Transfer/ Original
I. NORTHERN EUROPE				
A. ENGLAND (London)/ITV				
Catchphrase/IG	Sat	6 pm/30	M	O
Blind Date/SF	Sat	6:30 pm/60	F	T
Keynotes/IG	M-F	9:25 am/30	M	T
Talkabout/IG	Tu-F	2:50 pm/25	M	O
Blockbusters/IG	Tu-F	5:10 pm/30	M	T
Strike It Lucky/IG	Tu	8:30 pm/30	M	T
Everybody's Equal/IG	Th	8:30 pm/30	M	O
The Family Fortunes/IG	F	7 pm/30	M	T
You Bet (Wetten Das)/SF	F	7:30 pm/30	?	T
$64,000 Question/KQ?	F	7 pm/30	M	T
What's My Line/IG	M-Th	2:50 pm/25	F	T
Concentration/IG	Sun	7:15 pm/30	M	T
Pyramid Game/IG	M-F	9:25 am/30	M	T
Tell the Truth/IG	M-Th	2:50 pm/25	M	T
Wheel of Fortune/IG	M-F	?	M	T
15 to 1/IG	M-F	4:30 pm/30	M	O
Whose Line Is It Anyway?/SF	Th	10:30 pm/30	M	O
/BBC				
Call My Bluff/IG?	F?	4 pm/30	M	O
Have I Got News for You?/IG	F?	10 pm/30	M	O
Every Second Counts/UN	Sat	7:45 pm/30	M	T
Trivial Pursuit/UN	Tu	8 pm/30	?	?

Title/ Type	Day(s)	Time/min.	Host	Transfer/ Original
Four Square/UN	M-Th	2:50 pm/25	?	O
The Generation Game/UN	F	9:05 pm/90	M	O
Blankety Blank (*Match Game*) / IG	?	?	M	T
B. IRELAND/ **RTE 1**				
Where in the World?/IG	Su	??30	F	O
C. SWEDEN/SVERIGES TV				
Vem Tar Vem (*Dating Game*)/SF	F	?/45 ?	F	T
/ **SCANSAT**				
Lychohjulet (*Wheel of Fortune*) /IG	2 days/week/30		M	T
D. NORWAY/SCANSAT				
Lykkeehjulet (*Wheel of Fortune*) /IG	2 days/week/30		M	T
E. DENMARK/SCANSAT CHANNEL 3				
Knald Eller Fald (*Dating Game*)/SF	?	?	?	T
/TV2				
Lykkehjulet (*Wheel of Fortune*) /IG	?	?	?	T
F. FINLAND/MTV OY				
Dating Game/SF	?	?	F	T
II. WESTERN EUROPE				
A. FRANCE/TF 1				
La Roue de la Fortune/IG (*Wheel of Fortune*)	M-Sat	7:25 pm/30	M	T
La Chance aux Chansons/IG	M-F	4:35 pm/30	?	O

Title/ Type	Day(s)	Time/min.	Host	Transfer/ Original
Une Famille en Or/IG (*Family Feud*)	M-F	6:30 pm/30	M	T
Le Juste Prix/IG (*Price Is Right*)	W&F	12:30 pm/30	?	T
Intervilles/SF	F	8:35 pm/60	?	O
Tournez Manege/SF (*Dating Game*)	M-Sun	noon/varies	F+F	T
Jeopardy!/IG	M-F	11:30 am/30	M	T
/A 2				
Les Maries de l'A2/SF (*Newlywed Game*)	M-F	12:25 pm/30	M	T
Des Chiffes et des Lettres/KQ	M-F	5:10 pm/30	M	O
Les Clés de Fort Boyard/MX	Sat	8:40 pm/60	M&F	O
/FR 3				
Questions Pour un Champion/IG	M-F	6:30 pm/30	?	O
B. <u>ITALY</u>/CANALE 5				
La Routa de la Fortuna/IG (*Wheel of Fortune*)	M-F	?/30	M	T
OK Il Prezzo e Giusto/IG (*Price Is Right*)	M-Sa	11:45 am/60	F	T
Doppio Slalom/IG [*Double Slalom*] (*Blockbusters*)	M-Sa	5:20 pm/30	M	T
Cari Genitori/IG [*Dear Parents*] (*Family Feud*)	M-Sat	1:30 pm/30	M	T
Gioco dei 9/IG [*The Game of 9*] (*Hollywood Squares*)	M-Sat	7 pm/45	M	T
Tra Mogli e Marito/SF [*Between Husband & Wife*] (*Newlywed Game*)	M-Sun	7:45 pm/45	M	T

Title/ Type	Day(s)	Time/min.	Host	Transfer/ Original
Il Gioco della *Coppie*/SF	M-Sat	2:45 pm/15	M	T
[*The Couples Game*] (*Dating Game*)				
Babilonia/UN	M-F	5:30 pm/30	?	T
(*Hitman*)				
/RETE A SATELLITE				
Il Tesoro del Sapere/UN	Su-Sa	3 pm/30	?	O
[*Treasure of Knowledge*]				
Colpo Grosso/SF	weekend	late/60	M	O
[*Big Bang*]				
C. SPAIN				
Colpo Grosso/SF		late/60	M	T
[*Big Bang*]				
/TVE				
El Precio Justo/ IG	M	9 pm/90	M	T
/TELE 5				
Su Media Naranja/SF	M-F	9:15 pm/45	M	T
(*Newlywed Game*)				
V.I.P/IG	M-F	7 pm/30	M	T
(*Hollywood Squares*)	Sun	10 pm/105	M	T
/A 3				
Los Segundos Cuentan/UN	M-F	2 pm/30	?	T
(*Every Second Counts*)				
La Ruleta de la Fortuna/IG	M-F	?/30	F	T
D. PORTUGAL/RTP 1				
O Preco Certo/IG	?	?	M	T
(*Price Is Right*)				
Palavra puxa Palavra/IG	?	?	M	T
[*Word for Word*] (*Password*)				

Title/ Type	Day(s)	Time/min.	Host	Transfer/ Original
Roda da Sorte/ IG	?	?	M	T
(*Wheel of Fortune*)				
E. LUXEMBOURG/RTL TOI				
Coup de des/ MX	M-F	7:30 pm/35	M	O
Atoukado/ IG	Sun	5:30/60	M+F	O
F. BELGIUM/RTBF i (Walloon)				
Marmots/ MX	M-F	6:40 pm/20	M	T
(*Child's Play*)				
Genies en Herbe/				
KQ	W	5:20 pm/35	M	T
[*Budding Geniuses*]				
/ BRT 1 (Flemish)				
IQ/KQ	Sun	10 pm/30	M	O
Schoolslag/ MX	Sun	? pm/40	M	O
(*Battle of the Schools*)				
Van Pool tot				
Evenaar/ IG	Sun	6:05 pm/55	M	O
(*Between Pole*				
and Equator)				
De Drie Wijzen/				
IG	Tu	8 pm/40	M	T?
[*The Three Wizards*] (*To Tell the Truth*)				
/ VTM				
Rad van Fortuin/				
IG	M-F	? pm/30 min	M	T
(*Wheel of*				
Fortune)	Different host from RTL 4 version.			
Cijfers &				
Letters/KQ	M-F	? pm/25	M	T
(*Number and Letters*)				
Wie ben ik?/ IG	W	? pm/30	F	O
Wies Andersen				
Show/ IG	F	? pm/50	M	O
Waagstuk/ IG	Sat&Sun	? pm/30	M	T
(*Jeopardy!*)				

Title/ Type	Day(s)	Time/min.	Host	Transfer/ Original
De Juiste Prijs/IG	Sat	? pm/?	M	T
/BRT 2				
Ingrid, Ingrid!/ IG	M	8 pm/35	F	O
/BRT 1				
G. GERMANY/DEUTSCHLAND 2 ZDF				
Die Bessere Hafte (*The Better Half*)/IG	Th	8 pm/60	M	T
Die Pyramid/IG				
celeb guest	Sat	7:30 pm/45	M	T
regular	Tu	3:15 pm/45	M	T
/DEUTSCHLAND 1 ARD				
Geld oder Liebe/UN (*Love or Money*)	Tu	?	M	O
Dingsda/MX (*Child's Play*)	Tu	8:15 pm/? Tu	M	T
M*AZ ab!*/IG	Tu	8:15 pm/45	?	O
/DEUTSCHLAND 3 (WEST 3)				
Psst!/MX (*I've Got a Secret*)	M	9 pm/30	?	T
/RTL +				
Scrabble/IG	Sun	1 pm/30	?	T
Tutti Frutti/SF (*Colpo Grosso*)	Sun	10:35 pm/60	M	T
Riskant!/IG (*Jeopardy!*)	M-F	11:30 am/30	?	T
Der Preis ist Heiss/IG (*Price Is Right*)	M-F	noon/30	M	T
/SAT 1				
Glucksrad/IG	M-F	7:05 pm/45	?	T

Title/ Type	Day(s)	Time/min.	Host	Transfer/ Original
/ ZDF				
Wetten Dass/SF (*I'll Bet*)	Sat	8:15 pm/?	M	O
/ ARD				
Herzblatt/SF [*Hearthrob*] (*Dating Game*)	?	?	M	T
Grips/IG (*Blockbusters*)	?	?	M	T
Sag die Wahrheit/IG (*To Tell the Truth*)	?	?	M	T
H. SWITZERLAND/DRS (German-Swiss)				
Traumpaar/MX (*Dream Couple*)	Mon	8 pm/60	M	O
I. NETHERLANDS/RTL 4 NETHERLAND 1				
Rad van Fortuin/IG (*Wheel of Fortune*)	M-Sat	7:50 pm/30	M	T
Prijzenslag/IG [*Price Battle*] (*The Price Is Right*)	M-F	6:55 pm/30	M	T
Wie ben ik?/IG [*What Am I?*]	Tu	?/35	F	O
Ron's Honeymoon Quiz/MX	Th	?/90	M	O
/ NCRV NETHERLAND 1				
De Puzzel Kampioen/IG (*The Puzzle Champion*)	Sat	9:40 pm/25	M	T
/ KRO NETHERLAND 1				
Boggle/IG	M	8:15 pm/30	M	T
/ AVRO NETHERLAND 1				
12 Provincien-Spel/MX (*Game of 12 Provinces*)	M	? pm/60	M	O
/ NETHERLAND 2				
Op Goed Geluk/IG (*Good Luck*)	F	8:25 pm/45	F	O

Title/ Type	Day(s)	Time/min.	Host	Transfer/ Original
/NETHERLAND 1 & BRT 1				
Tien voor Taal				
/IG	M & Th	8:25 pm/60	M	O
(Contest between Netherlands and Flanders)				
III. EASTERN EUROPE				
A. USSR (1992)				
What, Where, When?/KQ	?	?	M	O
Quick Wits Club/MX	?	?	M	O
Trivial Pursuit/UN	Sat	once/month	?	T?
Field of Miracles/IG	F	9:50 pm/?	M	T?
(*Wheel of Fortune*)				
B. CZECHOSLOVAKIA/CST, PROGRAM I				
Videostop/IG	Sun	? pm/60	M	O
C. POLAND				
Wielka Gra/KQ	Sat	? pm/60	F	O
(*The Big Game*)				
Wheel of Fortune/ IG (1992)	M-F?	?	M	T
D. YUGOSLAVIA (1991)				
ZAGREB				
Kriskoteka/IG	Th	9 pm/90	M	O
TV BEOGRAD				
Trik Show/UN	F	8 pm/60	M	O
IV. NEAR EAST/MIDDLE EAST				
A. GREECE/ANTENNE TV				
O Trochos tis Hychis/IG	M-F	?	M	T
(*Wheel of Fortune*)				
B. TURKEY				
Carkifelek/IG (1992)	M-F	8:10 pm/30	M	T
(*Wheel of Fortune*)				

Title/ Type	Day(s)	Time/min.	Host	Transfer/ Original
/TRT CH. 1				
Bir Kelime, Bir Islem/KQ	Sun	2:45 pm/25	M	T?
[*One Word, One Operation*] (*Chiffres et Lettres*)				
/TRT CH. 2				
Hangisi/IG	M	9:25 pm/15	F	T?
[*Which One?*] (*To Tell the Truth*)				
C. ISRAEL/EDUCATIONAL TV				
Pitzuchim/IG	Th	3:25 pm/30	M	T
(*Blockbusters*)				
/ISRAEL TV				
Olympida-Science Quiz/KQ	Sun & Th	5:30 pm/30	M	O
D. SAUDI ARABIA (1985-86)				
Information Bank/KQ	once/week?/60 min		M	O
E. DUBAI, UAE				
Three x Three Quiz/KQ	M-F	6:50 pm/40	?	O
Children's Quiz/KQ	Sat	6 pm/30	?	O

V. AFRICA (NORTH AND SUB-SAHARAN)

Title/ Type	Day(s)	Time/min.	Host	Transfer/ Original
A. MOROCCO/RTM				
Yes/No/KQ	Th	?/15	M	O
B. TUNISIA/				
/CHANNEL 1 (1988)				
Jeux d'Afrique/KQ	Th	8:15 pm/40	F	O
C. EGYPT/CHANNEL 2				
Dowry ep Negoum /IG	M-Sun	? pm/45	M	O
[*The Stars Tournament*] (airs during month of Ramadan)				

Title/ Type	Day(s)	Time/min.	Host	Transfer/ Original
/ **CHANNEL 3**				
Numbers/IG	Th	? pm/45	F	O
(Educational children's show)				
D. KENYA/KENYA BROADCASTING CORP.				
Mix Them, Gather Them/KQ	1:45 pm Sun & 4:45 pm Th/30		M	O
(Educational children's show)				
Inter Primary School Quiz/KQ M	6 pm/30	M	O	
Sanaa ya Kiswahili/IG	Sun	3:40 pm/15	M	O
E. BOTSWANA/GBC				
Strike It Lucky/ IG	Sat	6 pm/30	M	T
F. SOUTH ARICA/TV 3 (for blacks)				
Ngogngibelo/MX [*On Saturday*] (Bilingual Zulu & Sotho)	Sat	7 pm/60	M+M	O
Pick a Box/UN	Th	7:15 pm/30	?	O
G. CAMEROUN (1991)				
Mister Word/KQ	Sun & Th	6 pm/30	F	O
Cherchez le Mot/ KQ	Sat & W	8 pm/30	F	O
H. GHANA (1991)				
Best Brain/KQ	F	8:30 pm/45	M	O
Kacici-Kacici/KQ (*In Hausa*)	W	4:30 pm/30	M	O
Name It/IG	?	?/30	M	O
I. IVORY COAST/RTI (1989)				
Les Genies en Herbe/ KQ [*Budding Geniuses*]	Sun	6:30 pm/30	M	T

Title/ Type	Day(s)	Time/min.	Host	Transfer/ Original
VI. SOUTH/SOUTHEAST ASIA				
A. INDIA/NEW DELHI				
What's the Good Word/IG	?	?	F	O
Alpha Plus/MX (Children's show)	Sun	10 am/22	M	O
Question Time/IG	Tu	10:20 pm/35	M	O
Mashour Mahal/IG	Sun	10 am/22	M	O
SAARC Quiz/KQ	?	?	?	O
B. MALAYSIA/TV 1 (RTM)				
More Jutaria/IG In Bahasa Malaysian.	Sun	8:25 pm/30	M	T
/TV 2 (RTM) Taped reruns of U.S. shows				
Give Us a Clue/SF	W	7:30 pm/30	M	T
Wheel of Fortune/IG	Th	7:30 pm/30	M	T
Win, Lose or Draw/IG	F	7:30 pm/30	?	T
$1 Million Chance of a Lifetime/ IG	Sat	7:30 pm/30	M	T
/TV 3				
Musik Musik 90/MX	Sun	6 pm/60	?	O
C. PHILIPPINES/IBC 13				
Uniwide Warehouse Club/SF	Sun	5 pm/60	M+M+F	O
/RPN 9				
Family Kuarta o Kahon/SF [*The Money or the Box*]	Sun	11:30 am/60	M	O
/ABS-CBN 2				
Sa Linggo na po Sila/MX [*They're on Sunday*]	Sun	noon/2 hrs	M+M+M	O
Eat Bulaga!/MX [*Lunchtime Surprise*]	M-Sat	noon/2 hrs	M+M+M	O

Title/ Type	Day(s)	Time/min.	Host	Transfer/ Original
D. THAILAND/CHANNEL 5				
Mar Tam Nad/IG [*Keep Your Appointment*]	M Tu W	9 pm/60	M+F	O
VII. EAST ASIA				
A. TAIWAN, REPUBLIC OF CHINA/TTV				
Chang Pan Tsuji/MX [*Unlucky Strike*]	M-F	6:30 pm/30	M+F	O
Wo Ai Hong Nyang/MX [*I Love the Matchmaker*]	Sat	5 pm/60	M+F	O
/ CTS				
Bai Tsan, Bai Seng/SF [*100 Battles, 100 Victories*] (Japan—*Takeshi's Castle*)	Sun	12:30 pm/90	M+M+F	T?
/ CTV				
Laiten/SF [*Sparks Fly*] (Japan—*Red Whale Tribe*)	Sun	12:30 pm/60	M+M+M	T?
B. PEOPLE'S REPUBLIC OF CHINA				
Tonight We Meet/ SF	F	10:19 pm/?	F	O
/ CCTV 1				
Tsong-i Ta Kuon /MX [*Entertainment Overview*]	Sat	? pm/60	M+F	O
/ CCTV 2				
Zhen Da Wen-i/MX [*Synthetic Entertainment*]	Sat	? pm/2.5 hrs	M+F	O
C. KOREA/KBS 2TV				
Family Quiz/MX	Tu	7:05 pm/55	?	O
100-year Quiz Show/IG	W	8 pm/50	?	O
Lucky Studio/SF	Sun	11:40 am/80	M+F	O

Title/ Type	Day(s)	Time/min.	Host	Transfer/ Original
/ MBC TV				
Let's Meet on Tuesday/IG	Tu	7:15 pm/50	?	O
Quiz of Love/SF	F	7:15 pm/45	?	O
Joyful Studio/SF	Sat	5:10 pm/50	M+F	O
Quiz Academy/KQ	Sun	5:10 pm/110	M+F	O
D. JAPAN (1992)				
TBS				
The Move/MX	M-F	7 pm/60	M+M	O
Shingo Yamashiro's Info Variety/IG	Sat	5 pm/30	M	O
Genius Quiz/KQ	Sat	5:30 pm/30	M+F	O
Quiz Derby/IG	Sat	7:30 pm/30	M	O
Discovering World's Mysteries/IG	Sat	9 pm/60	M+F	O
Sanma's Amateur Video Quiz/IG	Sun	7 pm/30	M	O
Look Out for Doubt/IG	Th	7 pm/60	M+M	O
Information Variety/IG	Th	9 pm/60	M	O
/ FUJI TV				
Takeshi & Itsumi's TV School/IG	Sat	7 pm/60	M+M	O
Tunnels Red Whale Tribe/SF	Sat	11 pm/30	M+M	O
Cult Quiz/IG	Sun	10 pm/30	M+F	O
Let's Go! the World/IG	Tu	9 pm/60	M+F	O
Young vs. Old Quiz/IG	Th	7 pm/60	M+F	O
Family Present Quiz/IG	F	9 pm/60	M+F	O
/ TV TOKYO				
Tamori's Music World/IG	Sat	10 pm/60	M	O

Title/ Type	Day(s)	Time/min.	Host	Transfer/ Original
World Gourmet Quiz/ IG	W	9 pm/60	M+F	O
TV Champion/ SF	Th	8 pm/60	M	O
Changing Locales Quiz/ IG	F	8 pm/60	M+F	O
/ ASAHI TV				
Attack 25/ IG	Sun	2:15/30	M	O
Kyosen's Useless English/ IG	Sun	7 pm/30	M	O
Hinto de Pinto/ IG	Sun	7:30 pm/30	M	O
Seeking Men's & Women's Hearts/ IG	Tu	7 pm/60	M+F	O
/ NHK				
Suzy Q Number Game/ IG	F	7:30 pm/30	M+F	O
That's Perfect/ KQ	Sun	7:30 pm/30	M	O
/ NIPPON TV				
Resemblance of Others/ IG	Sat	7:30 pm/60	M+F	O
Magical Brain Powers/ IG	Sat	8 pm/60	M+F	O
Teach Me! Galileo/ IG	Sun	7 pm/30	M+F	O
What's the Question?/ IG	Tu	7 pm/30	M+F	O
Interview Quiz/ IG	W	7 pm/30	M	O
World Professionals Quiz/ IG	W	8:30 pm/60	M	O
Trans-America Ultra Quiz/ MX	Th 4x/yr	8 pm/2 hrs	M	O

Title/ Type	Day(s)	Time/min.	Host	Transfer/ Original
VIII. PACIFIC				
A. AUSTRALIA/CHANNEL 7				
Family Feud/IG	M-F	5 pm/30	M	T
Celebrity Family Feud/IG	Sat	7:30 pm/30	M	T
Wheel of Fortune/IG	M-F	5:30 pm/30	M	T
Celebrity Wheel of Fortune/IG	Sat	8 pm/30	M	T
Now You See It/IG	M-F	4:30 pm/30	M	T
/ CHANNEL 9				
Sale of the Century/IG	M-F	7 pm/30	M	T
/ CHANNEL 10				
Double Dare/MX	M-F	4:30 pm/?	?	T
B. NEW ZEALAND/TV NZ				
Blind Date (*Dating Game*)/SF	?	?	?	T
IX. LATIN AMERICA				
A. BRAZIL (1992)/SBT				
Cocktail/SF (*Colpo Grosso*)	Tu	11 pm/60	M	T
Silvio Santos Show/MX	Sun	noon/10.5 hrs	M&M	O
/ GLOBO				
Domingao do Faustao/MX	Sun	3:35 pm/ 4.5 hrs.	M	O
Xuxa Show/MX (Children's show)	M-F	9:30 am/ 2.5 hrs.	F	O
Mallandro Show/MX (Children's show)	M-F	8:30 am/60	M	O
Roletrando Novelas/IG	M-F	6 pm/60	M	T

Title/ Type	Day(s)	Time/min.	Host	Transfer/ Original
/ **MANCHETE**				
Clube de Crianca/ MX (Children's Show)	M-F	4 pm/90	F	O
B. CHILE/CANAL 13				
Sabados Gigantes/ MX	Sat.	4 pm/4.5 hours	M	O
C. PERU/AMERICA TV, CHANNEL 4				
*Triki Trak/*MX	Sun	3 pm/5 hrs.	M+F	O
/ **PANAMERICANA TV, CHANNEL 5**				
*Alo, Gisela/*MX	M-F	noon/90	F	O
*Fantastico/*SF	M-Sat	8 pm/60	M+F	O
*Trampolina a la Fama/*SF	Sat	5 pm/3 hrs.	M	O
D. MEXICO/CH. 13				
*Familia Milionaria/*UN	Th	6 pm/60	M+F	O
/ **CH. 2**				
*En Familia/*MX (Children's show)	Sun	7 am/3.5 hrs.	M	O
X. NORTH AMERICA/CARIBBEAN				
A. JAMAICA/JBC				
*Schools Challenge Quiz/*KQ	M,Tu,Th	?/30	M	O
B. CANADA/TV 5				
*Des Chiffres et des Lettres/*KQ (Video from France)	M-F	6 pm/30	M	T
/ **CBFT**				
*Les Detecteurs de Mensonge/*IG	M-F	5 pm/30	M	O
/ **QUATRE SAISONS**				
Action-reaction/ UN	M-F	3 pm/30	?	O

Title/ Type	Day(s)	Time/min.	Host	Transfer/ Original
La Roue Chancuse /IG (*Wheel of Fortune*)	M-F	?	M	T
/25 MUCH MUSIC				
Test Pattern/MX	M-F	10:30/90	M	O
/TELEMETROPOLE				
Jeopardy!/IG	M-F	?/30	M	T

Note: most Canadians can get all U.S. network shows

C. UNITED STATES

Note: First airing of show is listed

Title/ Type	Day(s)	Time/min.	Host	Transfer/ Original
/ **ABC** (Ohio)				
Quiz Kids Challenge/KQ	M-F	10 am/30	M	O
Trump Card/IG	M-F	10:30 am/30	M	O
Love Connection/ SF	M-F	1:35 am/30	M	O
/ **CBS** (Ohio)				
Lottery Cash Explosion/UN	Sun	7:30 pm/30	M	O
Family Feud/IG	M-F	10 am/30	M	O
Wheel of Fortune/ IG (network version)	M-F	10:30 am/30	M	O
The Price Is Right/IG	M-F	11 am/60	M	O
Wheel of Fortune/ IG (syndicated version)	M-Sat	7 pm/30	M	O
Jeopardy!/IG	M-F	7:30 pm/30	M	O
/ **NBC** (Ohio)				
To Tell the Truth/IG	M-F	11 am/30	M	O
Challengers/IG	M-F	7 pm/30	M	O
Tic,Tac,Dough/IG	M-F	7:30 pm/30	M	O

Title/ Type	Day(s)	Time/min.	Host	Transfer/ Original
/ PBS				
Texaco Star Academic Championships/KQ	Sat	7:30 pm/30	M	O
Square 1 TV/IG	M-F	5:30 pm/30	M	O
/ USA CABLE (reruns)				
Name That Tune/IG	M-F	12:30 pm/30	M	O
Bumper Stumpers/ IG	M-F	1-1:30 pm/30	M	O
Hot Potato/IG	M-F	1:30 pm/30	?	O
Chain Reaction/IG	M-F	2 pm/30	?	O
Wipeout/IG	M-F	2:30 pm/30	?	O
Hollywood Squares/IG	M-F	3 pm/30	M	O
$25,000 Pyramid/ IG	M-F	3:30 pm/30	M	O
Press Your Luck/ IG	M-F	4 pm/30	?	O
High Rollers/IG	M-F	4:30 pm/30	M	O
/ NICKELODEON CABLE (Children)				
Think Fast/IG	Sat	11 am/30	M	O
Double Dare/MX	Sat	11:30/30	M	O
Make the Grade/IG	M-F	6:30 pm/30	M	O
/ OTHER CABLE				
Family Figures (BET)/IG	Sat	1 pm/30	M+M	O
Whose Line Is It Anyway? (HA!)/SF	Sat	10:30 pm/30	M	O
Clash (HA!)/UN	M-F	6:30 pm/30	?	O
Remote Control (MTV)/IG	M-F	noon/30	M	O
Turn It Up (MTV)/IG	M-F	midnite/30	?	O
Top Card (TNN)/ IG	M-F	12:30 pm/30	M	O

Title/ Type	Day(s)	Time/min.	Host	Transfer/ Original
Supermarket Sweep (Life)/MX	M-F	1 pm/30	M	O
Teen Win, Lose or Draw (Disney)/IG	M-F	4:30 pm/30	?	O

TNN = The Nashville Network
BET = Black Entertainment Television
Life = Lifetime Network

WORKS CITED

Adhoum, Mounir. Personal interview. Athens, OH, 1 Feb. 1991.

Altamirano, Juan Carlos. *Asi, Asi Se Mueve Don Francisco.* Santiago de Chile: VANSA, 1987.

Anderson, D.R., L.F. Alwith, E.P. Lorch, and S.R. Levin. "Watching Children Watch Television." *Attention and the Development of Cognitive Skills*. Eds. G. Hale and M. Lewis. New York: Plenum, 1979.

Andreae, Christopher. "It May Be Fun, But It's No Joke to Compile an Anthology of Humor." *Christian Science Monitor* 12 Apr. 1990: 14.

Ansah, Paul. "Mass Communication and Cultural Identity: Dilemmas and Prospects for Developing Nations." Paper presented to the 16th Conference, International Association for Mass Communication Research, Barcelona, 1988.

Artwick, Claudette. "Culture or Commerce: The European Community and 'Television without Frontiers.'" Paper presented to the Association for Education in Journalism and Mass Communication, annual convention, Minneapolis, 1990.

Austin, Bruce. "How Independent Affected People's Time TV Programs." *Journalism Quarterly* 60.1 (1983).

Bandura, Albert. *Social Foundations of Thought.* Englewood Cliffs, NJ: Prentice-Hall, 1986.

Bang, Jorgen, and Bo Fibiger. "The Television Screen as Medium for Education." Paper presented to the 17th Conference, International Association for Mass Communication Research, Bled, Yugoslavia, 1990.

Barnouw, Eric. *Tube of Plenty: The Evolution of American Television.* New York: Oxford UP, 1975.

Barnouw, Erik, and Catherine Kirkland. "Entertainment." *International Encyclopedia of Communications.* New York: Oxford UP, 1989.

Barwise, T.P., A.S.C. Ehrenberg, and G.J. Goodhardt. "Glued to the Box?: Patterns of TV Repeat-viewing." *Journal of Communication* 32.4 (1982): 22-29.

Beck, Kirsten. "American TV Loses Its Visa." *Channels* Dec. 1989.

Becker, Lee, and Pam Creedon. "Motivations for Watching Sports: Modeling and Spectating as Goals." Paper presented to the 17th conference, International Association for Mass Communication Research, Bled, Yugoslavia, 1990.

Belghith, Rached. Personal interview. Tunis, 21 June 1988.

Bell, Daniel. "Mediating Growth Tensions." *Society* 15 (Jan.-Feb. 1978): 34-38.

Beniger, James. "Who Are the Most Important Theorists of Communication?" *Communication Research* 17.5 (1990).

Berman, Ronald. *How Television Sees Its Audience.* Beverly Hills, CA: Sage, 1987.

Bernard, H. Russell. *Research Methods in Cultural Anthropology.* Newberry Park, CA: Sage, 1988.

Berry, Wendell. "Out of (Y)our Car, Off (Y)our Horse." *Atlantic Monthly* Feb 1991: 61-63.

Bishop, Robert L. *Qi Lai! Mobilizing One Billion Chinese: the Chinese Communication System.* Ames: Iowa State UP, 1989.

Bjork, Ulf Jonas. "Cultural Domination and Sovereignty: the Development of European TV Quotas, 1981-89." Paper presented to the Association for Education in Journalism and Mass Communication, Minneapolis, 1990.

Bloom, Allan. *The Closing of the American Mind.* New York: Simon and Schuster, 1987.

Boorstin, Daniel. "Americans Are 'Haunted by a Fear of Technology.'" *U.S. News and World Report* 17 Mar. 1980: 70.

Boulding, Kenneth. *The World as a Total System.* Beverly Hills, CA: Sage, 1985.

"Brazilian TV Host Out of Election." *Messenger* [Athens, OH] 10 Nov. 1989: 11.

Briggs, Asa. "Culture." *International Encyclopedia of Communication.* New York: Oxford UP, 1989.

Brookman, Faye. "U.S. Gameshows Fit Foreign Slots." *Variety* 18 Apr. 1990: 98.

Brown, Merrill. Personal interview. Chautauqua, NY, 10 July 1989.

Brown, William, and Arvind Singhal. "Ethical Dilemmas of Prosocial Television." *Communication Quarterly* 38.3 (1990): 268-80.

Browne, Donald. "Media Entertainment in the Western World." Eds. L. John Martin and Anju Grover Chaudhary. *Comparative Mass Media Systems.* New York: Longman, 1983: 187-208.

___. *Comparing Broadcast Systems: The Experiences of Six Industrialized Nations.* Ames: Iowa State UP, 1989.

Browne, Ray. "The Repressive Nature of TV Esthetics Criticism." *Journal of American Culture* 6.3 (1983): 117-22.

___. *Against Academia: The History of the Popular Culture Association/American Culture Association and Popular Culture Movement, 1967-1988.* Bowling Green, OH: Bowling Green State University Popular Press, 1989.

Browne, Ray, and Marshall Fishwick, eds. *Icons of Popular Culture.* Bowling Green, OH: Bowling Green State University Popular Press, 1972.

___. *The Popular Culture Explosion.* Bowling Green, OH: Bowling Green State University Popular Press, 1972.

Bryant, Jennings, and Dolf Zillman. "Using Television to Alleviate Boredom and Stress." *Journal of Broadasting* 28.1 (1984): 1-20.

Caillois, Roger. *Men, Play and Games.* Trans. by Meyer Barash. New York: Schocken Books, 1961.

Calvert, S., A.C. Huston, B.A. Watkins, and J.C. Wright. "The Effects of Selective Attention and Television Form on Children's Comprehension of Content." *Child Development* 53 (1981): 601-10.

Cambridge, Vibert. *Mass Media Entertainment and Human Resources Development: Radio Serials in Jamaica from 1962.* Unpublished Ph. D. dissertation. Ohio U, College of Communication, 1989.

Castellon-Aguayo, Lucia. Personal interview. Guaruja, Brazil, 19 Aug. 1992.

Castleman, Harry, and Walter J. Podrazik. *Watching TV: Four Decades of American Television.* New York: McGraw-Hill, 1982.

Cerf, Christopher. Speech. Chautauqua Institution, 11 July 1989.

Clark, Jennifer. "Italy: Europe's Exporter to the U.S." *Variety* 27 Jan. 1992: 40, 42.

Condry, John. *The Psychology of Television.* Hillsdale, NJ: Lawrence Erlbaum, 1989.

Cooper-Chen, Anne. "'Jumping into the Tube': The Content and Appeal of Television Game Shows." Paper presented to the International Communication Association annual convention, New Orleans, 1988.

___. "A Week of World News: TV Gatekeeping in Japan, the United States, Jamaica, Sri Lanka and Columbia." *Keio Communication Review* 14 (1992): 69-84.

___. "Pacific Play: Television Game Shows in Japan and the United States." *Chubu University International Relations Journal* 10 (1993): 143-56.

Coopman, Jeremy. "United Kingdom: Oh, Wow! Deja vu—the '60s Are Back." *Variety* 27 Jan. 1992: 37-38.

Cousins, Norman. "Art in the Age of a Great World Audience." *Christian Science Monitor* 17 Oct. 1989: 18.

Creedon, Pamela, ed. *Women, Media and Sport.* Newbury Park, CA: Sage, 1993.

Dassin, Joan. "The Brazilian Press and the Politics of *Abertura.*" *Journal of Interamerican Studies and World Affairs* 26.3 (1984): 385-414.

DeLong, Thomas. *Quiz Craze: America's Infatuation with Game Shows.* Westport, CT: Greenwood, 1991.

Dewey, John. *Experience and Nature.* New York: Dover, 1958.

Duncan, Amy. "Meet Brazil's Queen of Kid TV." *Christian Science Monitor* 22 Jan. 1991: 14.

Duncan, Margaret, and Barry Brummet. "Types and Sources of Spectating Pleasure in Televised Sports." *Sociology of Sport Journal* 6.3 (1989): 195-211.

Dupagne, Michel. "A Comparison of Televised International and Foreign News According to the Political Prominence of Four Western Countries." Paper presented to the Association for Education in Journalism and Mass Communication, Boston, 1991.

Edelstein, Alex. *Comparative Communication Research.* Beverly Hills, CA: Sage, 1982.

___. "Comparative Research." Presentation to Association for Education in Journalism and Mass Communication, Minneapolis, 1990.

Eiss, Harry. *Dictionary of Language Games, Puzzles and Amusements.* Westport, CT: Greenwood, 1986.

Ellis, Michael. *Why People Play.* Englewood Cliffs, NJ: Prentice-Hall, 1973.

Ellul, Jacques. *The Formation of Modern Culture.* New York: Knopf, 1986.

Fabe, Maxene. *TV Game Shows.* New York: Doubleday, 1979.

Fermaglich, Mollie. "Confessions of a TV Game Show Contestant." *Glamour* Aug. 1980: 72-78.

Ferry, Jeffrey. "Eyes on the Prize." *TWA Ambassador* June 1988: 26, 28.

Feuer, Jack. "The Meter Runs for Hispanic TV." *Channels Field Guide* 1990: 83.

Fiance, Beth. Personal communication to author, 1988.

Fischer, Hans-Dietrich, and Stephan Melnik. *Entertainment: A Cross-cultural Examination.* New York: Hastings House, 1979.

Fiske, John. *Television Culture.* New York: Methuen, 1987.

___. "Women and Quiz Shows: Consumerism, Patriarchy and Resisting Pleasures." *Television and Women's Culture.* Ed. Mary Ellen Brown. Newbury Park, CA: Sage, 1990: 134-43.

Fiske, John, and John Hartley. *Reading Television.* London: Methuen, 1978.

Flinn, John. "Beating Them at Their Own Game." *Channels* Dec. 1989: 74-75.

Fox, Richard W., and T. Jackson Lears. *The Culture of Consumption.* New York: Pantheon, 1983.

Freud, Sigmund. "Formulations Regarding the Two Principles in Mental Functioning." *Collected Papers* Vol. IV. New York: Basic Books, 1959.

Frye, Northrup. *Anatomy of Criticism.* Princeton, NJ: Princeton UP, 1957.

Fuller, Chris. "The Netherlands: Dutch Pack Their Schedules and Look for More." *Variety* 27 Jan. 1992: 38.

"Game's Over for Arrested 'Password' Player." *Messenger* [Athens, OH] 15 Jan. 1988: 1.

Garnham, Nicholas. "Raymond Williams, 1921-1988: A Cultural Analyst, a Distinctive Tradition." *Journal of Communication* 38.4 (1988): 123-31.

Geertz, Clifford. *The Interpretation of Cultures.* New York: Basic Books, 1973.

Gerard, Jeremy. Speech. Chautauqua Institution, 12 July 1989.

Gergen, David. Speech. Chautauqua Institution, 13 July 1989.

Germani, Clara. "Do You Get What You See?" *Christian Science Monitor* 16 July 1992: 13.

Giamatti, A. Bartlett. *Take Time for Paradise: Americans and Their Games.* New York: Summit Books, 1989.

Glick, Ira, and Sidney Levy. *Living with Television.* Chicago: Aldine, 1962.

Goodson, Mark. "Quiz Shows." *International Encyclopedia of Communications.* Ed Erik Barnouw. New York: Oxford UP, 1989.

Goonaskera, Anura. "Toward the Development of Mass Media for the Third World." *The Third Channel* 1.2 (1985): 230-41.

Graham, Jefferson. "Game Shows Win Heart of Heartland." *USA Today* 5 July 1985: 7-8.

___. *Come On Down!!!* New York: Abbeville, 1988.

Granville, Kari. "Nickelodeon Flexing Muscles." *Los Angeles Times* 28 Aug. 1989: 1, 8 VI.

Guttmann, Allen. *The Nature of Modern Sports.* New York: Columbia UP, 1978.

___. *Sports Spectators.* New York: Columbia UP, 1986.

___. *A Whole New Ball Game: An Interpretation of American Sports.* Chapel Hill: U of North Carolina P, 1988.

Hachten, William. *The World News Prism.* Ames: Iowa State UP, 1987.

Hardy, Phil. "They're Hot and Priced Right." *Variety* 27 Jan. 1992: 37.

Harris, Mike. "Australia: Still Crazy for 'em after All These Years." *Variety* 27 Jan. 1992: 42.

Head, Sydney. *World Broadcasting Systems.* Belmont, CA: Wadsworth, 1985.

Herold, Cacilda. "The 'Brazilianization' of Brazilian Television: A Critical Review." *Studies in Latin American Popular Culture* 7 (1988): 41-58.

Herzog, Herta. "What Do We Really Know about Daytime Serial Listeners?" *Radio Research, 1942-1943.* Eds. P. Lazarsfeld and F.N. Stanton. New York: Sloan and Pearce, 1944.

Hift, Fred. "What Do Europeans Want?" *Christian Science Monitor* 17 Jan. 1991: 14.

Himmelstein, Hal. *Television Myth and the American Mind.* New York: Praeger, 1984.

Hinds, Lynn. "Using Entertainment Television to Educate: A Case Study." *Journal of Popular Culture* 25.2 (1991): 117-26.

Hoggart, Simon. "A Nation's Culture is Always More Interesting than Its Politics." *Messenger* [Athens, OH] 22 Apr. 1990: A-10.

Holbrook, Morris. *Daytime Television Game Shows and the Celebration of Merchandise: The Price Is Right.* Bowling Green, OH: Bowling Green State University Popular Press, 1993.

Huizinga, Johan. *Homo Ludens.* 1938. New York: Roy, 1950.

Iwao, Sumiko; Ithiel Pool; and Shigeru Hagiwara. "Japanese and US Media: Some Insights into Violence." *Journal of Communication* 31 (1981): 28-36.

Iyer, Pico. *Video Night in Kathmandu.* New York: Vintage (Random House), 1989.

Jarvis, Jeff. "The Couch Critic; Family Feud." *TV Guide* 5 Sept. 1992: 5.

Johnson, Nicholas. Lecture at Cornell University Law School, 1978.

Johnson, Randal. "Popular Culture and the Political Transition in Brazil." *Studies in Latin American Popular Culture* 7 (1988): 1-16.

Kaminsky, Stuart, and Jeffrey Mahan. *American Television Genres.* Chicago: Nelson-Hall, 1985.

Kato, Hidetoshi. "Essays in Comparative Popular Culture." *Papers of the East-West Communication Institute* 13 (1975).

___."Japanese Popular Culture Reconsidered." *Handbook of Japanese Popular Culture.* Eds. R.G. Powers and H. Kato. New York: Greenwood, 1988: 301-18.

Katz, Elihu. "Can Authentic Culture Survive the Media?" *Journal of Communication* 27 (1977): 113-21.

Katz, Elihu, Michael Gurevitch, and Hadasah Haas. "On the Use of Mass Media for Important Things." *American Sociological Review* 38 (1973): 164-81.

Kitahara, Michio. "Popular Culture in Japan: A Psychoanalytic Interpretation." *Journal of Popular Culture* 17.1 (1983): 103-10.

Kottak, Conrad. *Prime Time Society: Anthropological Analysis of Television and Culture.* Belmont, CA: Wadsworth, 1989.

Kubey, Robert, and Mihaly Csikszentmihalyi. *Television and the Quality of Life.* Hillsdale, NJ: Erlbaum, 1990.

Land, Mitchell. "The Challenge of First World Industrialized Culture to Third World Cultures: Focus on Television in the Cote d'Ivoire." Paper presented to the 16th conference, International Association for Mass Communication Research, Barcelona, 1988.

Lang, Kurt. "Mass Appeal and Minority Tastes." *Mass Culture.* Eds. B. Rosenberg and D.M. White. Glencoe, NY: Free, 1957: 379-86.

Larson, James. *Television's Window on the World: International Coverage on the U.S. Networks.* Norwood, NJ: Ablex, 1984.

Lau, T.Y. "Audience Preference of Chinese Television: A Content Analysis of Letters to the Editor in the *Chinese Television Broadcasting Magazine,* 1983-1986." *Journal of Popular Culture* 24.4 (1991): 161-76.

Lewyn, Mark. "Is PBS Really Worth It?" *Newsweek* 24 Dec. 1990: 10.

Lieb, Rebecca. "Germany: Games' Gains Outrunning the Rest of the Pack." *Variety* 27 Jan. 1992: 38.

Liebes, Tamar, and Elihu Katz. *The Export of Meaning: Cross-cultural Readings of "Dallas."* New York: Oxford UP, 1990.

Linstrom, Barbara. "How is Former Athenian Doing on *Jeopardy*? Tune in Tonight." *Messenger* [Athens, OH] 12 Sep. 1990: 1.

Lippman, John. "Tuning in the Global Village." World Report Special Ed. *Los Angeles Times* 24 Oct. 1992.

Lull, James. "Constructing Rituals of Extension through Family Television Viewing." *World Families Watch Television.* Ed. James Lull. Beverly Hills, CA: Sage, 1988: 237-60.

___. "The Family and Television in World Cultures." *World Families Watch Television.* Ed. James Lull. Beverly Hills, CA: Sage, 1988: 9-21.

___. "Freedom, Democracy and Television in the People's Republic of China." Paper presented to the 17th Conference, International Association for Mass Communication Research, Bled, Yugoslavia, 1990.

___. *Inside Family Viewing.* New York: Routledge, 1990.

Lyons, Jeffrey. "TV *Can* be Good for Kids." *USA Weekend* 14-16 July 1989: 14.

Mahan, Elizabeth. "Popular Culture in the Production of Cultural Identity." *Studies in Latin American Popular Culture* 10 (1991): 1-8.

Makedon, Alexander. "Playful Gaming." *Simulation and Games* 15 (1984): 25-64.

Malley, Richard. "Changing Channels." *Omni* June 1990: 56-58+, 96.

Mandraud, Isabelle, and Phillippe Martinat. "Jeux Televises: Portrait de Famille." *Mediaspouvoirs* 19 (July-Sept. 1990): 13-19.

Martin, L. John. "The Contradiction of Cross-cultural Communication." *International and Intercultural Communi-*

cation. Eds. Heinz-Dietrich Fischer and John Merrill. New York: Hastings House, 1976: 424-34.

Martin, L. John, and Ray Hiebert. *Current Issues in International Communication.* New York: Longman, 1990.

May, William. "Seishin: Japanese Sports Newspapers and the Japanese Spirit during the 1988 Calgary Winter Olympic Games." Paper presented at the 17th conference, International Association for Mass Communication Research, Barcelona, 1988.

McAnany, Emile. "Television and Cultural Discourses: Latin American and United States Comparisons." *Studies in Latin American Popular Culture* 6 (1987): 1-21.

___."Wilbur Schramm, 1907-1987: Roots of the Past, Seeds of the Present." *Journal of Communication* 38.4: (1990): 109-17.

McLuhan, Marshall. *Understanding Media.* New York: Signet, 1964.

McPhail, Dennis. *Electronic Colonialism.* Beverly Hills, CA: Sage, 1981.

McWilliams, Alvi. *The Use of Entertainment for Social Change: A Literature Review.* Unpublished manuscript, Ohio University, College of Communication, 1989.

Meadowcroft, Jeanne, and Byron Reeves. "Influence of Story Schema Development on Children's Attention to Television." *Communication Research* 16.3 (1989): 352-74.

Meisler, Andy. "The Best Game Shows—and the Worst." *TV Guide* 13 Dec. 1986: 6-12.

___."A. Amazing, Brilliant, a Breed Apart. Q. What are *Jeopardy!* Champs?" *TV Guide* 7 Nov. 1987: 20-23.

Mendelssohn, Harold. *Mass Entertainment.* New Haven, CT: College and UP, 1966.

Merrill, Don. "Review: The New Newlywed Game." *TV Guide* 28 Feb. 1987: 40.

Merritt, Robert. "Experiment in Popular Culture Raises Questions." *Richmond Times-Dispatch* 10 Apr. 1978: A-6.

Meyer, Karl. "The Gaming of America." *Saturday Review* 28 Oct. 1978: 37.

Mondol, Harold. "The Emerging Role of TV in Asia." Paper presented to the 16th Conference, International Association for Mass Communication Research, Barcelona, 1988.

More, Linda. "Spain: Big Bucks Rule in Iberia." *Variety* 27 Jan. 1992: 42.

Muramatsu, Yasuko. "TV Dramas and Women." *NHK Hoso Bunka Kenkyu* 1978: 59-109.

Myers, Linnet. "The *Wheel of Fortune* Takes a Serious Spin on Polish TV." Raleigh, NC, *News and Observer* 8 Dec. 1992: 7A.

"NBC's Olympics Rating Slips." *Messenger* [Athens, OH] 2 Aug. 1992: D-6.

Nam, Sunwoo. "Media Entertainment in the Third World." *Comparative Mass Media Systems.* New York: Longman, 1983: 209-27.

Newton, Barbara, and Elizabeth Buck. "Television as Significant Other: Its Relationship to Self-Descriptors in Five Countries." *Journal of Cross Cultural Psychology* 16.3 (1985): 289-312.

Nisbett, Richard E., and Timothy Wilson. "Telling More than We Can Know: Verbal Reports on Mental Processes." *Psychological Review* 84 (1977): 231-59.

Noelle-Neuman, Elizabeth, E.R. Kocher, and P. Elliott. "Professional Views of Journalists: A German-English Study." Paper presented to the International Association for Mass Communication Research, Caracas, Venezuela, 1980.

Oh, Tojun. Personal communication to author, Nov. 1992.

Palm, Robert. "Why Pat and Vanna Have a W_NN_R." *TV Guide* 7 Mar. 1987:34-38.

Peng, Bonnie. Personal interview. Tapei, Taiwan, 28 Dec. 1991.

Pfeffer, Wendy. "Intellectuals Are More Popular in France: The Case of French and American Game Shows." *The Americanization of the Global Village: Essays in Comparative Popular Culture.* Ed. Roger Rollin. Bowling Green, OH: Bowling Green State University Popular Press, 1989: 24-32.

Piaget, Jean. *Play, Dreams and Imitation in Childhood.* London: Heinemann, 1951.

Picard, Christopher. "Xenxational Xuxa." *Rio Life* 4.11 (1990): 1, 3.

Poltrack, David. "Rating Systems: Radio and Television." *International Encyclopedia of Communications*. New York: Oxford UP, 1989.

Postman, Neil. *Amusing Ourselves to Death.* New York: Viking, 1985.

Powers, Richard Gid, and Hidetoshi Kato, eds. *Handbook of Japanese Popular Culture.* Westport, CT: Greenwood, 1989.

Poynton, Beverly, and John Hartley. "Male-gazing: Australian Rules Football, Gender and Television." *Television and Women's Culture.* Ed. Mary Ellen Brown. Newbury Park, CA: Sage, 1990: 144-57.

Real, Michael. *Supermedia.* Newbury Park, CA: Sage, 1989.

Revzin, Phillip. "La Boob Tube: Europe Complains about U.S. Shows." *Wall Street Journal* 16 Oct. 1989: 1.

Reynolds, Paul. *A Primer in Theory Construction.* Indianapolis: Bobbs-Merrill, 1971.

Rips, M. "In France, Hunting for les Bons Mots." *Channels* Oct. 1986: 77.

Roberts, John, and Brian Sutton-Smith. "Child Training and Game Involvement." *Sport, Culture and Society*. Eds. John Loy and Gerald Kenyon. New York: Macmillan, 1969: 120-31.

Robinson, John. "Leisure." *International Encyclopedia of Communications.* New York: Oxford UP, 1989.

Rollin, Roger. "On Comparative Popular Culture, American Style." *The Americanization of the Global Village: Essays in Comparative Popular Culture.* Ed. Roger Rollin. Bowling Green, OH: Bowling Green State University Popular Press, 1989: 1-10.

Rota, Josep. Personal interview. Athens, OH, 5 Apr. 1991.

Rota, Josep, and Denise Tremel. "Television Use and Its Impact on National Identity among Children in Rural Yucatan." Paper presented at the Sixth Annual Intercultural and International Communication Conference, Miami, 1989.

Rowland, Willard, and Bruce Watkins, eds. *Interpreting Television: Current Research Perspectives.* Beverly Hills, CA: Sage, 1984.

Rubin, Alan. "Ritualized and Instrumental Television Viewing." *Journal of Communication* 34.3 (1984): 67-77.

Rubin, Alan, and Rebecca Rubin. "Television Use and Contextual Age." Paper presented at Ohio University College of Communication Research Day, 1987.

Salomon, Gavriel. "The Study of Television in a Cross-cultural Context." *Journal of Cross-Cultural Psychology* 16.3 (1985): 381-97.

Salomon, Gavriel, and Tamar Leigh. "Predispositions about Learning from Television." *Journal of Communication* 43.2 (1984): 119-35.

Sanders, Keith, and Gamaleldin Hagamed. "Developmental Play: A New Approach to the Role of Mass Media in Developing Countries." Paper presented to the Association for Education in Journalism and Mass Communication, annual convention, Portland, 1988.

Sarrett, Carla, and Paul Messaris. "On the Consequences of Television-related Parent-child Interaction." *Human Communication Research* Spring 1981: 226-44.

"Le savior par le jeu." *Tele 7 Jours Week-end* (Tunis) July 1990: 10.

Schiffres, Manuel. 1987. "How to Ride TV's Wheel of Fortune." *U.S. News and World Report* 2 Feb. 1987: 54-55.

Schiller, Herbert. *Mass Communication and American Empire.* Boston: Beacon P, 1971.

___. *Communication and Cultural Domination.* White Plains, NY: International Arts and Sciences P, 1976.

___. *Who Knows: Information in the Age of the Fortune 500.* Norwood, NJ: Ablex, 1981.

___. *Information and the Crisis Economy.* Norwood, NJ: Ablex, 1984.

___. *Culture, Inc.* New York: Oxford UP, 1989.

Schramm, Wilbur. *One Day in the World's Press.* Stanford, CA: Stanford UP, 1959.

Schramm, Wilbur, J. Lyle, and E.B. Parker. *Television in the Lives of Our Children.* Stanford, CA: Stanford UP, 1961.

Sepstrup, Preben. *The Transnationalization of Television in Western Europe.* London: John Libbey, 1990.

Servaes, Jan. "Cultural Identity in East and West." Paper presented to the 16th Conference, International Association for Mass Communication Research, Barcelona, 1988.

Shaper, Laurel. "TV Math, but Not by the Numbers." *Christian Science Monitor* 31 Jan. 1990: 12.

Silva, Samuel. "The Latin Superchannels." *World Press Review* Nov. 1991: 56.

Singhal, Arvind. *Entertainment-education Strategies for Development.* Unpublished Ph. D. dissertation, U of Southern California, 1990.

Singhal, Arvind, and Everett Rogers. "Educating through Television." *Populi* 16.2 (1989a): 39-46.

___. *India's Information Revolution.* Newbury Park, CA: Sage, 1989b.

Singer, Jerome. "The Power and Limitations of Television: A Cognitive-affective Analysis." *The Entertainment Functions of Television.* Ed. P. Tannenbaum. Hillsdale, NJ: Lawrence Erlbaum, 1980: 31-66.

Smith, Anthony. *The Geopolitics of Information.* New York: Oxford UP, 1980.

Smith, Sally Bedell. *In All His Glory: the Life of William Paley.* New York: Simon and Schuster, 1990.

Sreberny, Annabelle, et al. *The World of the News: the News of the World.* Leicester, England: U of Leicester, 1986.

Stephenson, William. *The Play Theory of Mass Communication.* Chicago: U of Chicago P, 1967.

Stevenson, Robert. *Communication, Development and the Third World: The Global Politics of Information.* White Plains, NY: Longman, 1988.

Stevenson, Robert, and Donald Shaw. *Foreign News and the New World Information Order.* Ames: Iowa State UP, 1984.

Straubhaar, Joseph. "Brazilian Television: the Decline of American Influence." *Communication Research* 11.2 (1984): 221-40.

Straubhaar, Joseph, et al. "What Makes News: An Eight-country Comparison of Western, Socialist and Third World Television Newscasts." Paper presented to the International Communication Association, Chicago, 1986.

Streeter, Thomas. "An Alternative Approach to Television Research: Developments in British Cultural Studies at Birmingham." *Interpreting Television: Current Research Perspectives.* Eds. W. Rowland and Bruce Watkins. Beverly Hills, CA: Sage, 1984: 74-97.

Sutton-Smith, Brian. Introduction. *The Play Theory of Mass Communication.* By William Stephenson. New Brunswick, NJ: Transaction Books, 1988.

Sutton-Smith, Brian, and John Roberts. "The Cross-Cultural and Psychological Study of Games." *IRSS* 6 (1971): 79-87.

Szalai, Alexander, ed. *The Use of Time.* The Hague: Mouton, 1972.

"TV's Love Connection Is a Shocking Fraud." *Globe* 20 July 1993: 91.

Talbot, Paul. Telephone interview. New York, 29 Oct. 1990.

Tan, Alexis, and Gerdean Tan. "Television Use and Mental Health." *Journalism Quarterly* 63.1 (1986): 106-13.

Tannenbaum, Percy, ed. *The Entertainment Functions of Television.* Hillsdale, NJ: Lawrence Erlbaum, 1980.

Television without Frontiers. Catalogue no. CB-CO-84-270-EN-C. Luxembourg: Office for Official Publications of the European Communities, 1984.

Tempest, Rone. "*Wheel* Making a Fortune." World Report Special Ed., *Los Angeles Times* 24 Oct. 1992: 10A.

Thomas, Laurie. "Play, Social Integration and the Mass Media." Paper presented at the 20th Communication Week, Ohio University, 1988.

Tunstall, Jeremy. *The Media Are American.* New York: Columbia UP, 1977.

Ulin, Robert. *Understanding Cultures.* Austin: U of Texas P, 1984.

United States Commission on Civil Rights. *Window Dressing on the Set: an Update.* Washington, D.C., 1979.

Valenti, Jack. "Television with Manacles." *Washington Post* 1 Dec. 1989: A27.

Varis, Tapio. "Global Traffic in Television." *Journal of Communication* 24.1 (1974): 102-09.

___. "International Flow of Television Programs." *Journal of Communication* 34.1 (1984): 143-52.

Walley, Wayne, and Marcy Magiera. "Syndicators Feel New Puritanism." *Advertising Age* 2 Jan. 1990: 4.

Wang, Georgette, and Wimal Dissanayake. *Continuity and Change in Communication Systems: An Asian Perspective.* Norwood, NJ: Ablex, 1984.

Wartella, Ellen. Presentation to Leadership Institute, Freedom Forum, New York, 23 June 1992.

Waters, Harry. "What a Deal!" *Newsweek* 9 Feb. 1987: 62-68.

___. "Much Ado about TV's Mini Games." *Newsweek* 28 Mar. 1988: 72-73.

___. "Talking Back to the Tube." *Newsweek* 3 Dec. 1990: 56-57.

Weiss, Paul. *Sport: A Philosophic Inquiry.* Carbondale: Southern Illinois UP, 1969.

White, David Manning. "Mass Culture in America: Another Point of View." *Mass Culture.* Eds. D.M. White and B. Rosenberg. Glencoe: Free, 1957: 13-21.

White, David Manning, and Bernard Rosenberg, eds. *Mass Culture.* Glencoe: Free, 1957.

Wildman, Steven, and Stephen Siwek. *International Trade in Films and Television Programs.* Cambridge, MA: Ballinger, 1988.

Williams, Michael. "France: Craze of Recent Vintage Is up to a Dozen Shows." *Variety* 27 Jan. 1992: 38, 40.

Wilstein, Steve. "NFL America's Most Popular Spectator Sport." *Messenger* [Athens, OH] 24 Feb. 1991: 12.

Zillman, Dolf. "Anatomy of Suspense." *The Entertainment Functions of Television.* Ed. P. Tannenbaum. Hillsdale, NJ: Lawrence Erlbaum, 1980: 133-64.

Author Index

Subject Index

Bold page numbers refer to figures, tables and illustrations.